Misunderstanding Galatians

Misunderstanding Galatians

An Exegetical, Originalist Commentary

M. I. CHA

WIPF & STOCK · Eugene, Oregon

MISUNDERSTANDING GALATIANS
An Exegetical, Originalist Commentary

Copyright © 2021 M. I. Cha. All rights reserved. Except for brief quotations in critical publications or reviews, no part of this book may be reproduced in any manner without prior written permission from the publisher. Write: Permissions, Wipf and Stock Publishers, 199 W. 8th Ave., Suite 3, Eugene, OR 97401.

Wipf & Stock
An Imprint of Wipf and Stock Publishers
199 W. 8th Ave., Suite 3
Eugene, OR 97401

www.wipfandstock.com

PAPERBACK ISBN: 978-1-6667-1339-8
HARDCOVER ISBN: 978-1-6667-1340-4
EBOOK ISBN: 978-1-6667-1341-1

09/13/21

This commentary is dedicated to R. L. Thomas, J. Rosscup,
S. Toussaint, and R. Beacham

Contents

Introduction: Misunderstanding Paul		ix
1	Interpretive Presuppositions	1
2	Commentary on Galatians 1	28
3	Commentary on Galatians 2	49
4	Commentary on Galatians 3	82
5	Commentary on Galatians 4	128
6	Commentary on Galatians 5	148
7	Commentary on Galatians 6	156
Bibliography		163

Introduction: Misunderstanding Paul

STENDAHL AND CHRISTIAN INTROSPECTION

Christians have long misunderstood Paul. This misunderstanding is what Krister Stendahl labels "a major question in the history of mankind": "the West for centuries has wrongly surmised that the biblical writers were grappling with problems which no doubt are ours, but which never entered their consciousness."[1] This gross misappropriation arises from a common human tendency: "sayings which originally meant one thing later on were interpreted to mean something else, something which was felt to be more relevant to human conditions of later times."[2]

More specifically concerning the Pauline corpus of the New Testament (NT), Stendahl writes,

> Western interpreters have found the common denominator between Paul and the experiences of man, since Paul's statements about "justification by faith" have been hailed as the answer to the problem which faces the ruthlessly honest man in his practice of introspection. Especially in Protestant Christianity—which, however, at this point has its roots in Augustine and in the piety of the Middle Ages—the Pauline awareness of sin has been interpreted in the light of Luther's struggle with his conscience. But it is exactly at that point that we can discern the most drastic difference between Luther and Paul, between the 16th and the 1st century.[3]

---

1. Stendahl, "Introspective Conscience," 214.
2. Stendahl, "Introspective Conscience," 214.
3. Stendahl, "Introspective Conscience," 200.

Moreover, Stendahl raises the argument that "for the Jew the Law did not require a static or pedantic perfectionism but supposed a covenant relationship in which there was room for forgiveness and repentance."[4] His conclusion is accurate:

> The Reformers' interpretation of Paul rests on an analogism when Pauline statements about Faith and Works, Law and Gospel, Jews and Gentiles are read in the framework of late medieval piety. The Law, the Torah, with its specific requirements of circumcision and food restrictions becomes a general principle of "legalism" in religious matters. Where Paul was concerned about the possibility for Gentiles to be included in the messianic community, his statements are now read as answers to the quest for assurance about man's salvation out of a common human predicament. This shift in the frame of reference affects the interpretation at many points.[5]

Accordingly, the purpose of this originalist commentary on Paul's epistle to the Galatians is to redress the modernizing misappropriations of Western commentators. In order to restore an accurate understanding of Galatians, this commentary functions like Stendahl's ideal historian who "is rightly anxious to stress the value of having an adequate picture of what these people actually thought that they were saying. He will always be suspicious of any 'modernizing,' whether it be for apologetic, doctrinal, or psychological purposes."[6]

Stendahl concludes his essay on the misappropriation of Paul with an important insight. "We note how the biblical original functions as a critique of inherited presuppositions and an incentive to new thought. Few things are more liberating and creative in modern theology than a clear distinction between the 'original' and the 'translation' in any age, our own included."[7] The present commentary seeks to function as the "new thought" Stendahl mentions, ironically liberating modern theology from misinterpretations of the "biblical original" by returning to what the apostle Paul originally intended in his epistle to the Galatians.

---

4. Stendahl, "Introspective Conscience," 201.
5. Stendahl, "Introspective Conscience," 205–6.
6. Stendahl, "Introspective Conscience," 214.
7. Stendahl, "Introspective Conscience," 215.

2 PETER 3:15-17 AND MISUNDERSTANDING PAUL

Stendahl's concerns with misinterpreting Paul have a biblical basis. Second Peter 3:15-17 warns of the ease with which Paul's letters can be misconstrued.

> 15 just as also our beloved brother Paul, according to the wisdom given him, wrote to you, 16 as also in all *his* letters, speaking in them of these things, in which are some things hard to understand, which the untaught and unstable distort, as *they do* also the rest of the Scriptures, to their own destruction. 17 You therefore, beloved, knowing this beforehand, be on your guard so that you are not carried away by the error of unprincipled men and fall from your own steadfastness.[8]

In verse 17, Peter associates the error of misinterpreting Paul with those opposed to the law of God: "be on your guard so that you are not carried away by the error of lawless ones [τῶν ἀθέσμων] and fall from your own steadfastness." In the Septuagint, θεσμός is used to denote "ordinance," "rule," "instruction," or "custom" (Prov 1:8; 6:20; 3 Macc 6:36; 4 Macc 8:7; Wis 14:23). Albrecht Oepke defines ἄθεσμος primarily as "apart from or contrary to statute, illegal."[9] Although the translations "unprincipled" (NASB, NET) and "wicked" (KJV, NKJV) might be deduced from Peter's earlier usage of ἄθεσμος to refer to the Sodomites in 2 Peter 2:7, the translation "lawless" (ESV, NIV) better reflects its habitual usage and connection to the biblical commandments of God.

The preceding context supports the translation "lawless ones" in 2 Peter 3:17. Peter's statement, "what sort of people ought you to be in holy conduct and godliness [ἐν ἁγίαις ἀναστροφαῖς καὶ εὐσεβείαις]" in verse 11 would have evoked in its original hearers the image of a believer's faithful life lived in heart obedience to the covenant stipulations of Mount Sinai. Similarly, in verse 14, Peter's exhortation, "be diligent to be found by Him in peace, spotless and blameless [ἄσπιλοι καὶ ἀμώμητοι]" reflects a way of life that is measured by the standard of the law of God. Peter's mention of "the wisdom" (σοφίαν) given to Paul (v. 15) and "the rest of the Scriptures" (τὰς λοιπὰς γραφὰς, v. 16) further confirms the Torah perspective from which the apostle speaks. Thus Peter's warning not to "fall from your own steadfastness [ἐκπέσητε τοῦ ἰδίου στηριγμοῦ]" in verse 17 is a stern admonition

---

8. The preferred modern English translation for this commentary is the New American Standard Bible (NASB), 1995 update edition. Any adaptations or use of other translations will be noted.

9. Oepke, "ἄθεσμος," 1:167.

that to understand Paul as teaching against faithful law obedience is a distortion that leads to destruction.

Concerning στηριγμός ("steadfastness") in 2 Peter 3:17, Günther Harder writes,

> It denotes "perseverance" in the truth mentioned in 1:12, in orthodox teaching.... The context makes it clear what is at issue, for στηριγμός is threatened by a fall into error through ἀθέσμων πλάνῃ. στηριγμός is thus used in a transf. sense for "perseverance," "steadfastness" in the teaching which has been handed down; the same thing is expressed negatively by the metaphor of going away and not abiding in 2 Jn. 9: πᾶς ὁ προάγων καὶ μὴ μένων ἐν τῇ διδαχῇ.[10]

The "orthodox teaching" and "the teaching which has been handed down" that Peter originally had in mind in 2 Peter 3:17, to quote Harder, was not Christian doctrine or the body of apostolic teaching recorded in the NT, but rather the covenant stipulations of the OT law of God. Thus, "steadfastness" (στηριγμοῦ) in 2 Peter 3:17 refers to faithful adherence to the OT law of God (ἐκπέσητε τοῦ ἰδίου στηριγμοῦ—"fall from your firmness/steadfastness"). Peter sternly warns that to understand Paul as teaching against faithful obedience to the law of God is a grave error. David Stern comments, "The most common distortion is in the direction of antinomianism; this happens especially when Sha'ul's letters are read apart from their *Tanakh* and Gospels-Acts background."[11] According to Richard Bauckham, most commentators understand the misinterpretation of Paul in 2 Peter 3:15-16 to involve statements that could be used to support antinomianism (e.g., Rom 4:15; 5:20; 8:1; 1 Cor 6:12) and the false teachers' offer of "freedom" (cf. 2 Pet 2:19; Rom 8:2; 2 Cor 3:17).[12]

Yet most Christian commentators disregard Peter's warning in 2 Peter 3:16-17 by heralding Galatians as Paul's declaration of independence from enslavement to the (biblical) law of Moses. To Stendahl's chagrin, most modern Christian interpreters continue to dislodge Galatians from its historical context and obscure its original meaning.

---

10. Harder, "στηριγμός," 7:657.
11. Stern, *Jewish New Testament Commentary*, 767.
12. Bauckham, *Jude, 2 Peter*, 332.

MESSIANIC JUDAISM AND ANACHRONISM

Sensing Christianity's misunderstanding of Paul, some interpreters and the modern movement of Messianic Judaism have sought to interpret the apostle from a more Jewish perspective. In his commentary on Galatians, D. Thomas Lancaster, for example, contends,

> Christians in Galatia (Jews and God-fearing Galatians alike) were already a part of Judaism and had, in fact, never left Judaism. They worshiped on the Sabbath when Paul first found them and were doing so when he left them. They had never heard of a grace-versus-law dichotomy, nor had they heard of this Christianity-versus-Judaism dichotomy. Nor had Paul heard of these things. And they could not have considered themselves as a part of the Christian religion in antithesis to Judaism because that antithesis did not yet exist.[13]

The present commentary agrees with Lancaster here. Yet, when Lancaster notes that Jewish and Gentile believers in Galatia "were already a part of Judaism and had, in fact, never left Judaism," a few qualifications are in order. Throughout his commentary, Lancaster's references to "Judaism" often seem to present the religion in a monolithic sense, as if there has always been an official, orthodox Judaism with clear doctrinal boundary lines. The liability in this inaccurate oversimplification is the tendency to import contemporary practices and understandings of modern "Judaism" back into the historical reality of the Galatian believers and the issues Paul addressed in his epistle. What Lancaster means by "Judaism" may not be the same reality which Paul and the Galatians originally faced.

According to Jeff Anderson,

> It could even be affirmed that Judaism as we now understand it did not develop until the Rabbinic period, and only then as a direct result of the destruction of the temple in 70 C.E. Most of the socio-religious groups examined in this study, including Early Christianity, envisioned themselves as the legitimate expression of biblical Israel for their day, with many claiming that they alone were the sole legitimate expression of classical Yahwism. What flourished in the Second Temple Period was not a single, fixed, "normative" Judaism, but a developing, evolving religion. Nevertheless, no straight evolutionary line of the Jewish faith emerges. Consequently, it is preferable to speak of multiple Judaisms rather than a monolithic ideology that views

---

13. Lancaster, *Galatians*, 110.

one brand of Judaism as orthodox and the rest as "sects." All Judaisms, consequently, competed for an audience and for the authority that accompanies broad-based acceptance.[14]

Therefore, both Christian and Messianic Jewish interpreters of Paul must be wary of anachronism. All commentators must avoid transposing their own circumstances and personal theology back onto the text of Galatians. The present commentary endeavors to clarify the original meaning of Galatians with this noble principle in mind.

---

14. Anderson, *Second Temple Judaism*, 5–6.

1

Interpretive Presuppositions

This commentary approaches Paul's epistle to the Galatians with four hermeneutical presuppositions: (1) the perpetuity of the OT law of God; (2) Paul's nuanced understanding of "the law" in 1 Corinthians 9:20–21; (3) the historical reality of Jewish oral law; and (4) the central concern of gentile proselyte conversion in Galatians.

PERPETUITY OF THE OT LAW OF GOD

The Messiah taught the perpetuity of the OT law of God (Matt 5:17–19):

> 17 "Do not think that I came to abolish the Law or the Prophets; I did not come to abolish but to fulfill. 18 For truly I say to you, until heaven and earth pass away, not the smallest letter or stroke shall pass from the Law until all is accomplished. 19 Whoever then annuls one of the least of these commandments, and teaches others *to do* the same, shall be called least in the kingdom of heaven; but whoever keeps and teaches *them*, he shall be called great in the kingdom of heaven.

In *The Complete Jewish Study Bible*, David Stern offers the following helpful explanation of Matthew 5:17–20.

> These verses provide crucial insight into Yeshua's understanding of *Torah* and its meaning. Here he is not canceling the *Torah*;

instead he is stating that he came to interpret it correctly. Romans 10:4 is misinterpreted by many, making Yeshua's words in Matthew 5 difficult to understand ... the statement that Yeshua did not come to *abolish* the *Torah* is a first-century rabbinic idiom. To "abolish" the *Torah* meant to misinterpret it, not cancel it. Second, Yeshua's expression, to "complete" *Torah*, meant that he came to teach it correctly. David Friedman reinforces this: "Yeshua is here stating that it is not his intention to teach the *Torah* incorrectly, but quite the opposite, to affirm its fullness and truth by teaching all of it in a way that is true to its intended meaning" (Friedman, "Jewish Idioms in the New Testament"). In defense of this idiomatic usage in Matthew 5:17–20, *Shabbat* 116b states, "I have come not to take from the *Torah* of Moses [Moshe], but on the contrary; I have come to add to it." Yeshua's intent by reinforcing a correct understanding of *Torah* was to establish *Torah's* full and intended meaning so that his disciples would know how to follow God.[1]

In much agreement, J. Daryl Charles observes,

> What is striking [in Matt 5:17–20] is the degree to which the *halakah* advanced by Jesus himself appears to stand in continuity with the OT. The "greater righteousness" called for by Jesus does not stand in juxtaposition to the ethical standard enunciated in the law and the prophets. Rather, it is to be understood against the ethical deficiencies of contemporary establishment religion.[2]

Charles notes, "It has been said that Protestants have supreme difficulty in not underestimating the value of the Mosaic tradition in the corpus of divine revelation. Given the trajectory of much contemporary scholarship as it applies to Matt 5:17–48, it is difficult to disagree."[3] Charles shows that, according to Matthew, the first disciples of the Messiah traced their teaching back to the revelation imparted at Sinai, a standard reiterated by the Hebrew prophets. Charles concludes, "In the mind of Matthew, the question of discipleship could not be divorced from 'the core' of Jewish religion, which is *doing righteousness.*"[4]

1. Rubin, *Jewish Study Bible*, 1391.
2. Charles, "Disciple's Relationship to the Law," 1.
3. Charles, "Disciple's Relationship to the Law," 14.
4. Charles, "Disciple's Relationship to the Law," 14–15; similarly, Donald Hagner writes, "[The evangelist's] Jewish-Christian readers needed to know—especially in the light of repeated counter-claims—that the pattern for righteousness taught by Jesus reflects the true meaning of the Torah, and thus that the Torah in its entirety is preserved

Similarly, Noel Rabbinowitz offers a relevant study of Matthew 23:2–3.

> 2 "The scribes and the Pharisees have seated themselves in the chair of Moses; 3 therefore all that they tell you, do and observe, but do not do according to their deeds; for they say *things* and do not do *them*."

According to Rabbinowitz's reading, the Messiah *did* affirm the authority of the Pharisees and their *halakhic* teachings *in principle*: "This is not a blanket endorsement of all their teachings, but a qualified affirmation of the Pharisees in their role as teachers of the Law of Moses."[5] The Lord's command for his followers to do whatever the Pharisees taught was based on their legitimate occupation of the Seat of Moses, an actual chair in the synagogue and a symbol of their legal authority.[6] In commanding the disciples to do "all" that the Pharisees taught, the Lord meant they were to obey their teachings regarding the Torah and *halakah in principle*, not their hypocrisy or corrupt teaching, a fact supported by the Messiah's own basic observance of oral tradition.[7] "Jesus' condemnation of Pharisaic hypocrisy cannot be reduced to a black-and-white rejection of their authority. Jesus rebuked the Pharisees, not because of their *halakhah*, but because they had forsaken the greater commandments of justice, mercy, and faithfulness."[8]

In clear support of this Hebraic perspective are passages in the Hebrew Bible that describe the perpetuity of the Sinai covenant as "eternal/everlasting" (e.g., Exod 31:16; Lev 24:8; Num 18:19; Deut 4:10–14; 5:2–3; 30:1–10; 31:12–13; Isa 24:3–5; 66:16–17; Jer 32:40; 50:5; Ezek 16:60; 37:26; Zech 14:16–19). The permanently binding nature of passages like Deuteronomy 13:1–5 and 18:15–19 is consistent with the perpetuity of the OT law of God. Messianic passages like Isaiah 2:2–4 indicate that the Messiah will be the source of Torah instruction in the Messianic age to come. The substance of "My law/*torah*" in Jeremiah 31:33 and "My statutes/ordinances" in Ezekiel 36:27 is essentially the same as the covenant stipulations given at Sinai and expounded in Moab. Moreover, references to "commandments" (e.g., 1 John 2:3–8; 3:4; 5:1–4) and "Scripture" throughout the NT, when the NT canon was not yet finalized, further support the ongoing perpetuity of the OT law of God.

---

in and through the ethical teaching of the Church" (*Matthew 1–13*, 110).

5. Rabbinowitz, "Matthew 23:2–4," 423.
6. Rabbinowitz, "Matthew 23:2–4," 446.
7. Rabbinowitz, "Matthew 23:2–4," 446.
8. Rabbinowitz, "Matthew 23:2–4," 447.

Accordingly, Knox Chamblin has argued for continuity between the law of Moses and the law of Christ. A key point in Chamblin's argument is the continuity between the Abrahamic and Sinai covenants:

> There is the closest relationship between the Abrahamic Covenant (or "the covenant of promise") and the Sinaitic Covenant (or "the covenant of law"). It is precisely to honor the promises of Gen 12:2 ("I will make you into a great nation") and 12:7 ("To your offspring I will give this land") that Yahweh accomplishes the exodus (see Exod 3:6–8; 6:6–8). The great event which provides the setting for the Sinaitic Covenant is itself an *expression* of the Abrahamic Covenant. Far from being annulled or superseded by the Sinaitic Covenant, the Abrahamic Covenant remains in effect as the perpetual foundation for the latter covenant. Conversely, far from opposing the promise, the law *serves* the promise by guiding and protecting God's people until the promise finds fulfillment in the coming of Christ. In other words, at Sinai Yahweh does not replace one way of salvation (by grace through faith in God's promises) with another (by reward for obedience to God's commands). Promise always undergirds law; law always presupposes promise.[9]

Chamblin also explains the sanctifying effect of the Sinai covenant stipulations, and the meaning of being "holy" from the Hebrew perspective of the original hearers: "Because Yahweh is a holy God, his people must be holy too (Lev 11:44–45; 19:2; 20:7). The law, in all its particulars,[10] is God's appointed means for making Israel 'a holy nation' (Exod 19:6)."[11] Chamblin rightly contends that the "new covenant" of Jeremiah 31:31–34 is "not a new law but a new and more personal administration of the old (Mosaic) law," and will accomplish "that purpose for which the Sinaitic Covenant had been established and the Mosaic Law given—namely, the deepest mutual knowledge between Yahweh and his people."[12]

Furthermore, in Matthew 5–7, the Lord is not expounding a new law:

---

9. Chamblin, "Law of Moses," 184.

10. Chamblin asserts that the traditional division of the Mosaic Law into moral, ceremonial, and civil categories "can be misleading, because both OT and NT normally use the term 'law' to speak of the *whole* Mosaic Law rather than a particular aspect of it; and moral, ceremonial, and civil laws are inextricably bound together in the OT, each kind being intelligible and operable only in relation to the other two" ("Law of Moses," 183).

11. Chamblin, "Law of Moses," 185.

12. Chamblin, "Law of Moses," 187.

The disciples' "righteousness" comes about by fidelity to the ancient law (the subject of vv. 17–19) *as interpreted by Jesus* (vv. 21–48). This righteousness "surpasses that of the Pharisees and the teachers of the law" (v.20) *both* in that it marks the rediscovery of a quality of obedience which the champions of the law have lost, *and* in that it marks an intensifying or escalating of obedience owing to the dawn of the kingdom.[13]

Finally, Chamblin concludes, "The NT does not warrant the sweeping conclusion that the moral dimension of the Mosaic Law is safeguarded while the ceremonial and the civil dimensions are jettisoned. In *some* sense, the entirety of the law remains in force."[14] Therefore, believers are to reject the idea that only those particulars of the Mosaic law which the NT expressly reaffirms apply to believers today.

PAUL'S NUANCED UNDERSTANDING OF "LAW" (ΝΟΜΟΣ) IN 1 CORINTHIANS 9:20–21

> 20 To the Jews I became as a Jew, so that I might win Jews; to those who are under the law, as under the law though not being myself under the law, so that I might win those who are under the law; 21 to those who are without law, as without law, though not being without the law of God but under the law of Christ, so that I might win those who are without law.

In 1 Corinthians 9:20–21 Paul distinguishes between four different positions concerning "law" (νόμος): "not being myself under the law" (μὴ ὢν αὐτὸς ὑπὸ νόμον, v.20),[15] "as without law" (ὡς ἄνομος, v.21), "without the law of God" (ἄνομος θεοῦ, v.21), and "under the law of Messiah" (ἔννομος Χριστοῦ, v.21). The larger context of 9:19–23 and the apostle's purpose statement in verse 22 ("I have become all things to all men, so that I may by all means save some") suggest that the differing positions concerning the law focus on Jew-Gentile distinctions. Accordingly, "under the law" (ὑπὸ νόμον) would refer to religious Jews living under the *Jewish* law (including oral and written Torah plus ancestral traditions) while "without law" (ἄνομος) refers

---

13. Chamblin, "Law of Moses," 191.
14. Chamblin, "Law of Moses," 200.
15. This statement alone by Paul undermines the claims of modern Messianic Judaism that Paul "would have been understood to represent a lifestyle that we would today label Torah-observant, Orthodox, traditional—mutatis mutandis" (Nanos, "Torah-Observant Paul?").

to lawless gentiles and/or irreligious Jews. The phrase "though not being without the law of God" (μὴ ὢν ἄνομος θεοῦ) in this context, then, clarifies Paul's own position as no longer subject to the broader Jewish law, but adhering only to the biblical law of God as interpreted and explained by the Messiah ("under the law of Christ," ἔννομος Χριστοῦ).

Indeed, the Lord's instruction on the law of God did not denounce every Jewish teaching and custom, but it did severely condemn the hypocrisy of false teachers and everything within Judaism that distorted or nullified the biblical law of God (Matt 23:23, 28). Part of the difficulty in rightly interpreting Paul is the fact that the apostle's references to νόμος can refer to the wider Jewish law (with all its religious traditions and institutions) or the biblical law of God as taught and clarified by the Messiah.[16]

At least three NT passages support the thesis that νόμος in the NT can include Jewish oral tradition: Ephesians 2:15, Romans 9:31, and 1 Corinthians 9:20–21.

Ephesians 2:15

> 14 For He Himself is our peace, who made both *groups into* one and broke down the barrier of the dividing wall, 15 by abolishing in His flesh the enmity, *which is* the law of commandments *contained* in ordinances, so that in Himself He might make the two into one new man, *thus* establishing peace.

An important factor in determining how Paul uses νόμος in this passage is the identity of τὸ μεσότοιχον τοῦ φραγμοῦ ("barrier of the dividing wall") in Ephesian 2:14. Harold Hoehner provides four reasons why this phrase does not refer to the Jerusalem temple wall separating the court of the Gentiles from the court of the Jews.[17] The term μεσότοιχον is a *hapax* and does not appear in the LXX. It has been found in two inscriptions in the sense of "partition" or "barrier."[18] The term φραγμός is found three other times

---

16. The thesis that νόμος in the NT may include not only the written OT law of God but also the Jewish oral tradition has been argued in at least three scholarly works: Fuller, "Paul and 'The Works of the Law,'" 28–42; Davies, "Paul and the Law," 1459–504; Tomson, *Paul and the Jewish Law*. This author does not necessarily agree with all of these writers' arguments nor affirm all of their theological positions in other writings. Their scholarship is cited as evidence that arguments in support of a nuanced understanding of νόμος in the NT have undergone academic peer review.

17. Hoehner, *Ephesians*, 369; similarly, Lincoln, *Ephesians*, 141; Thielman, *Ephesians*, 165.

18. Schneider, "μεσότοιχον," 4:625.

in the NT, all with the sense of "fence."¹⁹ Thus, if the genitive is understood appositionally, τὸ μεσότοιχον τοῦ φραγμοῦ could be translated, "the barrier *consisting* of the fence."

For religious Jews, the idea of Jewish oral law acting as a fence around the biblical law is common. J. Israelstam, for example, explains why the written Torah needs the Jewish oral law as a fence around it in accordance with *Pirkei Avot* 1:1: "The Torah is conceived as a garden and its precepts as precious plants. Such a garden is fenced round for the purpose of obviating willful or even unintended damage. Likewise, the precepts of the Torah were to be 'fenced' round with additional inhibitions that should have the effect of preserving the original commandments from trespass."²⁰ *Avoth* 3.13 records, "R. Akiba said . . . 'Tradition is a fence to the Torah.'" In the Cairo Damascus document of the Dead Sea Scrolls, the rabbinic interpreters of the law are referred to as "builders of the wall" (*CD* 4.19; 8.12, 18), while *The Epistle of Aristeas* presents the oral law as the barrier separating Jew and non-Jew (139, 142). Thus, Lincoln writes, "The notion of the oral tradition as providing a fence for Torah was a familiar one (cf. *m. 'Abot* 1.1, 2; 3.18)."²¹ Therefore, the phrase τὸ μεσότοιχον τοῦ φραγμοῦ in Ephesians 2:14 likely refers to the protective barrier of Jewish oral law.

Along this trajectory of thought, τὴν ἔχθραν ("the enmity," 2:14) that was abolished in the flesh of Christ would also relate to rabbinic oral law. Against the rabbinic laws of separation that fostered hatred between Jew and gentile, Tim Hegg suggests that the OT law does not promote "enmity" between Jew and gentile:

> The foreigner who desired to worship the God of Abraham, Isaac, and Jacob was to be welcomed into the community and treated with the same respect as was given the native born (Ex. 22:21; 23:9; Lev. 19:33, 34; 25:35; Deut. 26:12). They were to be given full participation in matters of Torah and Torah-life (Sabbath, Ex. 23:12, cp. Is. 56:3ff; Gleanings, Lev. 19:10; Justice, Ex. 12:49; Lev. 24:22; Festivals, Deut. 16:11, 14; Worship and Prayer in the Temple, 1 Ki. 8:41-43, cp. 2 Chron. 6:32, 33). And the prophets pronounce judgment upon any who would neglect their God-given responsibilities to the "stranger," on the same grounds as neglect of orphans and widows (Ps. 94:6; Is. 56:3ff;

---

19. I.e., Matt 21:33; Mark 12:1; Luke 14:23; cf. Danker et al., "φραγμός," 1064: "a structure for enclosing an area, *fence, hedge.*"

20. See Israelstam, "Aboth I," 1n7, in Lazarus et al., *Soncino Babylonian Talmud*; cf. discussions of rabbinic oral law serving this function in *Pesachim* 2b; *Eruvin* 100b; *Sanhedrin* 46a.

21. Lincoln, *Ephesians*, 141.

Jer. 22:3; Zech. 7:10) . . . The practical outworking of the Rabbinic laws of purity, however, raised a strong wall of separation between the observant Jew and the non-Jew. With the emphasis put upon purity by the Rabbis, separation from those things which rendered a person unclean was inevitable. According to oral Torah mere contact with non-Jews could render a person unclean [*m.Pes.* 8:8; *m.Shek.* 8:1; *T.Yom HaKipp.* 4:20; Josephus, *Ant.* xviii, 90; Acts 10:28], as well as contact with the residence of a non-Jew [*m.Oholot* 18.7, 9; John 18:28] or with land outside the Land of Israel [*b.Shabbat* 14b; *y.Shabbat* I, 3c; *T.Parah* 3:10]. Contact with any object used for idolatrous worship was added to the list of what might render a person unclean [*m.Shabbat* 9:1; *m.Abodah Zarah* 3:6; *y.Pesach.* II, 36c]. Clearly, the oral Torah of the 1st Century functioned to separate Jew and Gentile in a dramatic way.[22]

A key interpretive issue is the precise referent of τὸν νόμον τῶν ἐντολῶν ἐν δόγμασιν καταργήσας in Ephesians 2:15. Hoehner notes that καταργήσας is either a participle of manner showing how τὸ μεσότοιχον τοῦ φραγμοῦ (2:14) was destroyed, or a participle of means.[23] Lincoln observes that τὸν νόμον stands in apposition to τὴν ἔχθραν (2:14).[24] Thus, the meaning of τὸν νόμον in 2:15 is governed by these two preceding phrases. This is a crucial point for the nuanced νόμος thesis because it constrains Paul's use of νόμος in this passage to the immediate context.

Hegg points out that δόγμα is never used in the LXX as a term for any of the commandments, judgments, statutes, or laws (e.g., Gen 26:5) of which the total written OT law consists.[25] The noun δόγμα is used five times in the NT (cf. Caesar's decrees in Luke 2:1; Acts 17:7; apostolic decree in Acts 16:4). In Colossians 2:14, God has destroyed τὸ καθ' ἡμῶν χειρόγραφον τοῖς δόγμασιν through Christ. Douglas Moo explains why χειρόγραφον in Colossians 2:14 cannot refer to the Mosaic law: "this last view fits a bit awkwardly with the basic sense of the word, since of course, an IOU is written not by the one to whom the obligation is due (God, the author of the law), but by the one who is in debt (human beings). And, on the whole, there is insufficient evidence to give to the word any nuance beyond its general well-attested meaning of 'IOU.'"[26]

---

22. Hegg, "Can We Speak of 'Law,'" 18.

23. Hoehner, *Ephesians*, 375.

24. Lincoln, *Ephesians*, 142.

25. Hegg, "Can We Speak of 'Law,'" 18; Bruce Metzger translates δόγμα in 3 Maccabees 1:3 as "ancestral traditions" (*Apocrypha of the Old Testament*, 295).

26. Moo, *Colossians*, 209–10; cf. Lohse (*Colossians and Philemon*, 108) for

On the basis of the removal of this certificate of indebtedness consisting of δόγμασιν (Col 2:14), Paul teaches his readers not to let others judge them in regard to "food or drink or in respect to a festival or a new moon or a Sabbath day" (v. 16). Hegg observes, "These were the very items which occasioned the attention of the Rabbis in their 'building fences,' and which had created the separation between Jew and non-Jew! Apparently, the abolishing of these decrees ought to have rendered the Colossian believers free from submitting to man-made fences such as 'do not handle, do not taste, do not touch' (v.20)."[27] In context, these decrees are associated with "philosophy and empty deception, according to the tradition of men" (Col 2:8), "in accordance with the commandments and teachings of men" (2:22), and "the appearance of wisdom in self-made religion and self-abasement and severe treatment of the body" (2:23). Dunn lends support to the nuanced νόμος thesis when he comments, "At all events this [τοῖς δόγμασιν] probably alludes to the halakhic rulings about to be denounced in 2:16, 21–22, which includes talk of 'judgment' (2:16) and uses the verbal equivalent (δογματίζω in 2:20)."[28]

Similarly, for Lincoln, δόγμασιν in Colossians 2:14 "refers not so much to the Torah as to ascetic regulations."[29] Therefore, Paul seems to have added the otherwise curious qualifiers τῶν ἐντολῶν ἐν δόγμασιν to τὸν νόμον in Ephesians 2:15 to identify the abolished law as the legal fence of the rabbis. Daniel Juster explains, "The commands and ordinances are not necessarily intrinsically Torah, but the oral extensions of these laws made Gentiles unclean and contact with Gentiles something to avoid. As well, it would abolish commands precluding a Jew worshipping in the most intimate way with a Gentile since the Gentile, in Yeshua, is no longer an idolatrous sinner."[30]

Others have argued that τὸν νόμον τῶν ἐντολῶν ἐν δόγμασιν in Ephesians 2:15 cannot refer to the entire Mosaic law, and so must refer to the "ceremonial law,"[31] misdirected human commandments,[32] or only those laws that marked Israel off from other nations.[33] Walter Kaiser observes, "Had the law in its entirety been intended in this 'abolishment,' Ephesians 6:2 would be somewhat of an embarrassment: 'Honor your father and

---

comparable themes of indebtedness to God in Jewish literature.
27. Hegg, "Can We Speak of 'Law,'" 19.
28. Dunn, *Colossians*, 165.
29. Lincoln, *Ephesians*, 142.
30. Juster, *Jewish Roots*, 113.
31. Eadie, *Ephesians*, 175; Hendriksen, *Ephesians*, 135.
32. Roetzel, "Discussion of Ephesians 2:15a," 86.
33. Balla, "Is the Law Abolished," 14–16.

mother.'"[34] This line of thought is consistent with Paul's statement in Romans 3:31: "Do we then nullify the law through faith? May it never be! On the contrary, we establish the law."

Romans 9:31

> 30 What shall we say then? That Gentiles, who did not pursue righteousness, attained righteousness, even the righteousness which is by faith; 31 but Israel, pursuing a law of righteousness, did not arrive at *that* law. 32 Why? Because *they did* not *pursue it* by faith, but as though *it were* by works.

Romans 9:31 also supports the thesis that νόμος in the NT can include Jewish oral tradition. Moo explains that νόμον δικαιοσύνης "has become a storm center of debate . . . its meaning is inherently unclear . . . The unusualness of the phrase has led to various suggestions for textual surgery, beginning with some early scribes."[35] Part of the debate is that since in the previous verse, "Gentiles, who did not pursue righteousness, attained righteousness," the deliberate parallelism should lead to Paul making "righteousness" the goal of Israel's pursuit in verse 31. Instead, the jarring contrast is that Israel was "pursuing" νόμον δικαιοσύνης, *not* δικαιοσύνη. This may hint that Paul is not using νόμος in this phrase to mean the Mosaic law (cf. Isa 51:7: "Listen to Me, you who know righteousness, a people in whose heart is My law").

Moo also observes that every time Paul uses νόμος in association with δικαιοσύνη or its cognates (Rom 3:21, 28; 4:13; 10:5; Gal 2:16, 21; 3:11, 21; 5:4; Phil 3:6, 9), "Such phrases always have a negative connotation . . . The consistently negative nuance of the association of righteousness and *nomos* in Paul renders it improbable that *nomon dikaiosynes* is used positively as an appropriate goal for Israel to pursue."[36] This is an important statement for the nuanced νόμος thesis since the law of God was precisely the goal which Israel was to pursue throughout the OT (cf. Deut 6:4–9). Moo concludes by understanding νόμον δικαιοσύνης in Romans 9:31 as "the law whose object is righteousness . . . the law 'promises' righteousness when its demands are met."[37]

---

34. Kaiser, *Old Testament Ethics*, 310; cf. Rom 3:31.

35. Moo, *Romans*, 622.

36. Moo, *Romans*, 623–24.

37. Moo, *Romans*, 625; cf. ἡ ἐντολὴ ἡ εἰς ζωήν ("the commandment which is intended to give life") in Romans 7:10.

C. K. Barrett views νόμον δικαιοσύνης as a qualitative genitive, translating it, "Israel, whose aim is a law purporting to give righteousness."[38] Moo and Barrett's observations on νόμον δικαιοσύνης in Romans 9:31 are significant for the nuanced νόμος thesis. While Moo and Barrett interpret νόμος in this phrase as referring to the Mosaic law, their comments are compatible with the argument that νόμος here could refer to the broader Jewish law that purported or promised to result in righteousness if kept scrupulously. Thus, Romans 9:31 indicates that Israel pursued *a* (Jewish) law *that promised* "righteousness" *if kept*, but they failed.

T. David Gordon argues that the elliptical phrase ὅτι οὐκ ἐκ πίστεως ἀλλ' ὡς ἐξ ἔργων in Romans 9:32 actually modifies νόμον in the preceding verse, and not διώκων.[39] Gordon's major support is that in Galatians 3:12, Paul employs the same negated prepositional phrase: ὁ δὲ νόμος οὐκ ἔστιν ἐκ πίστεως (Gordon notes many more similarities between the passages in the wider context of Gal 3:10-13). Another support for Gordon's thesis is the unbalanced parallelism between Romans 9:30 and verse 31, where gentiles who did not "pursue" righteousness attained it while Israel "pursued" a νόμος that promised righteousness but failed. The apparent answer to the question διὰ τί; at the beginning of verse 32 ("Why *did Israel not achieve righteousness?*") points to the source of their failure: the νόμον δικαιοσύνης that Israel pursued. This νόμος was οὐκ ἐκ πίστεως but ὡς ἐξ ἔργων (Rom 9:32; cf. Gal 3:12). In other words, when Paul asks "why" Israel did not attain unto the law, his answer addresses the *nature* of νόμον δικαιοσύνης, not the actual *pursuit* of law obedience. This is an important distinction that supports the nuanced νόμος thesis. Even if Gordon's position is rejected, Romans 9:32 is not condemning Israel's *pursuit* of the law, but the *manner* in which she pursued it.

Moreover, the occurrences of ὑπὲρ αὐτῶν in Romans 10:1 and αὐτοῖς in 10:2 indicate that Paul is continuing his discussion of Israel from 9:31. Moo suggests that τὴν δικαιοσύνην τὴν ἐκ νόμου in 10:5 parallels νόμον δικαιοσύνης in 9:31.[40] This is a significant observation since Paul's testimony about Israel in 10:2-3 then serves as further commentary on the statement Ἰσραὴλ δὲ διώκων νόμον δικαιοσύνης εἰς νόμον οὐκ ἔφθασεν in 9:31. Israel's διώκων νόμον δικαιοσύνης (9:31) is further elaborated by ζῆλον θεοῦ ἔχουσιν ἀλλ' οὐ κατ' ἐπίγνωσιν (10:2). Thomas Schreiner agrees: "10:2-3 parallel 9:31-32 in a remarkable way, i.e., Israel's 'zeal for God' (v.2) is

---

38. Barrett, *Romans*, 179.
39. Gordon, "Translation Note on Rom 9:32," 163-66.
40. Moo, *Romans*, 624.

another way of describing her pursuit of 'the law of righteousness' (9:31)."⁴¹ Dane Ortlund also observes that, just as zeal for God (10:2) parallels Israel's pursuit of νόμον δικαιοσύνης (9:31), so "not according to knowledge" in 10:2 parallels "not of faith but as of works" in 9:32.⁴² The phrase ἀλλ' οὐ κατ' ἐπίγνωσιν (10:2) is further explained (γὰρ) in 10:3.

The νόμον δικαιοσύνης that Israel pursued (9:31) was ὡς ἐξ ἔργων (9:32) and characterized by ζῆλον θεοῦ ἔχουσιν ἀλλ' οὐ κατ' ἐπίγνωσιν (10:2). Romans 10:3, then, further explains why Israel's νόμον δικαιοσύνης (9:31) was οὐ κατ' ἐπίγνωσιν (10:2). In 10:3, the "knowledge" that Israel lacked was a *true* knowledge of the righteousness that God required *in his law*.

Robert Jewett explains the key phrase τὴν ἰδίαν ζητοῦντες στῆσαι in Romans 10:3 as:

> a reference to the sense of ethnic or sectarian righteousness claimed by Jewish groups... The Pharisees taught that perfect obedience to the written and oral law would usher in the righteous messianic era... The Essenes argued that adherence to their calendar and cultic regulations for the temple would satisfy the conditions of righteousness... The Sadducees believed that maintaining the purity of the temple and following the laws of the Pentateuch would achieve righteousness... In their sectarian competition with each other, and their sense of superiority over the corrupt Gentile world, each of these groups sought to "validate their own righteousness."⁴³

Jewett's inclusion of the oral law and "cultic regulations" in his understanding of Romans 10:3 supports the thesis that νόμος in the NT often refers to the broader Jewish law that encompasses extrabiblical oral traditions.

Colin Kruse observes that τὴν ἰδίαν ζητοῦντες στῆσαι in Romans 10:3 resembles Paul's admission in Philippians 3:9: μὴ ἔχων ἐμὴν δικαιοσύνην τὴν ἐκ νόμου ("not having a righteousness of my own derived from *the* Law").⁴⁴ Peter O'Brien links Paul's own righteousness based on law in Philippians 3:9 to the three κατὰ clauses in 3:5–6: κατὰ νόμον Φαρισαῖος, κατὰ ζῆλος διώκων τὴν ἐκκλησίαν, κατὰ δικαιοσύνην τὴν ἐν νόμῳ γενόμενος ἄμεμπτος.⁴⁵ If these connections between Romans 10:3 and Philippians

---

41. Schreiner, "Israel's Failure," 215.
42. Ortlund, "Zeal Without Knowledge," 27–28.
43. Jewett, *Romans*, 618.
44. Kruse, *Romans*, 401; also Moo, *Romans*, 635; Schreiner, *Romans*, 553.
45. O'Brien, *Philippians*, 395–96.

3:5–6, 9 are valid, then the Philippians passage helps elucidate Israel's νόμον δικαιοσύνης in Romans 9:31.

O'Brien elaborates on κατὰ νόμον Φαρισαῖος in Philippians 3:5 by asserting that Paul "bound himself to obey not only the law of Moses but also the hundreds of commandments contained in the oral law, those interpretative traditions of the scribes which Pharisees regarded as equally binding. As a disciple of the great Pharisee Gamaliel (Acts 5:34; 22:3) he set himself to be the most zealous of all who kept the law."[46]

Moisés Silva adds that this Pharisaic perspective on the law, "which emphasized the 'ancestral traditions' (Gal. 1:14; this phrase corresponds to the *rabbinic oral law*), was widely perceived as the one most faithful to Scripture."[47] Similarly, Gerald Hawthorne offers the following interpretation of κατὰ νόμον Φαρισαῖος in Philippians 3:5:

> [W]ith regard to the Jewish Law I was a Pharisee . . . Not content merely to obey the Law of Moses, the Pharisees bound themselves also to observe every one of the myriad of commandments contained in the oral Law, the interpretive traditions of the Scribes. The most ardent of the Pharisees scrupulously avoided even accidental violations of the Law and did more than they were commanded to do (Caird; Jeremias, *Jerusalem*, 246–67; Moore, *Judaism*, 1, 66). Paul, a son of Pharisees (Acts 23:6), and a disciple of the great Pharisee, Gamaliel (Acts 5:34; 22:3), chose to be a Pharisee himself and set himself to be the most earnest of the earnest observers of the Jewish Law (Gal 1:14).[48]

Therefore, if κατὰ νόμον Φαρισαῖος in Philippians 3:5 helps inform Israel's misdirected pursuit of νόμον δικαιοσύνης in Romans 9:31, then Paul's use of νόμος in the NT does include not only the biblical law of Moses but also the Jewish oral law.

On κατὰ ζῆλος διώκων τὴν ἐκκλησίαν in Philippians 3:6, O'Brien clarifies,

> Phil. 3:6 does not state explicitly that Paul's persecution of the church was evidence of his zeal *for the law* and the ancestral traditions. The Greek is simply κατὰ ζῆλος ('in relation to zeal'), without any qualifiers. But it is correct, for (1) his parallel testimony in Gal. 1:13–14 makes plain that he persecuted the church beyond all measure and that this was evidence of his zeal for the law and the ancestral traditions. (2) According to Luke, Paul,

---

46. O'Brien, *Philippians*, 374.
47. Silva, *Philippians*, 150; emphasis added.
48. Hawthorne, *Philippians*, 133–34.

in his speech of defence to the inhabitants of Jerusalem, claims that he was a persecutor because of his zeal for God and his ardent devotion to the law given to the fathers and scrupulously observed by the Pharisees (Acts 22:3-4; cf. 23:6). (3) Zeal for the Torah was an important ideal among many Jews, even if it found different outward expression among the various parties (αἱρέσεις) of the first century A.D., that is, Pharisees, Zealots, and the Qumran community.[49]

O'Brien's repeated inclusion of "the ancestral traditions" and mention of Paul's "ardent devotion to the law given to the fathers and scrupulously observed by the Pharisees" are consistent with a broader use of νόμος in the NT that also covers Jewish oral law.

O'Brien understands δικαιοσύνην in the final κατὰ clause of 3:6 as "righteousness . . . with reference to the divine commands as amplified and applied through the *oral law*."[50] On ἄμεμπτος, O'Brien explains,

> 'Blameless' appears to describe an exemplary way of life that is in conformity with the OT as interpreted along Pharisaic lines. We may suppose that Paul's assertion was a right perception of his standing before others, at least in a quantifiable sense, since it could have been contradicted by his peers had it been false. The expression does not suggest that he was without sin or transgression (cf. Rom. 2)—we do at least know that he coveted (Rom. 7:7-9)—or that his careful obedience to the commandments was perfect.[51]

Gordon Fee interprets ἄμεμπτος in Philippians 3:6 as "he scrupulously adhered to the *pharisaic interpretation of the Law*, with its finely honed regulations for sabbath observance, food laws, and ritual cleanliness."[52] On Paul's use of νόμος in 3:6, Fee asserts, "Although 'the Law' cannot always be so narrowly defined in Paul, here he is probably referring to matters of 'food and drink' and 'the observance of days,' since, along with circumcision, these are the two items regularly singled out whenever discussion of Torah observance emerges in his letters."[53]

Silva also supports the nuanced νόμος thesis in his comments on Paul's use of νόμος in Philippians 3:6:

---

49. O'Brien, *Philippians*, 375-76; original emphasis.
50. O'Brien, *Philippians*, 379; emphasis added.
51. O'Brien, *Philippians*, 380.
52. Fee, *Philippians*, 309.
53. Fee, *Philippians*, 310.

[W]hen the apostle speaks about the law, he has in mind not the law in a historical vacuum but rather the law as it was understood and used in first-century Judaism. Calvin goes so far as to say: "Paul uses the word 'law' loosely for the teaching of religion, however much corrupted it was at that time, as Christianity is today in the Papacy." Without drawing the distinction that sharply, we must recognize that Paul had just spoken in verse 5 of his prior commitment to Pharisaism as providing the proper understanding of the law.... Implicit here [Phil 3:6] (and explicit elsewhere) is a "criticism" of the Torah that is difficult to reconcile with Paul's positive remarks in other passages. If Paul's negative comments refer to the OT law without qualifications, we face an unbearable tension within the pages of Scripture... some writers have argued that νόμος for Paul can be shorthand for Jewish legalism... this interpretation contains a measure of truth... Paul surely has in mind the OT law... but just as surely his negative remarks *reflect* the way that law was handled by his Jewish opponents.[54]

1 Corinthians 9:20-21

20 To the Jews I became as a Jew, so that I might win Jews; to those who are under the law, as under the law though not being myself under the law, so that I might win those who are under the law; 21 to those who are without law, as without law, though not being without the law of God but under the law of Christ, so that I might win those who are without law.

As noted earlier, Paul uses νόμος (and cognates) in four ways in 1 Corinthians 9:20-21: (1) τοῖς ὑπὸ νόμον ὡς ὑπὸ νόμον, μὴ ὢν αὐτὸς ὑπὸ νόμον (9:20); (2) τοῖς ἀνόμοις ὡς ἄνομος (9:21); (3) μὴ ὢν ἄνομος θεοῦ (9:21); and (4) ἀλλ' ἔννομος Χριστοῦ (9:21).

Gordon Fee notes on τοῖς ὑπὸ νόμον in 9:20, "the specific issue was related... especially to matters of Jewish (religious) legal requirements... it is a matter of religious obligation... For Paul the language 'being under (or "keeping") the law' has to do with being Jewish in a national-cultural-religious sense."[55]

Anthony Thiselton claims that τοῖς ἀνόμοις in 1 Corinthians 9:21 "clearly in this context denotes Gentiles who are outside the revealed law

---

54. Silva, *Philippians*, 152, 154; original emphasis.
55. Fee, *First Epistle to the Corinthians*, 428-30.

of the OT *and Judaism.*"⁵⁶ David Garland explains Paul's claim of being ὡς ἄνομος in 9:21 as "he did give up his zeal for *the tradition of the fathers* and righteousness earned under the law."⁵⁷ Thiselton's inclusion of Judaism's law in his interpretation of ἀνόμοις and Garland's addition of "the tradition of the fathers" for ὡς ἄνομος lend credence to the argument that νόμος in the NT can include Jewish oral tradition.

A crucial point for this perspective is Paul's implication in the phrase μὴ ὢν ἄνομος θεοῦ ("not being without the law of God"; 1 Cor 9:21) that ὡς ἄνομος ("as without law"; 9:21) is not identical to ἄνομος θεοῦ. In other words, being ὑπὸ νόμον (9:20) is not the opposite of ἄνομος θεοῦ. It seems clear, then, that Paul's use of νόμος in this passage is nuanced.

For D. A. Carson, the phrase ἔννομος Χριστοῦ in 1 Corinthians 9:21 "means, at the least, that Paul refuses to *identify nomos theou* with the law of Moses; and more, that the particular fashion in which he is himself obedient to the law of God is in the context of his relationship with Christ."⁵⁸ Carson's conclusion, that for Paul the Mosaic law is not the law of God, is astonishing, but he is correct in identifying the positive grammatical relationship between the law of God and ἔννομος Χριστοῦ. The νόμος of Christ *is* the νόμος of God which Paul insists he submits to, but the νόμος of Christ and God are not identical to the νόμος in the preceding phrase μὴ ὢν αὐτὸς ὑπὸ νόμον which Paul explicitly rejects. As Fee, Thiselton, and Garland seem to suggest in their commentaries, the νόμος that Paul is *not* under refers to the broader *Jewish* law (not only the biblical Mosaic law) that included ancestral traditions and rabbinic *halakah* not found in the OT. If Paul no longer views the Mosaic law as the νόμος of God, as Carson argues, then the apostle's earlier statement ἑορτάζωμεν [the Passover] . . . ἐν ἀζύμοις εἰλικρινείας καὶ ἀληθείας (1 Cor 5:8) and insistence upon τήρησις ἐντολῶν θεοῦ (7:19) are contradictory.

Michael Winger has also argued that Jewish oral traditions may be included in some of Paul's usages of νόμος in the NT.⁵⁹ Winger's premise is that, without a sound linguistical approach to analyzing νόμος, interpreters often force the evidence. Winger uses modern principles of linguistics to explain various possible uses of νόμος in the NT. By differentiating between meaning/sense and reference (the basic meaning of a word and how it might be used in a given context), Winger describes various components of the meaning of νόμος as used throughout the NT. He then applies these

---

56. Thiselton, *First Epistle to the Corinthians*, 703; emphasis added.
57. Garland, *1 Corinthians*, 431–32; emphasis added.
58. Carson, "Pauline Inconsistency," 12; original emphasis.
59. Winger, *Meaning of* Nomos, 100.

to Galatians 2:15–21 and Romans 7:14–25, demonstrating how Paul can use νόμος in a variety of ways. Winger disputes the notion that νόμος exclusively refers to the biblical law of Moses alone in every NT occurrence.[60]

Along the same line of thought, Jacob Neusner and William Green offer a Jewish understanding of νόμος:

> Although *nomos* overlaps *torah* and the English word "law" in meaning, it also has other connotations. An important additional concept was the idea of "custom" in a particular sense: the Greeks often considered their customs to be "natural law." Thus, obedience to the law meant more than honoring certain written regulations; it included an entire way of life. In Jewish writings in Greek, the term "the law" (*to nomos*) came to mean "Jewish religion."[61]

JEWISH ORAL LAW

A third interpretive presupposition of this commentary is the crucial role Jewish oral tradition plays in accurately understanding much of the NT and Paul in particular. The historical reality of Jewish oral law is undeniable (cf. "ancestral traditions," Gal 1:14; "the traditions of the elders," Mark 7:3). However, what modern interpreters understand as Jewish oral law may not be identical to the reality Paul addressed in Galatians. If the second-century rabbi Yehudah HaNasi, chief editor of the Mishnah,[62] was born in AD 135 and died in 217, and if the Mishnah, widely considered the first major work of Rabbinical Judaism, records the debates of the post-Temple sages from AD 70–200, then there is a significant time gap between Paul (ca. AD 5–67) and the completed Mishnah (ca. AD 200).[63]

Two factors within this significant time gap between Paul and the Mishnah altered traditional Judaism so that the oral Torah in Paul's time was probably different than the codified oral Torah that would develop from the Mishnah much later. These two factors are the destruction of the Second Temple in AD 70 and the growth of Christianity in the first and second centuries.[64]

60. Cf. Tomson, *Paul and the Jewish Law*, esp. "Chapter Three: The Halakha in First Corinthians," 97–150.

61. Neusner and Green, *Encyclopedia of Judaism*, 457.

62. Steinsaltz, *Essential Talmud*, 60.

63. Steinsaltz, *Essential Talmud*, 62.

64. Steinsaltz: "the destruction of the Temple by the Romans in 70 C.E. had made the reconstruction of the entire fabric of religious life an urgent necessity, while the

The destruction of the Second Temple was a catastrophic upheaval for the Jewish people. Without the temple, the heart of Jewish faith and practice, the vacuum of authority and leadership would be filled by rabbi Yohanan ben Zakkai,[65] a former student of Hillel, who would help establish a new center of Jewish learning in Yavneh.[66] The Council of Yavneh (ca. AD 70–90) essentially altered the course of Judaism by (1) decreeing that animal sacrifices and temple rituals could be replaced by prayer and "good deeds" (*mitzvot*); (2) rejecting Greek translations of the Hebrew Scriptures and establishing the OT canon; and (3) adding the *Birkat HaMinim*[67] to the *Amidah*.[68] Following Yohanan ben Zakkai and Yavneh, Rabbinical Judaism would become the mainstream religious system of Judaism following the destruction of the temple in AD 70.

A second factor that significantly altered Jewish oral law between the time of Paul and the completion of the Mishnah was the early growth of Christianity. The addition of the *Birkat HaMinim* in Yavneh points to the influence Christianity had on post-Second Temple Judaism. It seems likely, then, that the debates and commentary of the post-Second Temple Jewish sages recorded in the Mishnah were not only aware of the growth of Christianity but attempting to steer Judaism away from Jesus of Nazareth and the claims of his followers. Consequently, the continuity of Jewish oral law would experience a considerable change in the codification of the Mishnah. Over the next three centuries, generations of rabbis in both Israel and

---

minim (heretics, especially Gnostics) and Christian sects posed a grave threat to internal religious unity and the people suffered persecution at the hands of foreign oppressors" (*Essential Talmud*, 49).

65. Steinsaltz, *Essential Talmud*, 51.

66. Steinsaltz: "After the destruction of the Temple, the Jewish High Court (the Great Sanhedrin)—commonly referred to then as 'the Great Council' . . . since the Sanhedrin had ceased to operate with its full authority—became the recognized center of Jewish life. The head of the Sanhedrin, who was always chosen from among the descendants of Hillel the Elder, was recognized as the head of the Jewish community of Eretz Israel not only by the Jewish community, who gave him the title of Nasi, but also by the Roman authorities, who called him the Ethnarch. The scholars and the head of the Sanhedrin still retained the authority to fix the date of each new month (and thus the dates of the Festivals), to intercalate the years, and to ordain Rabbis . . . Ordination was only recognized when carried out by scholars of Eretz Israel (and, according to an ancient agreement, only with the authorization of the Nasi). The importance of these functions was so great that the Nasi was considered the spiritual leader not only of the Jews in Eretz Israel, but of all Jewry" (*Essential Talmud*, 14).

67. "Blessing on the heretics," understood to refer primarily to Jewish Christians (cf. Katz, "Rabbinic Response to Christianity," 290–93).

68. Or "Eighteen Benedictions," the central daily prayers of the Jewish liturgy at synagogues (*Essential Talmud*, 41–42); on Yavneh, cf. Lapin, "Rabbinic Movement," 206–12).

Babylonia would carefully study the Mishnah and compile their scholarship in the *Gemara* (Israeli Gemara, ca. AD 400; Babylonian Gemara, ca. AD 500).[69] The Mishnah combined with the Gemara would form the Talmud (both the *Talmud Bavli* and the *Talmud Yerushalami*), the backbone of contemporary traditional Judaism.[70]

The problem of Jewish oral law that Paul faced was a matter of authority and not necessity. Traditional Judaism teaches that when Moses was on Mount Sinai for forty days and nights writing down the words of the Torah, God also provided him with additional explanations that were not explicitly incorporated into the written text. The possibility, or even likelihood, of God's additional explanation of the written Torah to Moses on Sinai is not incredulous. The problems arise when this unrecorded instruction from God is officially labeled as *Torah she'bal peh* ("by mouth"), and claimed to have been preserved in its entirety and passed on to Joshua, the elders of Israel, the Hebrew prophets, the leaders of the Great Assembly,[71] and eventually to the Jewish sages and rabbis.[72] It is not difficult to imagine, then, how this concept of a preserved "oral law," given to Moses by God, could acquire its own authority, and how Maimonides (ca. AD 1135–1204), a medieval Jewish rabbi and scholar, could claim in his commentary on the Mishnah, "Every commandment which the Holy One, blessed be He, gave to Moses our teacher, was given with its clarification. First, he told him the commandment (written Torah) and then he expounded on its explanation and content including all that which is included in the Torah." This legendary conception of *Torah she'bal peh* would grow over time so that the oral Torah would become legally binding commentary on the written Torah with authoritative instructions on how the commandments were to be carried out. In other words, the oral Torah represented the religious authority that was allegedly transferred from Moses to Joshua through the laying on of hands

69. Steinsaltz, *Essential Talmud*, 12–13, 76–77.

70. Steinsaltz, *Essential Talmud*, 3; "If the Bible is the cornerstone of Judaism, then the Talmud is the central pillar, soaring up from the foundations and supporting the entire spiritual and intellectual edifice. In many ways the Talmud is the most important book in Jewish culture, the backbone of creativity and of national life. No other work has had a comparable influence on the theory and practice of Jewish life, shaping spiritual content and serving as a guide to conduct. The Jewish people have always been keenly aware that their continued survival and development depend on study of the Talmud, and those hostile to Judaism have also been cognizant of this fact . . . At times, talmudic study has been prohibited because it was abundantly clear that a Jewish society that ceased to study this work had no real hope of survival" (ibid., 3).

71. Steinsaltz, *Essential Talmud*, 39–40.

72. So Steinsaltz: "And almost from the first, the oral law, *Torah she-be-al-peh*, accompanied the written law, *Torah she-bi-khtav*" (*Essential Talmud*, 36).

(*semikhah*),⁷³ and ultimately onto the recognized sages and rabbis of post-Second Temple Rabbinical Judaism. Over time, the oral Torah included all the interpretations and conclusions that the sages developed from the written Torah, as well as the regulations instituted by them. Since Rabbinical Judaism posits a line of succession from Moses to the post-Temple rabbis, many rabbis and scholars retroject later Jewish traditions and institutions back into the Hebrew Scriptures, claiming that the essence of all later rabbinical teachings was all "given" to Moses on Mount Sinai (*Talmud Peah* 2:17a; *Berachot* 5a).

Despite these anachronistic retrojections, the reality of "oral Torah," in the sense of unrecorded instructions and commands given by God, is undeniable. Jewish scholars will argue that since God first spoke the Ten Commandments to Israel before Moses ascended Sinai to receive the stone tablets, oral Torah actually preceded the giving of the written Torah at Sinai. The same principle applies to God's instructions given to Adam, Cain and Abel, Noah, and Abraham. Genesis 4:3, for example, records, "So it came about in the course of time that Cain brought an offering to the LORD of the fruit of the ground." The strong implication is that prior to Cain and Abel's offerings, God had given them instructions on how to properly make these offerings. The statement, "If you do well . . . And if you do not do well . . ." in 4:7 indicates a God-given standard for the offerings that Cain and Abel were expected to abide by. In Genesis 5:24, "Enoch walked with God," and 6:9 records, "Noah was a righteous man, blameless in his time; Noah walked with God." This language depicts Enoch and Noah as faithful believers characterized by their heart obedience to the instructions and commands given by God. These instructions and commands to Enoch and Noah are not explicitly detailed in Scripture but are nonetheless understood as *oral* Torah from God. This seems to be the case in Genesis 26:5, which testifies that "Abraham obeyed Me and kept My charge, My commandments, My statutes and My laws" long before the Torah was given to Moses on Mount Sinai.

A case for oral Torah can be made when Moses descended from Sinai and explained the specific *mitzvot*, *mishpatim*, and *chukkim* to the seventy elders of Israel, thereby passing on the unrecorded explanation he received from God to the leadership of Israel. When Moses' father-in-law Jethro saw how the people came to Moses for help in interpreting and applying the Torah, he advised that Moses appoint various judges to help interpret and apply the written Torah to specific cases (Exod 18:20; Deut 16:18; 17:8–11). Later Moses anticipated the need for these judges to be appointed in every city in the Promised Land to decide disagreements and controversies

---

73. Steinsaltz, *Essential Talmud*, 50.

concerning the Torah of God. In Judaism, this biblical pattern is the origin of the *Bet Din* and Jewish law court system, which are all based on the fundamental idea of oral Torah.[74]

A case for the positive value of oral Torah is strengthened when it is acknowledged that the written Torah, like all other writings, is subject to interpretation. In Judaism, debates over interpretation have included topics like the Jewish calendar and appointed times, what is considered "work" on the Sabbath, laws of inheritance, execution of various civil laws, marriage, wearing of *tefillin*, and *mezuzah* on doorposts. Evidently, it is impossible to understand the commandments of the written Torah without making interpretative decisions about issues not explicitly addressed in it. It is argued, then, that in its best and most biblically-based articulations, oral Torah merely represented the most reliable and agreed upon interpretive decisions and applications concerning the written Torah.

In support of oral Torah, many would argue that the extant manuscripts of the Hebrew Scriptures themselves are based upon oral Torah. As the authoritative Hebrew and Aramaic text of the Tanakh for Rabbinic Judaism, the Masoretic Text (MT) was primarily copied, edited, and distributed by the Masoretes between the seventh and tenth centuries AD. Concerning the MT, the masorah (Jewish tradition) refers to the diacritic markings of the text and the marginal notes on textual details like precise word spelling. The masorah enables punctuation and vocalization of the text, and without it one could not properly define the usage of various obscure terms found in the OT. The combined efforts of the Masoretic scribes helped preserve the Hebrew Scriptures to this day, yet there are no explicit instructions or commands in the written Torah concerning scribal preservation.

Furthermore, many would argue that the Messiah acknowledged and even subjected himself to the idea of oral Torah. In Matthew 23:5, the Lord apparently endorses the custom of wearing phylacteries in modesty, an issue governed by the oral Torah of his time. In Matthew 9:20 (cf. Mark 6:56; Luke 8:44), when a sick woman reaches for the Lord, she "touched the fringe of His cloak," which a Jewish audience would have understood as the *tzitzit* (tassels or fringes) of a *tallit* (four cornered garment or prayer shawl) as prescribed in oral Torah. The observance of Hanukah, which the Lord apparently kept (John 10:22–23), is not required in the written Torah, but is described in oral Torah. The Lord's final Passover meal also indicates that he observed elements of Jewish oral tradition, such as the *seder* pattern of blessing the bread and cups that was endorsed by the sages of his day. The Lord recited *haftarah* (selected sections from the Prophets) in the

---

74. Steinsaltz, *Essential Talmud*, 39–40.

synagogue on the Sabbath according to the *parashah* divisions of oral Torah (Luke 4:16–22) and referred to the Hebrew Bible in the threefold division of Torah, Prophets, and Writings according to oral Torah. Much of the substance and methodology of the Lord's teachings had striking parallels in the matrix of Jewish oral tradition and various sects within the Judaism of his day.[75] Most conclusively, the Messiah explicitly instructed his followers to observe the teachings of the scribes and Pharisees with qualification in Matthew 23:2–3 (cf. Deut 17:8–13).

On the other hand, the Lord frequently opposed and rejected certain practices and teachings of the scribes and Pharisees. The NT records the Messiah's scathing rebuke of their hypocrisy, traditions that abrogated Torah, self-righteousness, and errant interpretations and misapplications of Scripture (Matt 15, 23; Mark 7; etc.). The Lord rejected their rules concerning purity (Matt 15:1–3; Mark 2:16) and Sabbath observance (Matt 12:10; Luke 6:1–4) and restored a proper understanding of the righteousness that God requires (Matt 5–7).

Admittedly, the NT describes many serious problems with the official Judaism in the time of the Lord and Paul that would later be codified in the Mishnah and worsen over time. Clearly, any elevation of oral Torah to equal authority with Scripture was a violation of adding to the word of God (Deut 4:2; 12:32; Prov 30:5–6). There is a tendency in many oral traditions to gradually move away from the clear revelation of Scripture into fanciful

---

75. For example, the Lord's teaching on prayer in Matthew 6:9–13 summarizes the third, fifth, sixth, ninth, and fifteenth of the Eighteen Benedictions (*Shimoneh Esrei*) or *Amidah* traditional prayer instituted by the sages. Other Jewish sages also practiced this method of combining elements of the *Amidah* in prayer, which is also recorded in the Talmud. The Lord's citation of Deuteronomy 6:5 and Leviticus 19:18 in response to questions concerning the greatest commandment was also the official answer of the house of Hillel according to oral Torah. The Lord's golden rule recorded in Matthew 7:12 is similar to the negatively stated teaching of Hillel: "Do not do to others as you would not have them do to you." The Lord's teaching on "turning the other cheek" in Matthew 5:39 is reflective of the sages' teaching that a person struck on the cheek should forgive the offending party even if he does not ask forgiveness (*Tosefta Baba Kanima* 9:29). The Talmud commends the person who accepts offense without retaliation and submits to suffering and insult cheerfully (Yoma 23a). The Lord's instruction on loving one's enemy (Matt 5:43) is also found in the Talmud (Yoma 23a; Giṭ 36b; Šabb. 88b). The Lord's teaching on looking upon a woman with lust (Matt 5:28) finds a parallel in *Kallah* chapter 1: "One who gazes lustfully upon the small finger of a married woman, it is as if he has committed adultery with her." Many have suggested parallels in oral Torah and rabbinic materials to almost all of the Messiah's teachings, but matters of origin and sources (who learned from or was influenced by whom) continue to be debated. The point, however, is that the Lord lived and taught within a continuous stream of Jewish tradition and thought that existed prior to the codification of the Mishnah, Gemara, and Talmud (cf. Rabbinowitz, "Matthew 23:2–4," 435–38).

speculations. Many have detected a pattern of revisionism in how the Talmud portrays Abraham, Moses, David, the prophets, and even the Messiah as practitioners and advocates of various oral Torah teachings. Often, God is depicted as warranting the authority of certain rabbis, like in the Talmud Bavli, B. Meṣ.59b:

> In response, R. Eliezer said to the Sages, "If the Halakhah agrees with me, let it be proved from heaven." Sure enough, a divine voice cried out, "Why do you dispute with R. Eliezer, with whom the Halakhah always agrees?" R. Joshua stood up and protested: "'The Torah is not in heaven!" (Deut 30:12). We pay no attention to a divine voice because long ago at Mount Sinai You wrote in your Torah at Mount Sinai, 'After the majority must one incline'. (Exod 23:2)"

This Talmudic revisionism served to secure sole authority to the rabbis in all of Jewish life. Over time, rabbinical consensus and their interpretations and applications of both Scripture and Jewish tradition would usurp the single authority of Scripture.

Nonetheless, the Messiah's conflict with certain errant religious leaders of a particular generation, and the increasing divergence of Jewish oral law with the completion of the Mishnah, do not require a complete abandonment of all Jewish tradition and oral Torah in their entirety. To understand how the concept and substance of oral Torah developed over time, and to be able to distinguish between Jewish traditions that upheld biblical truth and those that undermined Scripture, is to more fully comprehend the context in which the Messiah and his followers lived and taught. To denounce the entirety of oral Torah and Jewish traditions without careful qualification would lead to misunderstanding parts of the NT.

The Talmud offers invaluable insights into much of the written Torah, including many of the teachings and discussions about the meaning of Scripture that were prevalent in the time of the Messiah and the apostle Paul. These Jewish writings provide details about the culture and social life of Israel, the origins of various customs, and temple activities that are not recorded in Scripture. Often, additional insights from Jewish sages make difficult Scripture passages easier to understand, and grammatical observations shed light on important words and syntactical constructions. The Talmud helps contextualize the conflict between the Messiah and the religious leaders of his time, and the circumstances in which the first disciples advanced the gospel message.

It is evident that a distinction must be made between the clear teaching and exclusive authority of Scripture, and the religious system that resulted from the development of oral Torah and Jewish traditions over time. The teachings of the Mishnah and Talmud were not given to Moses by God on Mount Sinai, and both Jewish and gentile believers are not under the authority of rabbis who have rejected the Messiah of Israel. However, to disregard the entirety of oral Torah and Jewish tradition is to overlook invaluable sources of truth and insight concerning the word of God. According to the rabbis, the overriding intent of the oral Law is to elucidate the teaching of the written Law. From this ideal perspective, then, the best of Jewish oral law would be analogous to Christian commentaries and theologies, tools for more accurately understanding the word of God.

GENTILE PROSELYTE CONVERSION IN GALATIANS

Finally, a central interpretive presupposition in this commentary is that Paul was concerned primarily with gentile proselyte conversion into Pharisaic Judaism in Galatians, and not with whether gentile believers should obey the biblical commandments of God. D. Thomas Lancaster helps explain the background of this perspective by understanding the first biblical reference to "Christians" in Acts 11:26 from within a synagogue context:

> In those days each synagogue had a name like "Synagogue of the Hebrews," "Synagogue of the Freedmen," or something to denote their particular sect. Sociologist, historian, and scholar Magnus Zetterholm, in his book *The Formation of Christianity in Antioch*, suggests that originally our synagogue in Antioch was called the Synagogue of the *Christianoi*, i.e., the Synagogue of the Christians—or to put it in our English, the Synagogue of the Messianics.[76]

From this perspective, Lancaster discusses the importance of Paul's address in Acts 13:26: "Brethren, sons of Abraham's family, and those among you who fear God, to us the message of this salvation has been sent." The apostle's threefold address refers to the three types of people one might find in any diaspora synagogue of the first century, and to properly understand Paul's concern in Galatians, one must differentiate between these three groups.[77]

---

76. Lancaster, *Galatians*, 11–12; Lancaster cites Zetterholm, *Christianity in Antioch*, 37–38.

77. Lancaster, *Galatians*, 14.

In the context of the Pisidian-Antioch synagogue, Paul's "brethren" in Acts 13:26 were his fellow Jews.⁷⁸ "Sons of Abraham's family" (υἱοὶ γένους Ἀβραάμ) referred to gentile proselytes—those non-Jews who had, for one reason or another, made a formal conversion to Judaism, thus becoming legally Jewish.⁷⁹ A third type of congregant in the Pisidian-Antioch synagogue was "those among you who fear God," the gentile "God-fearer."

> They worshipped in the synagogue with Jewish people and proselytes, but chose not to undergo the ritual of conversion. They were not exactly pagans anymore, but they were not Jews either. While the synagogue community may have tolerated them and even appreciated their financial contributions to the community (as with the centurions in Luke 7 and Acts 10), they did not regard them as Jewish. The God-Fearers did not enjoy the rights and privileges of the Jewish people, nor did they have responsibilities within Judaism.⁸⁰

Subsequently, when Luke states in Acts 13:44 that "nearly the whole city assembled to hear the word of the Lord," the God-fearing gentiles had apparently invited their relatives, friends, and neighbors to attend, and the large crowd of gentiles in the synagogue irritated the Jewish community.

> From the Jewish perspective, however, a Gentile majority in the synagogue creates a serious threat to the integrity of the community's identity. Jewish identity is precarious enough in the face of assimilation in the Diaspora. The mainstream culture is always chipping away at the particulars of Jewish monotheism and Torah observance. A Gentile presence almost certainly would accelerate the tendency toward assimilation.⁸¹

---

78. Lancaster, *Galatians*, 14. Lancaster explains, "In the first century, the term 'Jew' did not specifically mean someone from the tribe of Judah. The term applied to all Israelites with legal standing in the Jewish community. Thus, Paul referred to himself as Jewish, though he was actually a Benjamite."

79. Lancaster, *Galatians*, 15; "According to the Jewish law, they were no longer regarded as Gentiles, but through the rituals of circumcision and immersion (and sacrifice when possible), they had taken on the religious and legal status of Israel. The Jewish community referred to them as 'sons and daughters of Abraham.' This conversion process was based upon biblical texts which speak about the stranger who undergoes circumcision as a member of Abraham's household (Genesis 17) or as a sojourner who desires to eat of the Passover sacrifice (Exodus 12). In the days of the apostles, the biblical 'stranger who dwells among you' was understood by the Jewish world to refer primarily (though not exclusively) to the formal, legal proselyte to Judaism."

80. Lancaster, *Galatians*, 15.

81. Lancaster, *Galatians*, 16.

Therefore, when Luke states in Acts 13:45, "when the Jews saw the crowds, they were filled with jealousy and *began* contradicting the things spoken by Paul, and were blaspheming," the Jews were jealous that the message of the gospel was compromising the particularity of Jewish identity. "The message of the gospel seemed to be throwing the doors of Judaism wide open to the Gentile world."[82]

Lancaster concludes, "Paul and his colleagues in Antioch wrote the epistle of Galatians to the God-fearing Gentile believers whom they left behind in the territory of Galatia."[83] Upon returning to Antioch, Paul received word from the God-fearing gentile believers whom he had left behind in Pisidian Antioch and Iconium that a number of them had apparently succumbed to some type of pressure to go through conversion and become full proselytes and to achieve status as legal Jews.[84] "[T]he Galatian Gentiles had decided to undergo legal conversion to become Jewish because it had entered their heads that, unless they did, they would not obtain a share in the kingdom and the world to come. They had come to believe that only Israel proper, i.e., the Jewish people, could be saved."[85]

Along the same line of thought, Shaye Cohen lists three elements of conversion to Judaism in antiquity: practice of the Jewish laws, exclusive devotion to the God of the Jews, and integration into the Jewish community.[86] Cohen demonstrates that the first-century Jewish historian Josephus singled out circumcision as the central component of conversion to Judaism.

> For him [Josephus] "to adopt the customs of the Jews" and "to be circumcised" are synonymous expressions (cf. *Vita* 23 § 113 with 31 § 149). In the second century BCE circumcision achieved prominence, for Jews and gentiles alike, as *the* Jewish ritual, and in subsequent centuries many gentile writers (for example, Tacitus and Juvenal) confirmed Josephus's (and Paul's!) view that the acceptance of circumcision is the acceptance of Judaism . . . The Greek-speaking Jews of the second temple period and the Hebrew- (and Aramaic-) speaking Jews after 70 CE debated the meaning of circumcision and the ritual's exact place in the conversion process, but as far as is known no (non-Christian) Jewish community in antiquity accepted male proselytes who were not circumcised. Perhaps the god of the Jews would be pleased with gentiles who venerated him and practiced some of

---

82. Lancaster, *Galatians*, 17.
83. Lancaster, *Galatians*, 18.
84. Lancaster, *Galatians*, 18.
85. Lancaster, *Galatians*, 18–19.
86. Cohen, "Becoming a Jew," 26.

his laws, and perhaps in the day of the eschaton gentiles would not need to be circumcised to be part of god's holy people; but if those gentiles wanted to join the Jewish community in the here and now, they had to accept circumcision.[87]

Accordingly, Paul's polemic against circumcision in Galatians addresses the very same issue the Jerusalem council faced in Acts 15: gentile proselyte conversion and inclusion within the believing covenant community. As Cohen has demonstrated, the term "circumcision" most likely functions as shorthand for proselyte conversion in both Galatians and Acts 15. Like the Jerusalem Council, Paul is not dealing with the question of whether a gentile should obey the OT law of God. He is arguing against the belief that a gentile needed to undergo proselyte conversion under rabbinic authority to become a true member of the covenant nation.

Stendahl's sobering criticisms are valid: self-absorbed Western introspection has severely blurred the original meaning of Paul's writings. Moreover, the apostle Peter warns us in 2 Peter 3:15–17 that Paul's epistles require careful interpretation and must not be understood as opposing faithful obedience to the biblical law of God. Apparently, misguided teachers have long distorted Paul to advocate lawlessness (2 Pet 3:16–17). Proponents of a more "Jewish" Paul, however, may overcompensate by anachronistically forcing the apostle into later rabbinic and more modern molds. The present commentary hopes to clarify Paul's originally intended meaning in Galatians by acknowledging the perpetuity of the OT law of God, Paul's nuanced use of νόμος, the role of Pharisaic oral tradition, and the apostle's chief concern with gentile proselyte conversion.

---

87. Cohen, "Becoming a Jew," 27.

2

Commentary on Galatians 1

¹:¹ Παῦλος ἀπόστολος οὐκ ἀπ' ἀνθρώπων οὐδὲ δι' ἀνθρώπου ἀλλὰ διὰ Ἰησοῦ Χριστοῦ καὶ θεοῦ πατρὸς τοῦ ἐγείραντος αὐτὸν ἐκ νεκρῶν, ² καὶ οἱ σὺν ἐμοὶ πάντες ἀδελφοὶ
ταῖς ἐκκλησίαις τῆς Γαλατίας

¹:¹ Paul, an apostle (not *sent* from men nor through the agency of man, but through Jesus Christ and God the Father, who raised Him from the dead), ² and all the brethren who are with me,
To the churches of Galatia:

Paul's role as an ἀπόστολος (v.1) ought to be compared to the Hebrew שָׁלִיחַ.[1] In the LXX ἀποστέλλειν is used to translate the Hebrew verb שלח. God "sent" (שלח) his prophets to his people as authorized representatives and official messengers (cf. Exod 3:10; Judg 6:8, 14; Isa 6:8; Jer 1:7; Ezek 2:3; Hag 1:12; Zech 2:15 [Eng. 2:11]; 4:9; Mal 3:2–3 [4:4]).[2] The Latin theologian Jerome (ca. 347–420 AD) compared the Jewish title שָׁלִיחַ to the ἀπόστολοι, and in the Syrian Church an apostle was called שְׁלִיחָא.[3] In m. Ber. 5:5, the rabbis taught "the one sent by a man is as the man himself" (שְׁלוּחוֹ שֶׁל אָדָם

---

1. Rengstorf, "ἀπόστολος," 1:414.

2. Avi ben Mordechai explains that Paul's official role as a *shaliach* of the Messiah and God the Father meant his message was subject to the tests recorded in Deuteronomy 13 and 18, where if someone who claimed to speak for God was found leading people away from the written commandments, he was a false prophet requiring execution (*Galatians*, 119).

3. Rengstorf, "ἀπόστολος," 1:414.

כְּמוֹתוֹ), meaning the שָׁלִיחַ is as good as the שֹׁלֵחַ in all that he says and does in execution of his commission.[4] In m. Roš Haš. 1:3, official messengers (הַשְּׁלוּחִין) are sent out by the Sanhedrin to announce the new moon and thus the official beginning of Tishri.[5]

Kyu Kim has demonstrated the OT/Jewish background in Paul's use of ἀδελφοὶ ("brothers") in Galatians 1:2.[6] All the descendants of Jacob belong to the one family of God (cf. Exod 4:22; 6:6-8; Jer 31:9, 20; Hos 11:1; Amos 5:25). In Amos 3:2 God tells the sons of Israel, "You only have I chosen among all the families of the earth." Thus gentiles were distinguished from, and not referred to as, a "brother" (e.g., Exod 2:11; Deut 3:18; 15:2-3; 17:5; 23:20-21; 24:14; Neh 5:1; Isa 66:20; cf. 1 Macc 2:40; 2 Macc 1:1). In 2 Maccabees 1:1 Jews in Israel address Jews in Egypt as "brothers," indicating that the term connotes shared ethnic origin apart from regional or political affiliation (cf. also Tob 1:3, 16).[7] Since Paul was aware of the ethnic significance of Jewish sibling language, Kim concludes that Paul's usage of "brother" indicated that Jewish and gentile Christians alike are members of God's reconstituted family.[8] The status of Paul's gentile believers was the same as Jewish proselytes in Judaism who were addressed by Jews with sibling language.

Paul's defensiveness about his authority as an apostle of the Messiah and God the Father (v. 1) probably concerns the issue of gentile proselyte conversion into Judaism (cf. Acts 15:1-2).

The term ἐκκλησία in Galatians 1:2 is used in the LXX to translate the Hebrew קָהָל. James Dunn notes, "'Churches' might be better translated 'assemblies'... the assemblies so designated were continuous with 'the assembly of Israel' in the Jewish Scriptures."[9] The connection between ἐκκλησία in Galatians 1:2 and the קָהָל of Israel (cf. Exod 12:6; Lev 16:17; Num 14:5; Deut 31:30) is strengthened by Stephen's use of ἐκκλησία in Acts 7:38 for the assembly of Israel in the wilderness.

In Matthew 16, following the Jewish leaders' rejection of the Messiah (Matt 16:1-4) and Peter's accurate identification (v. 16), the Lord promises,

---

4. Rengstorf, "ἀπόστολος," 1:415.

5. Hegg, *Galatians*, 23.

6. Kim, "Paul's Sibling Language," 1-8.

7. Concerning Paul's use of "brethren" in Galatians 1:2, Hegg sees continuity with the synagogue: "The term 'brother'... was also used among the Jewish communities. It was therefore not a term coined by The Way, nor something that identified the emerging Christian Church as distinct from the Jewish communities out of which it grew" (*Galatians*, 24).

8. Cf. Gal 1:11; 3:15; 4:12, 28, 31; 5:11, 13; 6:1, 18.

9. Dunn, *Galatians*, 30.

"I will build my ἐκκλησία" (v. 18). Although the leaders and majority of the assembly of Israel reject the Messiah, the Lord will build his own assembly with the faithful remnant of his disciples. Later in Matthew 18:15–18 the Lord instructs his followers on how to resolve sin issues within the ἐκκλησία (v. 17). In Matthew 18:16 the Lord applies Deuteronomy 19:15 and if the "brother" is still unrepentant, "let him be to you as a Gentile and a tax collector" (v. 17). The mention of "Gentile" and "tax gatherer" indicates that the rebellious person who rejects Deuteronomy 19:15 is deemed to be outside of the community of true Israel.

According to Ralph Korner at least three ancient Jewish writers utilized ἐκκλησία to refer to Jewish synagogue-like assemblies: Ben Sira (Sir 15:5; 21:17; 38:33), Josephus (*Ant.* 3:84; 12.164; 13.216), and Philo (*Virt* 108; *Spec.* 1:324–25).[10] At a minimum, these three witnesses indicate that publicly accessible Jewish assemblies called ἐκκλησία existed contemporaneously with early Christ-followers.[11] For Korner, Paul's use of ἐκκλησία suggests that "Pauline Christ-followers would not have seen themselves as some sort of new, a-cultural, universal association of Jesus worshippers disconnected from their Jewish roots."[12] Rather, regional ἐκκλησία designated Jewish associations and public gatherings in Paul's time that were a part of, and in continuity with, the greater קָהָל of Israel.

> ³ χάρις ὑμῖν καὶ εἰρήνη ἀπὸ θεοῦ πατρὸς ἡμῶν καὶ κυρίου Ἰησοῦ Χριστοῦ ⁴ τοῦ δόντος ἑαυτὸν ὑπὲρ τῶν ἁμαρτιῶν ἡμῶν, ὅπως ἐξέληται ἡμᾶς ἐκ τοῦ αἰῶνος τοῦ ἐνεστῶτος πονηροῦ κατὰ τὸ θέλημα τοῦ θεοῦ καὶ πατρὸς ἡμῶν, ⁵ ᾧ ἡ δόξα εἰς τοὺς αἰῶνας τῶν αἰώνων, ἀμήν.
> ³ Grace to you and peace from God our Father and the Lord Jesus Christ, ⁴ who gave Himself for our sins so that He might rescue us from this present evil age, according to the will of our God and Father, ⁵ to whom *be* the glory forevermore. Amen.

Most commentators understand the opening greeting χάρις as a form of the standard salutation χαίρειν in Greek letter writing.[13] However, χάρις often translates the Hebrew term חֶסֶד which especially signifies the covenant

---

10. Korner, "*Ekklēsia* as a Jewish Synagogue," 64–66.
11. Paul never uses the term συναγωγή in his canonical writings, but is quoted as using the term in his self-defenses in Acts 22:19; 24:12; 26:11. Possible reasons for Paul's preference of ἐκκλησία over συναγωγή are stylistic choice, emphasis on a physical meeting location or structure, and/or a distinction between the ἐκκλησία of the Messiah (cf. Matt 16:18) and the συναγωγή institution of Judaism.
12. Korner, "*Ekklēsia* as a Jewish Synagogue," 71.
13. E.g., Bruce, *Galatians*, 74; Moo, *Galatians*, 71; Keener, *Galatians*, 52.

love of God for the children of Israel. In view of 6:16 Paul seems to be using χάρις/חֶסֶד in a covenantal sense in 1:3.

Douglas Moo explains that Paul's greeting of εἰρήνη in 1:3 "is not a wish that they enjoy a quiet, happy life or that their souls may find rest but that they might experience the full measure of God's eschatological *shalom*."[14]

The phrase "God our father" (θεοῦ πατρὸς ἡμῶν) in 1:3 evokes the theme of God's fatherhood to the nation of Israel in the OT (cf. Deut 32:6; 1 Chr 29:10; Isa 63:16; 64:8; Jer 3:19; 31:9; Mal 1:6; 2:10; Ps 68:6; 103:13; Prov 3:12).[15] The nation of Israel is distinctly the "sons/children" of God (cf. Exod 4:22-23; Deut 14:1; Isa 1:2; Hos 1:10; 11:1; Ps 82:6).

Paul's use of κύριος in the phrase κυρίου Ἰησοῦ Χριστοῦ in 1:3 is debated. Some commentators reason that since κύριος is used in the LXX to render the divine name יהוה, Paul is identifying Jesus as YHWH of the OT (cf. Mark 1:3; Acts 2:34; 1 Cor 12:3; Phil 2:9-11). Still, κύριος is also used in the LXX to translate אָדוֹן. When used of God, אֲדֹנָי/אָדוֹן emphasizes the lordship and sovereign power of YHWH over all creation, and is similar to מֶלֶךְ (cf. הָאָדֹן יְהוָה, "the Lord GOD" in Exod 23:17; 34:23). Although the plurality of God is certainly implied throughout the OT (e.g., Gen 1:26-27; Exod 3:1-6, 13-16), what Paul may be emphasizing in the phrase κυρίου Ἰησοῦ Χριστοῦ in 1:3 is the supreme lordship of Jesus as the promised Messiah and kingly agent of YHWH's rule over all creation. This is not to deny the deity or preexistence of the Messiah (cf. Gen 1:26-27 with John 1:1-3; 8:58; Col 1:15-17; Paul's use of Joel 2:32 in Rom 10:13), but to clarify Paul's intended emphasis in 1:3.[16] As the Messiah, Jesus holds the same authority and position as God the Father, and will rule over all creation on his behalf.

The imagery of the Messiah "who gave Himself for our sins" (τοῦ δόντος ἑαυτὸν ὑπὲρ τῶν ἁμαρτιῶν ἡμῶν) (v. 4a) recalls LXX Isaiah 53:5-6, 12 (cf. 1 Cor 15:3, "according to the Scriptures").[17] The imagery of an animal sacrifice bearing the sins of the people in Isaiah 53 may allude to Abraham's offering of Isaac (Gen 22:8), the Passover lamb (Exod 12), the daily *Tamid* sacrifice (Exod 29:38-42), the guilt offering (Isa 53:10; cf. Lev 5; 14:12-13; Num 6:11-12), and the scapegoat on the Day of Atonement (Lev 16:6-10). The picture of the gentle lamb led to slaughter in Isaiah 53:7 is a striking

---

14. Moo, *Galatians*, 71.

15. Hegg (*Galatians*, 27) and Keener (*Galatians*, 53n45) note the widespread references to God as "Father" in rabbinic literature and Jewish prayers.

16. Daniel Boyarin has demonstrated a belief in the plurality of divine beings in Jewish thought and ancient rabbinic literature ("Gospel of the *Memra*," 248; "Divine Polymorphy of Ancient Judaism," 323-24).

17. So Moo, *Galatians*, 72; Keener, *Galatians*, 53.

echo of the prophet Jeremiah (Jer 11:18–19). The reference to "the lamb of God who takes away the sin of the world" in John 1:29 also points to the Servant of YHWH in Isaiah 53 who will "sprinkle many nations" (Isa 52:15).

In Isaiah 42:6; 49:8 God states that he will give his unique servant as "a covenant" to the people of God. This language echoes the imagery of Exodus 24:5–8 where "the blood of the covenant" sacrifices were "sprinkled" (v. 8) on the altar and people in ratifying the Sinai covenant. Isaiah 49:5–6 describes a key reason for the giving of the servant as a covenant sacrifice: "to bring Jacob back to Him, so that Israel might be gathered to Him" (v. 5) and "to raise up the tribes of Jacob and to restore the preserved ones of Israel" (v. 6). This servant of YHWH will also be "a light to the nations" (Isa 42:6; 49:6). In Isaiah 52, the "good news" of God's "salvation" concerns the establishment of the kingdom of God (v. 7), the restoration and redemption of Zion/Jerusalem (vv. 8–9), God's regathering of the scattered exiles of his people (vv. 11–12), the exaltation of the servant of YHWH (v. 13), and the sprinkling of many nations through the destruction of this servant (vv. 14–15). This stream of theology concerning the servant of YHWH in Isaiah 42–53 seems to be in Paul's mind in Galatians 1:4 when he alludes to the imagery of the Messiah "who gave Himself for our sins" in LXX Isaiah 53:5–6, 12.

The purpose of the Messiah's giving of himself for sin (1:4) is "so that He might rescue us from this present evil age" (ὅπως ἐξέληται ἡμᾶς ἐκ τοῦ αἰῶνος τοῦ ἐνεστῶτος πονηροῦ). The rare verb ἐξαιρέω means "to remove something from its place, take out, tear out."[18] English translations of this verb seem to avoid the sense of "remove," allowing instead for the idea of spiritual deliverance (e.g., "deliver us" in ESV, KJV/NKJV; "set us free" in NRSV; "rescue us" in NASB, NIV, NET). F. F. Bruce represents this perspective well when he comments, "Christ's self-oblation not only procures for his people the forgiveness of their past sins; it delivers them from the realm in which sin is irresistible into the realm where he himself is Lord."[19]

However, Dunn makes an important point: "The verb (*exairein*) is not much used in Greek writing in the sense of 'rescue, deliver from', but occurs

---

18. Bruce: "This is the only occurrence of ἐξαιρέομαι in Paul: he prefers σῴζω, ῥύομαι, ἐλευθερόω, or (ἐξ)αγοράζω to express the saving act of God in Christ" (*Galatians*, 75).

19. Bruce, *Galatians*, 75. Cf. Moo: "the cross of Christ is the decisive and uniquely sufficient means to rescue sinners from death. Embracing Christ's cross through faith is all that is needed to effect this rescue and to bring believers into the 'new creation' (6:15)" (*Galatians*, 71). Similarly, Dunn: "In earliest Christian understanding, Christ's death was the key to deliverance from the seductive and corrupting introversion of this age's self-delusion, since by his death he broke both the power of sin and the power of death" (*Galatians*, 36).

frequently in the LXX in this sense, particularly as a physical act of release from enemies and troubles (regularly in the idiom, 'rescue from the hand of . . .')."[20] Understanding ἐξαιρέω in 1:4 as a "physical act of release from enemies" seems to be more in line with the regathering of exiles motif in Isaiah 49:5-6; 52:11-12. The phrase "this present evil age" (τοῦ αἰῶνος τοῦ ἐνεστῶτος πονηροῦ) in 1:4 then refers to the evil world nations and powers that oppose the will of God and obstruct the full restoration of Israel. Keener articulates this perspective well when he explains, "Especially in Judea and Galilee, many Jews believed that the present age was under the dominion of evil forces, but that God would exalt his people in the age to come . . . God would bring to an end this age and deliver his people in the coming era, when present roles would be reversed."[21]

Concerning Galatians 1:4, Bruce rightly observes that, "The pattern of this form of words, in which the statement about Christ's self-giving is followed by a clause of purpose, is followed closely in Tit. 2:14."[22] He wrongly concludes, however, that, "The deliverance of which Paul speaks is not out of the material world but from the evil which dominates it." Titus 2:14 alludes to the Second/Eschatological Exodus motif found in passages like Isaiah 52:1-12. Bruce's spiritual interpretation is understandable when the purpose clause ἵνα λυτρώσηται ἡμᾶς ἀπὸ πάσης ἀνομίας in Titus 2:14 is rendered "to redeem us from every lawless deed" (cf. NIV: "from all wickedness"). A better translation of the purpose clause in Titus 2:14 that is consistent with the Second Exodus motif in Isaiah 52:1-12 emphasizes the *spatial* aspect of ἀπὸ: "to redeem us [out] from all lawlessness" (ESV). The "all lawlessness" (πάσης ἀνομίας) in Titus 2:14 corresponds to "this present evil age" in Galatians 1:4—the evil world nations and powers that defy the law of God and prevent the full restoration of Israel and the kingdom of God. This spatial dimension of redemption during the Second Exodus is reflected in Isaiah 52:11: "Depart, depart, go out from there, touch nothing unclean; go out of the midst of her, purify yourselves, you who carry the vessels of the LORD." This is not to deny that the Messiah gave himself for the

---

20. Dunn, *Galatians*, 35.

21. Keener, *Galatians*, 55; similarly, Moo: "New Testament scholars generally recognize that the NT language of a 'present age' (Mark 10:30) versus 'the age to come' (Matt. 12:32) reflects apocalyptic Judaism, which divided history sharply into two phases and looked for a decisive intervention of God to end the present age and usher in the new age of salvation" (*Galatians*, 72-73). Moo (*Galatians*, 71) rightly cites Hays ("Galatians," 202) in describing the self-giving of Christ in Galatians 1:4 as an "apocalyptic rescue operation" but overlooks the Second Exodus and regathering of the exiles motifs in the OT prophets. For Moo and Hays the "apocalyptic rescue operation" is spiritual deliverance of the individual believer from the consequence and power of sin.

22. Bruce, *Galatians*, 75.

forgiveness of sins or spiritual deliverance, but Paul's emphasis in Galatians 1:4 (and Titus 2:14) seems to be the corporate redemption and restoration of Israel.[23]

The phrase "according to the will of our God and Father" (κατὰ τὸ θέλημα τοῦ θεοῦ καὶ πατρὸς ἡμῶν) at the end of Galatians 1:4 affirms that the self-giving of the Messiah for sin was in accordance with Isaiah 53. This would be the equivalent of the phrase "according to the Scriptures" in 1 Corinthians 15:3 (cf. Rom 1:1–2). More specifically, Paul may have Isaiah 53:10 in mind: "But the LORD was pleased to crush Him, putting *Him* to grief." In Isaiah 53:10, the servant's offering of himself as a guilt offering to YHWH for the sins of the people was not an accident but a part of God's plan. God will accept the destruction of the servant as a propitiatory sacrifice that wipes away his indignation toward the sins of the people.

> [6] Θαυμάζω ὅτι οὕτως ταχέως μετατίθεσθε ἀπὸ τοῦ καλέσαντος ὑμᾶς ἐν χάριτι [Χριστοῦ] εἰς ἕτερον εὐαγγέλιον, [7] ὃ οὐκ ἔστιν ἄλλο, εἰ μή τινές εἰσιν οἱ ταράσσοντες ὑμᾶς καὶ θέλοντες μεταστρέψαι τὸ εὐαγγέλιον τοῦ Χριστοῦ.
>
> [6] I am amazed that you are so quickly deserting Him who called you by the grace of Christ, for a different gospel; [7] which is *really* not another; only there are some who are disturbing you and want to distort the gospel of Christ.

The OT background for the substantive εὐαγγέλιον and its related verb forms begins in Isaiah 40:9 which speaks of the good news of Israel's liberation from exile and the restoration of the kingdom of God. The Hebrew participle מְבַשֶּׂרֶת in Isaiah 40:9 ("bearer of good news") is translated in the LXX as ὁ εὐαγγελιζόμενος. This theme of the "good news" of Israel's restoration is continued in Isaiah 52:7: "How lovely on the mountains are the feet of him who brings good news (מְבַשֵּׂר), who announces peace and brings good news (מְבַשֵּׂר) of happiness, who announces salvation, *and* says to Zion, 'Your God reigns!'" (cf. Rom 10:15). In Isaiah 61:1 a unique servant of YHWH is anointed with the spirit of God "to bring good news (לְבַשֵּׂר) to the afflicted." Thus Paul's εὐαγγέλιον in Galatians 1:6–7 is based upon the future return of Israel from exile and the long-awaited restoration of the kingdom of God described in Isaiah 40–66 through the person and work of a unique servant of YHWH (cf. Isa 42:1–9; 49:1–13; 50:4–11; 52:13—53:12; 61:1–3).[24]

---

23. Cf. ben Mordechai, *Galatians*, 126–29; Sedaca, "Salvation and the People of Israel," 4.

24. Mark Nanos observes the same Isaianic "good news" theme of Israel's endtime restoration in Jewish groups contemporary with Paul (e.g., Pss. Sol. 11.1 [ca. first

The phrase "Him who called you by the grace of Christ" (τοῦ καλέσαντος ὑμᾶς ἐν χάριτι [Χριστοῦ]) in Galatians 1:6 is debated. The majority of manuscript witnesses (𝔓51vid ℵ A B F^C Ψ 33 81 614 1175 1505 1739 1881 2464 𝔐 f vg syr^(p, h, pal) cop^bo goth arm al) read ἐν χάριτι Χριστοῦ ("in/by the grace of Christ").[25] A few manuscripts and other witnesses (𝔓46vid F* G H^vid it^(g, ar) Marcion Tertullian Cyprian Ambrosiaster Marius Victorinus Lucifer Ephraem Pelagius) have only ἐν χάριτι. This shortest reading seems best in explaining the rise of the other expansive alternates.[26]

If the shorter reading ἐν χάριτι is assumed, Galatians 1:6 states, "I am amazed that you are so quickly deserting Him who called you *in grace* for a different gospel." Based on the phrase τὸ εὐαγγέλιον τοῦ Χριστοῦ at the end of 1:7, the implied subject who is "calling" in 1:6 seems to be the Messiah. Thus the conflict in Galatians 1:6-7 is between τὸ εὐαγγέλιον τοῦ Χριστοῦ (v.7) that is characterized by the Messiah's "calling . . . in grace" (ἐν χάριτι, v.6) and the distortion of this calling/gospel by Paul's opponents. Paul seems to emphasize this grace-centered contrast in Romans 6:14-15 where he repeatedly declares that believers are "not under law but under grace" (οὐ/οὐκ . . . ὑπὸ νόμον ἀλλὰ ὑπὸ χάριν).

The phrase "him who called you" (τοῦ καλέσαντος ὑμᾶς) in Galatians 1:6 is significant. God uniquely "called" Israel out of Egyptian bondage to become his covenant nation (Hos 11:1; Isa 48:12).[27] In Isaiah 40:1-11; 41:9; 43:1-7 God will "call" the exiles of Israel again in a greater Exodus event to permanently restore the nation of Israel and the kingdom of God. In Isaiah 55 God's gracious call of redemption focuses in verse 5 on a future Davidic king's "calling": "Behold, you [sing.] will call a nation you do not know, and a nation which knows you not will run to you, because of the LORD your

---

century BC]: "Sound in Zion the signal trumpet of the sanctuary; announce in Jerusalem the voice of one bringing good news [εὐαγγελιζομένου]"; Qumran texts 1QH 18.14-15; 11QMelch 2.15-24; 4Q 521.12; CD 2.12 (*Irony of Galatians*, 290-91).

25. Alternate readings include χάριτι Ἰησοῦ Χριστοῦ (D 326 1241S itd syrh with *), χάριτι Χριστοῦ Ἰησοῦ (copsa Jerome), and χάριτι θεοῦ (7 327 336 Origenlat Theodoret).

26. Bruce Metzger: "The Committee found it difficult to decide whether transcriptional probabilities or external evidence should be allowed the greater weight in choosing among the five variant readings. On the one hand, the absence of any genitive qualifying ἐν χάριτι . . . has the appearance of being the original reading, which copyists supplemented . . . On the other hand however, a majority of the Committee was unwilling to adopt a reading that is supported by only part of the Western tradition" (*Textual Commentary*, 520).

27. Cf. God's "calling" of Abraham to a redemptive and covenantal relationship (Isa 51:2) and the call of God to repentance (cf. Isa 50:2; 65:12; Jer 7:13; Hos 11:2). Paul's "calling" language elsewhere (e.g., Rom 9:7, 12, 25; 11:29) seems to emphasize inclusion among faithful Israel, the covenant people of God who will experience the end-time redemption/salvation.

God, even the Holy One of Israel; for He has glorified you." The Messiah's calling of the nations in Isaiah 55:5 likely undergirds Paul's "calling" language in Galatians 1:6.

Some characteristics of the opponents' "different gospel" (ἕτερον εὐαγγέλιον, 1:6) and their "distortion of the gospel of Christ" (μεταστρέψαι τὸ εὐαγγέλιον τοῦ Χριστοῦ, 1:7) are implied in the rest of the epistle: perfection in the flesh (3:3), the observance of days, months, seasons, and years (4:10), circumcision (5:2-4; 6:12-13), and seeking to be justified by law (5:4). Thus, most commentators view the error of Paul's opponents as requiring the observance of the Mosaic law in addition to belief/faith in Jesus as the Messiah.

However, if Paul's first missionary journey in Acts 13-14 is the background for his epistle to the Galatians, then Acts 15:1 captures the heart of the conflict in the epistle: "Some men came down from Judea and *began* teaching the brethren, 'Unless you are circumcised according to the custom of Moses, you cannot be saved.'"[28] Although most interpreters understand the language of "being saved" as the spiritual experience of individual conversion, the OT basis of Israel's eschatological "salvation" points to the idea of becoming a part of faithful Israel and experiencing the nation's future/eschatological salvation/restoration.

In Paul's time, a prevailing Jewish belief was that only Jews had a future inheritance in the Messianic age since God had established his covenant with Israel alone.[29] This explains why the rabbis believed that the only way

---

28. The connection between Paul's opponents in Galatians and the Jerusalem leadership (cf. "the coming of certain men from James," 2:12) suggests that the matters concerning gentile believers which were resolved in Acts 15 were not yet resolved at the time Paul wrote Galatians. If Paul wrote Galatians after the Jerusalem Council, then his opponents were undermining the apostolic resolutions of Acts 15. If Paul wrote Galatians to the churches in South Galatia prior to the Jerusalem Council in Acts 15, then the apostle's visit described in Galatians 4:13 is the same one described in Acts 14:21. The issues Paul addresses in Galatians are the same issues debated at the Jerusalem Council in Acts 15 concerning the inclusion of gentile believers in the covenant community. In Acts 15:24 the Jewish leaders write to the gentile believers, "we have heard that some of our number to whom we gave no instruction have disturbed (ταράσσω) you with *their* words, unsettling your souls" while in Galatians 1:7 Paul is upset that "there are some who are disturbing (ταράσσω) you and want to distort the gospel of Christ." Keener: "It is probably no coincidence that the same Greek term also appears in the Jerusalem Council's public disavowal of some law-demanding Jerusalemite believers (*tines*, "certain persons") who had earlier disturbed believers in the province directly to Galatia's south and east (Acts 15:24). By speaking of *some who are unsettling you*, Paul may directly evoke the language of the widely circulated Jerusalem decree that he either had delivered or soon would deliver among them (Acts 16:4)" (*Galatians*, 63).

29. E.g., m. Sanh. 10.1: "All Israel/Jews have a share in the world to come, as it says (Isaiah 60:21), 'Your people are all righteous; they shall inherit the land forever, the

a gentile could secure an inheritance in the world to come was by legally becoming a Jew through proselyte conversion. Paul's opponents may have understood Isaiah's good news of Israel's restoration differently, with the subjugation of gentile nations (e.g., Isa 49:22; 54:3; 60:5, 11–16; 61:6; 64:2; 66:20) and only the circumcised becoming part of the people of God.[30]

Accordingly, the requirement of "circumcision" in Acts 15:1 is a reference to legal proselyte conversion. Paul's opponents from Judea were merely contending for the prevailing Jewish theology of their day. Gentile believers needed to undergo proselyte conversion to be a part of Israel and thus receive an inheritance in the coming Messianic age. Therefore, the core issues debated at the Jerusalem Council in Acts 15 concerned the legal status and covenant membership of gentile believers according to Jewish tradition. Paul would argue that allegiance to the Messiah and his teachings, rather than proselyte conversion required by Jewish law, is the basis for salvation and an inheritance in the coming Messianic kingdom.

Some may argue that "circumcision" in Acts 15:1 refers to the Mosaic law because of the phrase τῷ ἔθει τῷ Μωϋσέως ("according to the custom of Moses"). Yet the meaning of ἔθος here is debated. In Acts 6:14, a false witness accused Stephen of claiming that the Messiah will "alter the customs which Moses handed down to us" (ἀλλάξει τὰ ἔθη ἃ παρέδωκεν ἡμῖν Μωϋσῆς). At first glance, this also seems to refer to the Mosaic law, but the use of ἔθος ("custom, manner of behavior") for the law of God is unnatural. Instead, the idea of "customs" being "handed down to us" from Moses at Sinai is reminiscent of rabbinic claims concerning the origin of Judaism's Oral Torah (cf. "walk according to the customs" in Acts 21:21; "customs . . . among the Jews" in Acts 26:3; "the customs of our forefathers" in Acts 28:3). Elsewhere in Acts, ἔθος is used to denote Roman traditions (16:21; 25:16) and Paul's customary practices (17:2). Therefore, the phrase τῷ ἔθει τῷ Μωϋσέως in Acts 15:1 likely refers to a traditional procedure of circumcision according to Jewish law that was believed to have originated from Moses and was "handed down" and preserved through oral tradition.

For some, Peter's words in Acts 15:10 ("why do you put God to the test by placing upon the neck of the disciples a yoke which neither our fathers nor we have been able to bear?") prove that the issue at hand in Acts 15 is gentile observance of the Mosaic law. However, the common Jewish metaphor of the "yoke" of God's commandments emphasizes the various rabbinic applications of the Torah more than the plain requirements of

---

branch of my planting, the work of my hands, that I may be glorified'" (כָּל יִשְׂרָאֵל יֵשׁ לָהֶם חֵלֶק לָעוֹלָם הַבָּא שֶׁנֶּאֱמַר ישעיה ס וְעַמֵּךְ כֻּלָּם צַדִּיקִים לְעוֹלָם יִירְשׁוּ אָרֶץ נֵצֶר מַטָּעַי מַעֲשֵׂה יָדַי לְהִתְפָּאֵר).

30. Keener, *Galatians*, 61.

the biblical law itself (cf. Matt 23:4). According to Pharisaic Judaism, one was not keeping God's commandments properly unless he kept them as prescribed by the religious authorities—according to approved *halakah* (Hebrew "way of walking" or rule of faith). In this way, the Messiah could claim that his "yoke" was lighter than his religious contemporaries (Matt 11:29–30). Evidently, the "yoke" of God's commandments could become a heavier burden than the written law of God itself.

It seems that in Paul's time the Jewish oral traditions and official *halakah* were perceived as having the same authority as the written/biblical law of God—the two had become indistinguishable. In the Jewish mindset, "Torah" and "the law" of God included both the written Torah (Scripture) and the oral Torah (religious traditions). This perspective explains Paul's distinctions of "law" in 1 Corinthians 9:20–21 ("under the law" and "without law" versus "the law of God" and "the law of Christ"), and why some NT passages describe the "law" negatively.

It is also important to note that the four prohibitions for gentile believers in Acts 15:20, 29 are not a maximal, comprehensive list of stipulations, but rather a minimal foundation from which converts could begin to participate in the covenant community. The new gentile converts who were formerly pagan idolaters needed to cease their idolatrous practices immediately in order to begin participating in the covenant community. The four immediate prohibitions, clearly based on OT commandments, addressed their former lifestyles as idol-worshiping pagans and the practices associated with idolatry. The reason for starting (only) with these four prohibitions is recorded in 15:21: "for Moses from ancient generations has in every city those who preach him, since he is read in the synagogues every Sabbath." The implication is that these gentile believers would continue to learn and grow in the Mosaic law of God as they participated in the synagogues every Sabbath. No further requirements were necessary for the new gentile believers to begin integrating into the community of believers. This was the apostles' response to the claim that gentile believers first needed to be "circumcised" and undergo official proselyte conversion.

> ⁸ ἀλλὰ καὶ ἐὰν ἡμεῖς ἢ ἄγγελος ἐξ οὐρανοῦ εὐαγγελίζηται [ὑμῖν] παρ' ὃ εὐηγγελισάμεθα ὑμῖν, ἀνάθεμα ἔστω. ⁹ ὡς προειρήκαμεν καὶ ἄρτι πάλιν λέγω, εἴ τις ὑμᾶς εὐαγγελίζεται παρ' ὃ παρελάβετε, ἀνάθεμα ἔστω.
>
> ⁸ But even if we, or an angel from heaven, should preach to you a gospel contrary to what we have preached to you, he is to be accursed! ⁹ As we have said before, so I say again now, if any man is preaching to you a gospel contrary to what you received, he is to be accursed!

Paul's reference to "an angel from heaven" (ἄγγελος ἐξ οὐρανοῦ) in 1:8 is consistent with much Jewish literature describing heavenly angels delivering new revelations.[31] In Colossians 2:18 false teachers were "delighting in . . . the worship of the angels, taking his stand on *visions* he has seen." Paul's opponents may have argued that their position was based on heavenly revelation. In Galatians 3:19 the law was "ordered/administered through angels in/by the hand of an intermediary" (διαταγεὶς δι' ἀγγέλων ἐν χειρὶ μεσίτου).

The phrase "even if we, or an angel from heaven" (ἐὰν ἡμεῖς ἢ ἄγγελος ἐξ οὐρανοῦ) functions as a rabbinic "*kal va-chomer*" (קל וחומר, "lesser to greater") argument. If the teaching of a heavenly messenger is to be scrutinized, how much more the message of mere humans.

The phrase "as we have said before" (ὡς προειρήκαμεν) in 1:9 suggests that during Paul's initial visit to the Galatians he had warned them about those who were teaching the need for proselyte conversion in order to obtain covenant status.

A common understanding of the phrase ἀνάθεμα ἔστω ("he is to be accursed") in 1:8 is that the errant messengers are to be "delivered over to God's wrath for final judgment . . . to suffer the eternal retribution and judgment of God."[32] However, an alternate approach would center on the Hebrew word חֵרֶם that may be behind ἀνάθεμα in Galatians 1:8-9.[33] Leon Wood renders the basic meaning of the root חרם as "the exclusion of an object from the use or abuse of man and its irrevocable surrender to God . . . devoting it to the service of God or putting it under a ban for utter destruction."[34] This is the primary sense of חֵרֶם in the accounts of Jericho and Achan's sin in Joshua 6-7. If this original OT meaning of חֵרֶם is carried

---

31. E.g., 2 Enoch 1:4; Apoc. of Zeph. 2:1; 4 Ezra 2:44. Keener lists 1 Enoch 1:2; 72:1; 74:2; Jub. 4:21; 32:21; 4 Ezra 4:1; 3 Bar. 1:8; 5:1; 6:1; 4 Bar. 6:15; T. Reu. 5:3; T. Jud. 15:5; Ps.-Eup. in Eusebius, *Praep. ev.* 9.17.9; b. Ber. 51a; b. Ned. 20ab; Gen. Rab. 50:9; 68:12; 78:2 (*Galatians*, 66n68).

32. George, *Galatians*, 98. NIV translates ἀνάθεμα as "eternally condemned," NET—"condemned to hell." Bruce explains, "But why should he express himself so vehemently against those who preached a different message from his own? Partly because he held the preaching of salvation by law-keeping to be a snare and a delusion, which put the souls of men and women in jeopardy; partly, also, because of its adverse implications for the authenticity of Christ. In Paul's eyes, the acknowledgement of Jesus as Messiah logically implied the abrogation of the law . . . If Christ displaced the law as the activating centre of Paul's own life, he equally displaced the law in the economy of God, in the ordering of salvation-history. Therefore, if the law was still in force as the way of salvation and life, the messianic age had not yet dawned, and Jesus accordingly was not the Messiah. In that case Jesus had been rightly convicted and sentenced because his messianic claims were false" (*Galatians*, 83-84).

33. Hegg, *Galatians*, 35.

34. Wood, "חֵרֶם," 1:324.

through to Galatians 1:8–9, then Paul's use of ἀνάθεμα in that passage may emphasize more the notions of *exclusion* and *avoidance*. Tim Hegg explains, "Since the Hebrew word *cherem* meant that the object could not be acquired, and that all were to separate from it, the word *anathema* may also emphasize Paul's desire that the Galatians separate themselves from those teachers who might be offering this contrary message."[35]

Consignment to "hell" and the eternal wrath of God may be a result of חֵרֶם but is not an accurate definition. The original meaning seems to center on *exclusive dedication* to God, thereby prohibiting any human use/contact and resulting in *exclusion* and *avoidance*. In Galatians 1:8–9 Paul sternly warns the Galatians to avoid and mark out for exclusion the false teachers with the implication that they would be judged by God if they did not repent. Paul seems to use ἀνάθεμα similarly in Romans 9:3: ηὐχόμην γὰρ ἀνάθεμα εἶναι αὐτὸς ἐγὼ ἀπὸ τοῦ Χριστοῦ ὑπὲρ τῶν ἀδελφῶν μου ("For I could wish that I myself were accursed, *separated* from Christ for the sake of my brethren"). The idea of *exclusion* is consistent with the spatial nuance of ἀπὸ τοῦ Χριστοῦ—the apostle is contemplating his exclusion *away from* or *apart from* Christ if only his fellow Jews could be saved thereby.

Another perspective is to see ἀνάθεμα in Galatians 1:8–9 as referring to the covenant curses of Leviticus 26 and Deuteronomy 28. Paul's warning is not a pronouncement of God's eternal condemnation in hell, then, but an affirmation that those demanding proselyte conversion remain under the covenant-cursed condition of that generation. The apostle seems to express a similar sentiment later in Galatians 3:10: "as many as are of the works of the law are under a curse (ὑπὸ κατάραν)."

> [10] Ἄρτι γὰρ ἀνθρώπους πείθω ἢ τὸν θεόν; ἢ ζητῶ ἀνθρώποις ἀρέσκειν; εἰ ἔτι ἀνθρώποις ἤρεσκον, Χριστοῦ δοῦλος οὐκ ἂν ἤμην. [11] Γνωρίζω γὰρ ὑμῖν, ἀδελφοί, τὸ εὐαγγέλιον τὸ εὐαγγελισθὲν ὑπ' ἐμοῦ ὅτι οὐκ ἔστιν κατὰ ἄνθρωπον· [12] οὐδὲ γὰρ ἐγὼ παρὰ ἀνθρώπου παρέλαβον αὐτὸ οὔτε ἐδιδάχθην ἀλλὰ δι' ἀποκαλύψεως Ἰησοῦ Χριστοῦ.
>
> [10] For am I now seeking the favor of men, or of God? Or am I striving to please men? If I were still trying to please men, I would not be a bond-servant of Christ. [11] For I would have you know, brethren, that the gospel which was preached by me is not according to man. [12] For I neither received it from man, nor was I taught it, but *I received it* through a revelation of Jesus Christ.

The beginning ἄρτι ("now") in 1:10 might suggest that formerly Paul was influenced by the approval of man. This may refer to the apostle's

---

35. Hegg, *Galatians*, 35–36.

"former manner of life in Judaism" (v. 13) and his past zeal for Jewish "ancestral traditions" (v. 14). Galatians 5:11 indicates that Paul used to "preach circumcision" (εἰ περιτομὴν ἔτι κηρύσσω).

The tension between "seeking the favor of men" and being "a bondservant of Christ" in 1:10 arose from the issue of forcing gentile believers to undergo proselyte conversion (Acts 15:1). Like the Messiah, Paul conflicted with the Jewish religious authority of his time. If Paul, like his opponents, taught that gentile believers were to complete their conversion by undergoing the proselytization process (starting with the rite of circumcision) required by Judaism, he could earn favor with fellow Jewish believers and the greater Jewish community. If Paul had agreed with his opponents' position, he may not have been forced out of the synagogue in Pisidian Antioch, run out of Iconium, or stoned in Lystra.

On the contrary, the gospel Paul preached was not in accordance with Jewish religious authorities or oral traditions. Paul's gospel was received directly from the Messiah and centered on allegiance to the Messiah's teachings. Still, the apostle is not expressing a clean break from Judaism nor abandoning his Jewish heritage.[36] Paul was arguing that gentile believers did not need to undergo proselyte conversion according to Jewish tradition to be saved. Salvation was found in the person, work, and teaching of the Messiah alone for all believers.

Paul uses the same language of "receiving" (παραλαμβάνω) in 1:12 in 1 Corinthians 11:2, 23; 15:1, 3 to refer to teaching that has been passed on through human agents.[37] In Mark 7:4, concerning the Pharisees and Jews, "there are many other things which they have received [παραλαμβάνω] in order to observe, such as the washing of cups and pitchers and copper pots," which in the following verse is called "the tradition of the elders" (τὴν παράδοσιν τῶν πρεσβυτέρων). This phrase parallels Paul's reference to "my ancestral traditions" (τῶν πατρικῶν μου παραδόσεων) in Galatians 1:14. Paul formerly followed human tradition like his opponents (cf. Mark 7:8; Col 2:8), but now he proclaims the message he received directly from the Messiah and not religious traditions passed down from man.

¹³ Ἠκούσατε γὰρ τὴν ἐμὴν ἀναστροφήν ποτε ἐν τῷ Ἰουδαϊσμῷ, ὅτι καθ' ὑπερβολὴν ἐδίωκον τὴν ἐκκλησίαν τοῦ θεοῦ καὶ ἐπόρθουν αὐτήν, ¹⁴ καὶ προέκοπτον ἐν τῷ Ἰουδαϊσμῷ ὑπὲρ

---

36. Cf. Longenecker: "Paul, of course, does not deny that he himself continued as a Christian to live a basically Jewish lifestyle (cf. 1 Cor 9:19–23), or that he saw it as legitimate for Jewish believers in Jesus to continue to express their faith in the traditional forms of Judaism (cf. 1 Cor 7:17–20)" (*Galatians*, 18).

37. Keener, *Galatians*, 72.

πολλοὺς συνηλικιώτας ἐν τῷ γένει μου, περισσοτέρως ζηλωτὴς ὑπάρχων τῶν πατρικῶν μου παραδόσεων.
¹³ For you have heard of my former manner of life in Judaism, how I used to persecute the church of God beyond measure and tried to destroy it; ¹⁴ and I was advancing in Judaism beyond many of my contemporaries among my countrymen, being more extremely zealous for my ancestral traditions.

Paul supports his argument against "seeking the favor of men" and "striving to please men" (v. 10) by pointing out his "former manner of life in Judaism" (v. 13) and his "advancing in Judaism beyond many of my contemporaries among my countrymen" (v. 14). The apostle's former advancement in "Judaism" (τῷ Ἰουδαϊσμῷ, vv. 13–14) amounted to extreme zeal for "my ancestral traditions" (τῶν πατρικῶν μου παραδόσεων, v. 14).³⁸ Just as these Jewish ancestral traditions caused conflict between the religious leaders and the Messiah (e.g., Mark 7:1–13), Paul also "persecuted the church of God beyond measure and tried to destroy it" (v. 13).

Hegg sees the Jewish concept of הֲלָכָה (*halakah*) behind the term "way of life" (ἀναστροφή) in 1:13.³⁹ Keener compares the use of ἀναστροφή here to the same term in 2 Maccabees 6:23 that describes another pietist's lifestyle of faithfulness and devotion to the law of God from childhood.⁴⁰ The apostle was not abandoning all aspects of Judaism in general, nor the OT law in particular, but was expressing a specific disagreement with Pharisaic *halakha* concerning gentile associations. Hegg further discerns a parallel between Paul's usage of συνηλικιώτας ("contemporaries") in verse 14 and the Pharisees' common practice of referring to each other as *chavarim* (חברים, "friends, associates"). The apostle "still considers his former associates . . . as 'my countrymen' . . . showing clearly that he had no intention of distancing himself from his own people in spite of the fact that his primary mission was to the Gentiles."⁴¹

Keener compares Paul's persecution (διώκω) of the church of God in 1:13 to the Maccabees who pursued/persecuted (διώκω) those who violated

---

38. This seems consistent with Paul's repeated and emphatic use of the article in "*the* Judaism," perhaps signaling the particularly strict sect of Pharisaic Judaism. Keener: "*Judaism* here refers not to a former ethnicity or faith, as if Paul became a gentile or stopped following the God of Israel when he became a Christian. It refers to Jewish practice and appears especially in contexts of nationalistic resistance against foreign cultural impositions (2 Macc. 2:21; 8:1; 14:38), even when some tried to 'compel' abandonment of Jewish practice (4 Macc. 4:26)" (*Galatians*, 79).

39. Hegg, *Galatians*, 42–43.
40. Keener, *Galatians*, 78n37.
41. Hegg, *Galatians*, 43.

(1 Macc 2:46–47; 3:5) or militarily opposed (3:24; 5:22; 10:49) the Jewish law.[42] Paul may have been emulating the Maccabees who courageously fought for the Jewish way of life (Ἰουδαϊσμός) and pursued their foes (2 Macc 2:21). In this manner some Jews persecuted some of Jesus's followers in this period (1 Thess 2:14–16) and other minority Jewish sects.[43]

The phrase "the assembly of God" (τὴν ἐκκλησίαν τοῦ θεοῦ) in 1:13 recalls the covenant community of Israel, the people of God (Judg 20:2; 1 Chr 28:8; Neh 13:1). Many commentators may see a contrast between "Judaism" and "the assembly of God" in this passage so that Paul no longer considers those within Judaism as members of "the assembly of God." However, the apostle's point seems to be that those he formerly persecuted were actually *fellow members* and *included* in the covenant people of God.

It is important to reemphasize that Paul is not denouncing all aspects of Judaism in general. Nor is he teaching the abrogation of the Mosaic law or that gentile believers need not obey the OT commandments of God. Paul's issue is narrowly focused on the matter of proselyte conversion in the Judaism of his time and whether gentile believers are required to comply with traditional religious requirements. Paul's concern is chiefly with the "ancestral traditions" of "Judaism" (v. 14). These Jewish traditions refer to what later came to be called the Oral Torah (תורה שבעל פה) that was eventually compiled in the Mishnah and, after several centuries, resulted in the literature of the Talmud. In Paul's time these ancestral traditions were called "the traditions of the fathers," or sometimes just "the traditions," and were stewarded and passed on by the Pharisees.[44] The Pharisees were known for their meticulous faithfulness to ancestral traditions.[45] Keener demonstrates that Jewish heroes of the past were prepared to die even by torture for the religious traditions and customs of their ancestors (cf. 1 Macc 2:50; 2 Macc 6:1; 7:2, 8, 24, 30, 37; 4 Macc 5:33; 8:7; 9:1, 24, 29; 18:5).[46] Jews also despised apostates who departed from these traditional practices (3 Macc 1:3).[47]

42. Keener, *Galatians*, 79–80.

43. Keener cites 1QpHab 8.8–12; 9.4–7; 12.5; 4Q169 1.11; Josephus, *Ant.* 18.17; m. Yad. 4:7; t. Hag. 3:35; t. Nid. 5:3; Josephus, *Life* 272–75, 302–3 (*Galatians*, 80n44).

44. Lancaster, *Galatians*, 34. Paul identified as a Pharisee when necessary (Acts 23:6) but prioritized his allegiance to the Messiah (Phil 3:5–8; cf. 1 Cor 9:19–23).

45. Keener, *Galatians*, 83; "Mark 7:3, 8–9; Josephus, *Ant.* 13.297, 408; cf. *b. Sukkah* 28a . . . Because they often saw many of their traditions already implicit in the law of Moses (*m. ʾAbot* 1:1; *Sipre Deut.* 313.2.4), some successors of Pharisaic teachers suggested that the oral traditions even equaled (*Sipra Behuq.* par. 2.264.1.1; pq. 8.269.2.14; *Sipre Deut.* 115.1.1–2; 306.25.1; 351.1.2–3) or outranked (*m. Sanh.* 11:3) the written law" (*Galatians*, 83n81).

46. Keener, *Galatians*, 83n85.

47. Keener, *Galatians*, 83n85.

Even after his encounter with the Messiah in Acts 9, Paul identified with Pharisaic Judaism to some extent (Acts 23:6; 28:17). In Acts 28:17 Paul contended that he did not violate "the customs of our fathers" (τοῖς ἔθεσι τοῖς πατρῴοις). In Acts 22:3 Paul defends himself against Jewish accusers by asserting, "I am a Jew... educated under Gamaliel, strictly according to the law of our fathers [τοῦ πατρῴου νόμου]." Here the phrase "law of our fathers" probably refers to the Jewish law of the Pharisees that interpreted and applied the OT law according to the "ancestral traditions" of "Judaism" (Gal 1:14). Paul did confront errors of the established Judaism of his time (e.g., Col 2:8, 16–23), but these shortcomings did not diminish Paul's understanding of Israel's unique covenant privilege, the future fulfillment of God's covenant promises to Israel, and hope in the nation's eschatological restoration (Rom 3:1–2; 9:4–5).

Noel Rabbinowitz has demonstrated that the Messiah himself practiced elements of Pharisaic *halakah*. Rabbinowitz contends that the Lord's participation in the synagogue service (cf. Luke 4:14–21) and the manner in which he observed the Passover meal indicate his adherence to *halakic* principles of the oral law.[48] Rabbinowitz understands Matthew 23:2–4 as the Lord's acknowledgement of the Pharisees' legitimate occupation of the Seat of Moses, an actual synagogue chair and symbol of authority based on Deuteronomy 17:11. Although the Lord regularly attacked the Pharisees for their hypocrisy and false teachings, this was not an absolute rejection of their authority, and his disciples were to obey Pharisaic teachings regarding the Torah and *halakah* in principle.[49]

"Zeal" (ζηλωτὴς) for God and his written law is commendable throughout Scripture (Num 25:11–13; 1 Kgs 19:10; Ezra 7:23; Ps 69:9; 119:139; Acts 21:20; Tit 2:14; 1 Pet 3:13). However, Paul's extreme zeal for his "ancestral traditions" (Gal 1:14) was akin to "a zeal for God, but not in accordance with knowledge" (Rom 10:2; cf. Phil 3:6). According to Keener, Paul's violent zeal for the purity of Jewish ancestral traditions against the contamination of Hellenism and gentile influence may have been modeled after the Maccabees (1 Macc 2:26, 54).[50] Paul's violent zeal was directed against those who undermined the established Jewish religion and authority, such as the Hellenist Jewish Christians (Acts 6:13–14; 8:1–3; 11:19–20). His family's diaspora background may have made Paul even more eager to identify with his Jewish heritage.[51]

---

48. Rabbinowitz, "Matthew 23:2–4," 436.
49. Rabbinowitz, "Matthew 23:2–4," 446–47.
50. Keener, *Galatians*, 84.
51. Keener, *Galatians*, 85–86.

¹⁵ ὅτε δὲ εὐδόκησεν [ὁ θεὸς] ὁ ἀφορίσας με ἐκ κοιλίας μητρός μου καὶ καλέσας διὰ τῆς χάριτος αὐτοῦ ¹⁶ ἀποκαλύψαι τὸν υἱὸν αὐτοῦ ἐν ἐμοί, ἵνα εὐαγγελίζωμαι αὐτὸν ἐν τοῖς ἔθνεσιν, εὐθέως οὐ προσανεθέμην σαρκὶ καὶ αἵματι ¹⁷ οὐδὲ ἀνῆλθον εἰς Ἱεροσόλυμα πρὸς τοὺς πρὸ ἐμοῦ ἀποστόλους, ἀλλὰ ἀπῆλθον εἰς Ἀραβίαν καὶ πάλιν ὑπέστρεψα εἰς Δαμασκόν.

¹⁵ But when God, who had set me apart *even* from my mother's womb and called me through His grace, was pleased ¹⁶ to reveal His Son in me so that I might preach Him among the Gentiles, I did not immediately consult with flesh and blood, ¹⁷ nor did I go up to Jerusalem to those who were apostles before me; but I went away to Arabia, and returned once more to Damascus.

The statement "set me apart from my mother's womb and called me" in 1:15 echoes similar language in Isaiah 49:1 and Jeremiah 1:5. Paul's being "set apart" by God from his mother's womb (1:15) parallels Jeremiah's being "consecrated" by God from the womb (Jer 1:5). The prophet's calling in Jeremiah 1:5 includes "I have appointed you a prophet to the nations" which parallels Paul's calling in Galatians 1:16: "I might preach Him among the Gentiles" (cf. Rom 11:13). Keener draws attention to other parallels between Paul's calling and OT prophets: allusions to Jeremiah's call in Acts 9:15-16; Acts 26:18 alludes to Isaiah 42:6-7 (perhaps by way of 49:6); in Acts 13:47 Paul cites Isaiah 49:6 to his first audience in Galatia.[52] These allusions to OT prophets reflect Paul's self-understanding of his unique calling.[53]

In Jeremiah 3:11-12 God instructs the prophet to "proclaim these words toward the north . . . 'Return, faithless Israel . . . I will not look upon you in anger for I am gracious.'" In Jeremiah 3:14 God promises to restore the scattered northern kingdom of Israel and "bring you to Zion." At that time "all the nations will be gathered" to the exalted throne of YHWH in Jerusalem (v. 17) and "the house of Judah will walk with the house of Israel, and they will come together from the land of the north to the land that I gave your fathers as an inheritance" (v. 18). Mordechai suggests that Paul and Jeremiah may have traveled into similar regions north and west of Israel as appointed messengers of God to the nations.[54]

---

52. Keener, *Galatians*, 86.

53. Keener compares Jer 1:5 with Rom 11:13; Jer 1:8 with Acts 18:9-10; 26:17; Jer 1:10 with 2 Cor 10:8; 13:10; Isa 49:8 in 2 Cor 6:2 (*Galatians*, 86n115).

54. ben Mordechai, *Galatians*, 160. "Paul was on a mission to seek out the Gentiles of the exiled house of Israel, to let them know that *teshuva* (repentance) was possible and that YHWH had taken note of their captivity and wanted to return them to the covenant of Torah, as prophecy candidly speaks about: [Isa 42:1-3]" (*Galatians*, 160).

Paul insists that he "did not immediately consult with flesh and blood, nor did I go up to Jerusalem to those who were apostles before me" (vv. 16–17). Paul's opponents may have claimed that Paul's teaching was secondary to that of Jerusalem's true apostles, and thus the opponents' doctrine reflected a direct connection with the Messiah's original apostles.

The only two occurrences of "Arabia" (Ἀραβία) in the NT are found in Galatians (1:17; 4:25), and in 4:25 Mount Sinai is located in Arabia, possibly at modern-day Jabal al-Lawz in Saudi Arabia. Two reasons may explain Paul's trip to Arabia in 1:17. First, given the archetypal zeal of Phinehas and Elijah in Jewish tradition, Paul may have been emulating Elijah who also received a direct revelation from God related to his zeal (1 Kgs 19:5–10) and was directed to Mount Sinai (1 Kgs 19:8, 11).[55] Perhaps Paul went to Mount Sinai/Arabia to "consult" with God first before any "flesh and blood" or human apostles (Gal 1:16). Like Elijah (1 Kgs 19:15), Paul also returned to Damascus following his visit to Mount Sinai/Arabia (Gal 1:17). N. T. Wright offers an explanation of the Elijah motif in Galatians 1:13–17: "I stood in the tradition of 'zeal' going back to Phinehas and Elijah, the tradition that the Maccabean martyrs so nobly exemplified. Indeed, my persecution of the church was inspired by exactly this tradition. But the God of Israel called me, like Elijah, to step back from this zeal and to listen to him afresh."[56]

Second, Paul may have visited Arabia because of Isaiah. Keener explains that if Paul understood his calling partly in line with that of Isaiah's servant (cf. echo of Isa 49:1 in Gal 1:15), nearby Nabatea may have been an attractive mission field, if he construed Isaiah's Kedar and Nebaioth (Isa 42:11; 60:7) as Nabatea, as Josephus did (*Ant.* 1.220–21).[57] Following the servant's mission to be "a light to the nations" in Isaiah 42:6 (cf. Acts 13:47), verse 11 records, "Let the inhabitants of Sela sing aloud," which could be a reference to "Petra" located in Paul's "Arabia." Since native Nabateans spoke an ancient dialect of Arabic and were entrenched in polytheism, Paul probably began his evangelism among the substantial communities of Hellenistic and irreligious Jews throughout the Decapolis and Nabatean region east of the Jordan River.[58]

¹⁸ Ἔπειτα μετὰ ἔτη τρία ἀνῆλθον εἰς Ἱεροσόλυμα ἱστορῆσαι Κηφᾶν καὶ ἐπέμεινα πρὸς αὐτὸν ἡμέρας δεκαπέντε, ¹⁹ ἕτερον δὲ τῶν ἀποστόλων οὐκ εἶδον εἰ μὴ Ἰάκωβον τὸν ἀδελφὸν τοῦ κυρίου. ²⁰ ἃ δὲ γράφω ὑμῖν, ἰδοὺ ἐνώπιον τοῦ θεοῦ ὅτι οὐ

---

55. Cf. Wright, "Paul, Arabia, and Elijah," 686.
56. Wright, "Paul, Arabia, and Elijah," 689.
57. Keener, *Galatians*, 92.
58. Keener, *Galatians*, 95–96.

ψεύδομαι. ²¹ ἔπειτα ἦλθον εἰς τὰ κλίματα τῆς Συρίας καὶ τῆς Κιλικίας· ²² ἤμην δὲ ἀγνοούμενος τῷ προσώπῳ ταῖς ἐκκλησίαις τῆς Ἰουδαίας ταῖς ἐν Χριστῷ. ²³ μόνον δὲ ἀκούοντες ἦσαν ὅτι Ὁ διώκων ἡμᾶς ποτε νῦν εὐαγγελίζεται τὴν πίστιν ἥν ποτε ἐπόρθει, ²⁴ καὶ ἐδόξαζον ἐν ἐμοὶ τὸν θεόν.

¹⁸ Then three years later I went up to Jerusalem to become acquainted with Cephas, and stayed with him fifteen days. ¹⁹ But I did not see any other of the apostles except James, the Lord's brother. ²⁰ (Now in what I am writing to you, I assure you before God that I am not lying.) ²¹ Then I went into the regions of Syria and Cilicia. ²² I was *still* unknown by sight to the churches of Judea which were in Christ; ²³ but only, they kept hearing, "He who once persecuted us is now preaching the faith which he once tried to destroy." ²⁴ And they were glorifying God because of me.

The solemn oath statement in 1:20 focuses attention to Paul's concern throughout this section: the minimal contact he had with the Jerusalem apostles so that no one could accuse him of having learned his gospel from them (1:1, 12, 17). Evidently Paul's opponents were claiming that Paul's apostleship came from the Jerusalem leaders and that his understanding of the Messiah was received secondhand. Therefore, Paul ought to defer to the authority of the Jerusalem apostles and their associates.

Dunn explains the oath statement in 1:20 by suggesting that Paul's version of what had happened on his first visit to Jerusalem was being challenged (cf. Acts 9:27).[59] The apostle's claim to have met only two of the Jerusalem leadership during a fifteen-day visit seemed unlikely. Therefore, Paul needed to convince the Galatians that he had only gone to Jerusalem to get to know Peter and that he had seen no one else of significance except James in passing.

τὴν πίστιν ("the faith") in 1:23 refers to a core body of truth that followers of the Messiah received and affirmed (cf. Rom 1:5; 1 Tim 1:19; 4:1, 6; 6:10). Rather than later creeds or doctrinal formulations, τὴν πίστιν here seems to refer to the Messiah's teachings on the OT law of God (cf. Matt 5:17-19; 28:19-20).[60] Dunn observes that in Paul's Jewish background, "the characteristic usage of the most closely related concept [τό πίστις] denotes

---

59. Dunn, *Galatians*, 78.

60. William Baird understands τὴν πίστιν in 1:23 as "the proclamation of the living Son who has been revealed to Paul" ("What Is the Kerygma," 187); similarly, Hegg: "confessing Yeshua as the true Messiah" (*Galatians*, 55). Moo: "'Faith' in Paul normally refers to the act of believing . . . 'faith' in Christ, came to be a way of referring, objectively, to the movement itself" (*Galatians*, 114).

rather 'faithfulness' (אֱמוּנָה) ... in LXX *pistis* mostly translates *emunah*."[61] Keener notes the possibility that Paul's "preaching the faith" in 1:23 at this point may have included the rite of circumcision (cf. 5:11).[62]

The combination of δοξάζω + ἐν + personal pronoun in 1:24 is comparatively rare. Thus Paul seems to be alluding to the same formulation in LXX Isaiah 49:3: "and he said to me, 'You are my servant Israel, and in you I will be glorified'" (καὶ εἶπέν μοι δοῦλός μου εἶ σύ Ισραηλ καὶ ἐν σοὶ δοξασθήσομαι).[63] Paul alluded to this same Servant passage earlier in describing his "call" (v.15, Isa 49:1; cf. Isa 49:6 in Acts 13:47). These allusions suggest that Paul views his mission to the gentiles in terms of the prophecies about the Servant in Isaiah.

---

61. Dunn, *Galatians*, 84.
62. Keener, *Galatians*, 107.
63. Moo, *Galatians*, 115.

3

Commentary on Galatians 2

> ²:¹Ἔπειτα διὰ δεκατεσσάρων ἐτῶν πάλιν ἀνέβην εἰς Ἱεροσόλυμα μετὰ Βαρναβᾶ συμπαραλαβὼν καὶ Τίτον· ² ἀνέβην δὲ κατὰ ἀποκάλυψιν· καὶ ἀνεθέμην αὐτοῖς τὸ εὐαγγέλιον ὃ κηρύσσω ἐν τοῖς ἔθνεσιν, κατ' ἰδίαν δὲ τοῖς δοκοῦσιν, μή πως εἰς κενὸν τρέχω ἢ ἔδραμον.
>
> ²:¹ Then after an interval of fourteen years I went up again to Jerusalem with Barnabas, taking Titus along also. ² It was because of a revelation that I went up; and I submitted to them the gospel which I preach among the Gentiles, but *I did so* in private to those who were of reputation, for fear that I might be running, or had run, in vain.

In 1:6 the threat against Paul's "gospel" is the turning away from "Him who called you in/by grace" (τοῦ καλέσαντος ὑμᾶς ἐν χάριτι). Hence the essence of Paul's gospel seems to be the OT call of repentance and restoration for dispersed Israel, issued by the Messiah, "in/by grace." This call of restoration is "in/by grace" in that it is not encumbered by religious rites or Jewish tradition. Similarly, at the Jerusalem Council in Acts 15 James decided, "it is my judgment that we do not trouble (παρενοχλέω, *cause unnecessary difficulty*) those who are turning to God from among the Gentiles" (v. 19), and "to lay upon you no greater burden than these essentials" (v. 28). The Messiah's call of salvation is graciously based on faithfulness to him and his teaching.

Nevertheless Paul needed the Jerusalem leadership's approval for credibility. The apostle may have been concerned that after having preached his gospel to the gentiles, the Jerusalem community and her leaders might not approve their membership in the visible covenant community.

It is important to note that James (1:19) was one of "those who were of reputation" (2:2). In the Epistle of James, the phrases νόμον τέλειον τὸν τῆς ἐλευθερίας ("the perfect law, the law of liberty," Jas 1:25) and νόμον . . . βασιλικὸν ("the royal law," 2:8) indicate James's affirmation of the OT law of God.[1] Against those who argue that Paul's gospel message was "justification by faith alone" with no regard for the law of God, it is unreasonable to think that Paul could have disagreed with James on the perpetuity of the OT law. If Paul would have "submitted" (2:2) a gospel that abrogated the law of God, it would not have been approved by James nor any other Jerusalem leader.

> [3] ἀλλ' οὐδὲ Τίτος ὁ σὺν ἐμοί, Ἕλλην ὤν, ἠναγκάσθη περιτμηθῆναι· [4] διὰ δὲ τοὺς παρεισάκτους ψευδαδέλφους, οἵτινες παρεισῆλθον κατασκοπῆσαι τὴν ἐλευθερίαν ἡμῶν ἣν ἔχομεν ἐν Χριστῷ Ἰησοῦ, ἵνα ἡμᾶς καταδουλώσουσιν, [5] οἷς οὐδὲ πρὸς ὥραν εἴξαμεν τῇ ὑποταγῇ, ἵνα ἡ ἀλήθεια τοῦ εὐαγγελίου διαμείνῃ πρὸς ὑμᾶς.
>
> [3] But not even Titus, who was with me, though he was a Greek, was compelled to be circumcised. [4] But *it was* because of the false brethren secretly brought in, who had sneaked in to spy out our liberty which we have in Christ Jesus, in order to bring us into bondage. [5] But we did not yield in subjection to them for even an hour, so that the truth of the gospel would remain with you.

When Paul writes that Titus was not compelled to be circumcised (2:3), he means that Titus was not forced to undergo proselyte conversion according to Jewish legal requirements of the time.[2] Paul never denied that

---

1. Regarding νόμον τέλειον τὸν τῆς ἐλευθερίας in James 1:25, Peter Davids explains, "there is absolutely no question that Jews saw their law as perfect (Pss. 19:7; 119; Aristeas 31; Rom. 7:12), that they found joy in its observance (Pss. 1:2; 19:7-11; 40:6-8; Pss 119; Sir. 6:23-31; 51:13-22), and even that they saw the law giving freedom ([*Mishna Aboth*] 3:5; 6:2; [*Baba Kamma*] 8:6; [Babylonian Talmud *Baba Metzia*] 85b). E. Stauffer, 'Gesetz,' claims to find the very expression 'law of freedom' in 1QS 10:6, 8, 11, and this has been supported by S. Légasse, 338-339 . . . It is within this Jewish world that one can understand the phrase. For the Jewish Christian the law is still the will of God, but Messiah has come and perfected it and given his new law . . . one must agree with Davies that James sees Jesus' reinterpretation of the law as a new law (cf. 2:8, royal law . . .)" (*James*, 99-100).

2. E.g., Talmud tractate Yebam. 46b: "Our Rabbis taught: 'If a proselyte was circumcised but had not performed the prescribed ritual ablution,' R. Eliezer said, 'Behold he

circumcision was a commandment of God (Gen 17) or that new believers would eventually practice circumcision as they matured in faith (cf. Acts 15:21). In 2:3 there seems to be a distinction between the commandment of God regarding circumcision and the rite of proselyte circumcision built upon Jewish tradition (cf. 1 Cor 7:19: "Circumcision is nothing, and uncircumcision is nothing, but *what matters is* the keeping of the commandments of God"). Paul was not teaching the abolition of the commandment of circumcision but resisting the notion that righteousness and covenant membership could be merited through Jewish religion.

During the Maccabean revolt, Jewish identity was a life or death matter, and the Greek Seleucids prohibited Jewish circumcision with the death penalty. In response, Jewish religious leaders decided that circumcision for proselytes was the only acceptable way for a gentile convert to be considered an equal member of the Jewish community. Greek and Roman culture viewed proselyte circumcision as an irrevocable rejection of the gods, and so for the Jewish person of the first century, a gentile undergoing proselyte circumcision expressed an undeniable commitment and loyalty to the Jewish people.

Traditional Christian interpreters tend to understand καταδουλώσουσιν ("bondage") in 2:4 and ζυγῷ δουλείας ("yoke of slavery") in 5:1 as the OT law of Moses. Thus Paul seems to be urging the Galatians to leave the enslaving OT law behind and move on to "the liberty which we have in Christ Jesus" (2:4). In the preceding context, however, the "bondage" and "yoke of slavery" probably refer to "my former manner of life in Judaism" (1:13) and "my ancestral traditions" (1:14)—the burdensome stipulations of the Jewish religious authorities in Paul's time.

Avi ben Mordechai clarifies that the liberty and bondage spoken of in Galatians 2:4 refer to Jewish oral law. Pharisees who came to believe in the Messiah also brought with them their entrenched religious ideologies concerning the traditions (*takanot, gezerot, ma'asim,* and *minhagim*) of the Jewish elders, including what was called *Torah Sh'ba'al Peh*, the oral law.[3] According to ben Mordechai, the oral law was an accumulation of religious enactments, precedents, and traditions not found in the OT Scriptures, but

---

is a proper proselyte; for so we find that our forefathers were circumcised and had not performed ritual ablution.' If he performed the prescribed ablution but had not been circumcised, R. Joshua said, 'Behold he is a proper proselyte; for so we find that the mothers had performed ritual ablution but had not been circumcised.' The Sages, however, said, 'Whether he had performed ritual ablution but had not been circumcised or whether he had been circumcised but had not performed the prescribed ritual ablution, he is not a proper proselyte, unless he has been circumcised and has also performed the prescribed ritual ablution.'"

3. ben Mordechai, *Galatians*, 173.

vigorously promoted by Hillel and Shammai a full generation before Paul.[4] ben Mordechai demonstrates the prevalence of Pharisaic oral law in the time of Paul by citing Josephus[5] and Eusebius,[6] and concludes,

> [T]o say to a Jew inside or outside of *Eretz Israel*, "We all need Torah Judaism," or "We need to return to the Torah," it is automatically understood to mean, "We must follow and obey the Rabbis." There is no line of demarcation separating between the Written Law and Rabbinic Law; they are understood to be one and the same. Outside of *Eretz Israel*, this is not so well defined. But, in *HaAretz*, it is well defined. Generally speaking, eight out of ten Israelis want nothing to do with the religion of Jewish Orthodoxy. For the *am haaretz* (common people) of Israel, they see a religion that is impossible to keep, and since this religion calls itself "Torah Judaism," they therefore conclude that the Torah is impossible to observe, and so they run from it.[7]

⁶ ἀπὸ δὲ τῶν δοκούντων εἶναί τι,—ὁποῖοί ποτε ἦσαν οὐδέν μοι διαφέρει· πρόσωπον [ὁ] θεὸς ἀνθρώπου οὐ λαμβάνει—ἐμοὶ γὰρ οἱ δοκοῦντες οὐδὲν προσανέθεντο, ⁷ ἀλλὰ τοὐναντίον ἰδόντες ὅτι πεπίστευμαι τὸ εὐαγγέλιον τῆς ἀκροβυστίας καθὼς Πέτρος τῆς περιτομῆς, ⁸ ὁ γὰρ ἐνεργήσας Πέτρῳ εἰς ἀποστολὴν τῆς περιτομῆς ἐνήργησεν καὶ ἐμοὶ εἰς τὰ ἔθνη, ⁹ καὶ γνόντες τὴν χάριν τὴν δοθεῖσάν μοι, Ἰάκωβος καὶ Κηφᾶς καὶ Ἰωάννης, οἱ δοκοῦντες στῦλοι εἶναι, δεξιὰς ἔδωκαν ἐμοὶ καὶ Βαρναβᾷ κοινωνίας, ἵνα ἡμεῖς εἰς τὰ ἔθνη, αὐτοὶ δὲ εἰς τὴν περιτομήν· ¹⁰ μόνον τῶν πτωχῶν ἵνα μνημονεύωμεν, ὃ καὶ ἐσπούδασα αὐτὸ τοῦτο ποιῆσαι.

---

4. ben Mordechai cites the Babylonian Talmud *Shabbat* 31a for support: "Our Rabbis taught: A certain heathen once came before Shammai and asked him, 'How many Toroth have you?' 'Two,' he replied: 'the Written Torah and the Oral Torah.' 'I believe you with respect to the Written, but not with respect to the Oral Torah; make me a proselyte on condition that you teach me the Written Torah [only].' [But] he scolded and repulsed him in anger. When he went before Hillel, he accepted him as a proselyte. On the first day, he taught him, *Alef, Beth, Gimmel, Daleth*; the following day he reversed [them] to him. 'But yesterday you did not teach them to me thus,' he protested. 'Must you then not rely upon me? Then rely upon me with respect to the Oral [Torah] too'" (*Galatians*, 173).

5. "The Pharisees have delivered to the people a great many observances by succession from their fathers, which are not written in the law of Moses, and for that reason it is that the Sadducees reject them, and say that we ought to esteem those observances to be obligatory which are in the written word, but are not to observe what was derived from the tradition of our fathers" (*Ant.* 13, 10:6).

6. "And he mentions other matters as taken from the oral tradition of the Jews" (*Hist. eccl.* 4:22).

7. ben Mordechai, *Galatians*, 176.

⁶ But from those who were of high reputation (what they were makes no difference to me; God shows no partiality)—well, those who were of reputation contributed nothing to me. ⁷ But on the contrary, seeing that I had been entrusted with the gospel to the uncircumcised, just as Peter *had been* to the circumcised ⁸ (for He who effectually worked for Peter in *his* apostleship to the circumcised effectually worked for me also to the Gentiles) ⁹ and recognizing the grace that had been given to me, James and Cephas and John, who were reputed to be pillars, gave to me and Barnabas the right hand of fellowship, so that we *might go* to the Gentiles and they to the circumcised. ¹⁰ *They* only *asked* us to remember the poor—the very thing I also was eager to do.

2:6. "God shows no partiality" (πρόσωπον θεὸς ἀνθρώπου οὐ λαμβάνει): The expression πρόσωπον λαμβάνω is a literal rendering of the Hebrew phrase פָּנִים נָשָׂא, "lift the face" (e.g. of a suppliant) and thus "show favor."[8] Deuteronomy 10:17 records that God "does not show partiality nor take a bribe." In the OT and Judaism it is axiomatic that God does not judge unjustly by outward appearance alone nor exhibit self-serving prejudice (cf. 2 Chr 19:7; Job 13:10; 34:19). Here Paul means that God is not unfairly biased toward the Jerusalem apostles, relatives and disciples of the Messiah during his earthly ministry.

2:6. "those who were of reputation added nothing to me" (ἐμοὶ γὰρ οἱ δοκοῦντες οὐδὲν προσανέθεντο): Moo observes that this is the main point of the paragraph (vv. 6–10, a single sentence in the Greek text).[9] The Jerusalem leaders did not add any requirements like circumcision to Paul's evangelism ministry among Gentiles. Later in 2:10, their "only" request was to remember the poor.

2:7. "I had been entrusted with the gospel to the uncircumcised" (πεπίστευμαι τὸ εὐαγγέλιον τῆς ἀκροβυστίας): Paul's unique calling to "the foreskin" has historically been understood as evangelism among non-Israelite "gentiles." Some suggest that Paul has in mind gentile "God-fearers" who practice Judaism in varying degrees but have not undergone the final step of circumcision as required in the official proselyte conversion process of that time. However, the prophecy of Hosea (1:9–10; 7:8; 8:8, 10; 9:1, 3, 6, 17), which Paul cites in Romans 9:25–26, indicates that the group Paul has in mind in the phrase τῆς ἀκροβυστίας in Galatians 2:7 are diaspora Israelites who either were not circumcised at birth or underwent the surgical

---

8. Bruce, *Galatians*, 118.
9. Moo, *Galatians*, 131, 133.

procedure of epispasm due to Hellenistic pressures.[10] Paul's intent to seek out secularized diaspora Israelites did not preclude the opportunity for non-Israelite gentiles to embrace the Messiah of Israel and be grafted into the faithful remnant by grace through faith.

Craig Keener makes a helpful observation: "Paul's wording in 2:7 presumably implies the feature of his gospel for the gentiles that was most distinctive, or at least most relevant for the matter at hand: it was good news *for the uncircumcised*, precisely *as* those who were *uncircumcised*."[11] Yet Paul's distinctive calling is easily steered toward supersessionism.

> Paul's preaching to Gentiles would require that he make clear to them that the gracious nature of the gospel means that they should not be circumcised or put themselves under the law of Moses. Peter, on the other hand, while also making clear to a Jewish audience the gracious character of the gospel, would not necessarily bring up circumcision or the law in the same manner.[12]

According to commentators like Moo, then, Paul's distinct gospel for the uncircumcised would amount to further lawlessness. Unfortunately, Moo misunderstands the "gracious nature of the gospel"; mental affirmation of creedal dogma does not replace the need for heart obedience to the law of God. Paul's uniquely gracious gospel for uncircumcised gentiles is that Jesus of Nazareth is the promised Messiah of Israel and his death on the cross was the atoning sacrifice for the future ratification of the New Covenant with the restored nation of Israel. Secularized Israelites in exile, and even believing non-Israelite gentiles, can be forgiven of their sins and restored to a covenant relationship with God by embracing the Messiah in faith. Moreover, secularized Israelites and non-Israelite gentiles do not need to undergo proselyte conversion into Judaism to become a citizen of true Israel. They are justified by their faithfulness to the Messiah and his teachings. Therefore, if τῆς ἀκροβυστίας in Galatians 2:7 originally referred to secularized diaspora Israelites, or even gentile "God-fearers" who had not fully completed Jewish proselyte conversion, then Paul's primary concern seems to be acceptance within Judaism and proselyte conversion, and not whether "gentile" believers should obey the OT commandments.

---

10. Hall, "Epispasm," 52–57; Hall, "Circumcision," 1:1027–29; cf. ἀκροβυστία in Rom 2:25–27; 3:30; 4:9; 1 Cor 7:18–19; Eph 2:11; Col 3:11.

11. Keener, *Galatians*, 125; original emphasis.

12. Moo, *Galatians*, 134.

2:9. "James and Cephas and John, who were reputed to be pillars" (Ἰάκωβος καὶ Κηφᾶς καὶ Ἰωάννης, οἱ δοκοῦντες στῦλοι εἶναι): Commentators have suggested a deeper meaning in the word "pillars."

> [T]he word 'pillars' appears most frequently in the LXX in reference to the supports of the tabernacle and pillars of the temple ... It is likely then that the reference here is to the three as 'pillars in the temple' (as in Rev. iii.12) ... C. K. Barrett is probably correct in the further suggestion that the reference was eschatological ... there was speculation in second-Temple Judaism about the destruction and reconstitution of the Temple in the new age ... In short, James, Cephas and John were probably regarded by the Jerusalem church as pillars of the eschatological temple of God's people, that is, as the main support on which their own community was built, 'the church of God' (i.13; 1 Cor. xv.9).[13]

Dunn's implication that the new community of the eschatological temple (Christian church) replaces the old tabernacle/temple (Israel) is similar to rabbinical literature describing Abraham and Moses as "pillars of the world" (Exod. Rab. 2:13 on Exod 3:4).[14]

However, in Revelation 3:12 the overcoming believer is promised, "He who overcomes, I will make him a pillar (στῦλος) in the temple of my God." The idea of the presence of God dwelling inside/among faithful believers recalls passages like Isaiah 66:1–2 which carry no supersessionist overtones. The Hebrew Bible eagerly anticipates a new temple in the Messianic kingdom where faithful believers will gather to worship in the presence of God (Ezek 40–48).

2:10. *They* only *asked* us to remember the poor—the very thing I also was eager to do (μόνον τῶν πτωχῶν ἵνα μνημονεύωμεν, ὃ καὶ ἐσπούδασα αὐτὸ τοῦτο ποιῆσαι): In the OT, the "poor" (עֲנָוִים) were faithful believers who often lacked worldly resources because of their complete dependence upon God for their needs. Because of their uncompromising adherence to the commandments of God the "poor" are often pictured as the righteous in contrast to the rich and powerful, especially in times of gentile usurpation and religious corruption (e.g., Isa 29:19; 61:1). Dunn observes,

> Active concern for the poor was a particular and distinctive feature of Jewish law and tradition (e.g. Deut. xxiv.10–22; Pss. x.2, 9; xii.5; xiv.6; etc.; Isa. iii.14–15; x.1–2; lviii.6–7; Amos viii.4–6 ...). More to the point, however, almsgiving was widely understood within Judaism as a central and crucial expression of

---

13. Dunn, *Galatians*, 109–10.
14. Bruce, *Galatians*, 122.

covenant righteousness (Dan. iv.27; Sir. iii.30; xxix.12; xl.24; Tob. iv.10; xii.9; xiv.11) . . . What the 'pillars' asked for was that an obligation characteristically understood as a primary expression of Jewish covenant piety should be given high priority by Paul and Barnabas . . . the principle of covenant obligation on those claiming membership of the assembly of God's people should be safeguarded and affirmed at least to this, significant extent.[15]

Keener adds that religious diaspora Jews regularly sent money to Jerusalem and that accepting offerings from uncircumcised Gentiles would imply their equal status.[16] In Judaism, obedience to laws concerning care for the poor constituted a major test of a proselyte's acceptance of Torah.[17] Requiring Paul and gentile believers to care for the poor signified adherence to Jewish ethical standards based on Scripture (e.g., Deut 15:11; 24:10–22; Prov 29:7; Ezek 16:49).[18] Paul's affirmation in the phrase, "the very thing I also was eager to do" (Gal 2:10) reveals that the apostle's faith in the Messiah did not diminish his Jewish piety in any way, but extended it to uncircumcised "gentile" believers as equally part of the nation of Israel.

[11] Ὅτε δὲ ἦλθεν Κηφᾶς εἰς Ἀντιόχειαν, κατὰ πρόσωπον αὐτῷ ἀντέστην, ὅτι κατεγνωσμένος ἦν. [12] πρὸ τοῦ γὰρ ἐλθεῖν τινας ἀπὸ Ἰακώβου μετὰ τῶν ἐθνῶν συνήσθιεν· ὅτε δὲ ἦλθον, ὑπέστελλεν καὶ ἀφώριζεν ἑαυτὸν φοβούμενος τοὺς ἐκ περιτομῆς. [13] καὶ συνυπεκρίθησαν αὐτῷ [καὶ] οἱ λοιποὶ Ἰουδαῖοι, ὥστε καὶ Βαρναβᾶς συναπήχθη αὐτῶν τῇ ὑποκρίσει. [14] ἀλλ᾽ ὅτε εἶδον ὅτι οὐκ ὀρθοποδοῦσιν πρὸς τὴν ἀλήθειαν τοῦ εὐαγγελίου, εἶπον τῷ Κηφᾷ ἔμπροσθεν πάντων, Εἰ σὺ Ἰουδαῖος ὑπάρχων ἐθνικῶς καὶ οὐχὶ Ἰουδαϊκῶς ζῇς, πῶς τὰ ἔθνη ἀναγκάζεις Ἰουδαΐζειν;

[11] But when Cephas came to Antioch, I opposed him to his face, because he stood condemned. [12] For prior to the coming of certain men from James, he used to eat with the Gentiles; but when they came, he *began* to withdraw and hold himself aloof, fearing the party of the circumcision. [13] The rest of the Jews joined him in hypocrisy, with the result that even Barnabas was carried away by their hypocrisy. [14] But when I saw that they were not straightforward about the truth of the gospel, I said to Cephas in the presence of all, "If you, being a Jew, live like the Gentiles and not like the Jews, how *is it that* you compel the Gentiles to live like Jews?

15. Dunn, *Galatians*, 112–13.
16. Keener, *Galatians*, 132n480.
17. Keener, *Galatians*, 135; Keener cites Schiffman, "Jewish Christian Schism," 124.
18. Keener, *Galatians*, 135–36.

Moo observes that "this text was seen as one important indicator of a fundamental theological split between Paul and Peter, a split that cleaved the early church into two parts."[19] This grave misunderstanding, however, arises when Jewish purity laws are falsely equated with biblical dietary commandments. The conflict in this text arises from Peter's oversensitivity to Pharisaic Judaism, not the biblical law of God.

A likely factor in Peter's visit to Antioch (v. 11) was the region's large diaspora Jewish population.[20] Keener explains, "Its ties to the east and the proximity of Judea, then governed as part of Syria, probably gave Antioch's Jewish community stronger Judean connections than most other Diaspora cities. Jews and Christians continued in active contact in Antioch at least into the fourth century."[21] Interestingly, Josephus claims, "They [Jews of Antioch] also made proselytes of a great many of the Greeks perpetually, and thereby, after a sort, brought them to be a portion of their own body."[22] While most Christian interpreters would understand Josephus's statement here as describing the proselyte conversion of non-Israelite Greek gentiles into Judaism, the precise ethnicity of these "Greeks" is not specified. While non-Israelite gentiles were probably included, Josephus may also be describing Hellenized/secularized Jews/Israelites who lived like "Greeks" undergoing proselyte conversion to officially become part of or rejoin the religious Jewish community.

The phrase τοὺς ἐκ περιτομῆς in Galatians 2:12 probably refers to the faction described in Acts 15:1: "Some men came down from Judea and *began* teaching the brethren, 'Unless you are circumcised according to the custom of Moses, you cannot be saved'" (cf. Acts 10:45; 11:2; Rom 4:12; Col 4:11; Titus 1:10).

Dunn helpfully points out that Jewish eating was not only governed by the biblical food laws, but also by "various traditions which had grown round these."[23] For the religious, eating moved beyond straightforward matters of unclean foods (Lev 11, Deut 14) and animal sacrifice/blood (Lev 17:10-14; Deut 12:16, 23-24) to a self-isolating fear of being contaminated by gentile idolatry (4 Macc 5.2; cf. 1 Cor 8-10). So for Peter, the issue in Galatians 2:11-14 is not whether he could violate the law of God and consume

---

19. Moo, *Galatians*, 146.
20. Josephus, *J.W.* 7.43-45; Dunn, *Galatians*, 116.
21. Keener, *Galatians*, 144.
22. Josephus, *J.W.* 7.45.
23. Dunn, *Galatians*, 118.

unclean animals or blood. The tension centers on strict adherence to Jewish purity traditions that were intended to safeguard law compliance.[24]

> The importance of these laws and traditions within second-Temple Judaism should not be underestimated . . . As with circumcision, the Maccabean crisis made the food laws a test case of national loyalty and religious faithfulness (1 Macc. i.62-3; 2 Macc. v.27) . . . At this time the Pharisees were already noted for their concern to erect a purity hedge round their table-fellowship (see again Mark vii.2) . . . In this context it is no surprise that Jesus was remembered as causing no little surprise and offence by the fact that he evidently ignored at least some aspects of these various rulings and traditions (e.g. Mark ii.16; Matt. xi.19; Luke xiv.12-24).[25]

Thus the issue in Galatians 2:11-14 is not obedience to the biblical dietary laws, but contact with those who may not have adhered to an acceptable level of Jewish purity. As Dunn shows, Jewish texts like *Jubilees* 22.16 ("Eat not with them [Gentiles] . . . for their works are unclean") and m. 'Ohal. 18.7 ("the dwelling-places of Gentiles are unclean") suggest that the general practice for pious Jews was to refrain from all social contact with gentiles who, as a whole, were perceived to be "unclean" (cf. Acts 10:14; 11:3, 8).[26]

The purity of table fellowship was of central concern for Pharisaic Judaism.[27] According to *Tosefta 'Abodah Zarah* 4.6, diaspora Jews who attended gentile banquets were idolaters even if they brought their own kosher food and drink.[28] According to *'Abot de Rabbi Nathan* 32, §72B, a pious Jew should not eat the food of an *'am ha'ares*, a Jewish commoner not educated in the law (cf. also 31, §68; *b. Berakot* 43b; *y. Demai* 2.3), since his food must be presumed to be untithed (*t. Demai* 3.7).[29] A pious person who oversaw such a person's banquet must be able to certify that all the food had been properly tithed. Some later rabbis compared eating with uncircumcised

---

24. Dunn explains, "The designation of various foods as 'unclean' brought table-fellowship very much within the realm of purity, where further rulings (as in Mark vii.2-4) would be an obvious way to safeguard still more effectively the purity of the meal table . . . devout diaspora Jews were purity conscious (Philo, *Spec. Leg.* iii.205-6; *Sib. Or.* iii.591-2), and the policy of 'separation' from table-fellowship is clearly motivated by the same fundamental purity concerns" (*Galatians*, 118).

25. Dunn, *Galatians*, 118-19.

26. Dunn, *Galatians*, 119.

27. Cf. *Pesikta de-Rav Kahana*; *Seder Eliahu Rabba*, "Aggadat Bereshit"; Tacitus, *Histories* 5.5.1-2.

28. Keener, *Galatians*, 149n598.

29. Keener, *Galatians*, 154.

persons to eating unclean flesh (*Pirqe Rabbi Eliezer* 29).³⁰ The Qumran sect was even more extreme than the Pharisees, insisting on separating from the rest of Israel, the "perverse" community (1QS 5.1-2, 10; 8.13; 9.20; 4Q259 3.3-4; 4.1; CD 8.8; 19.20).³¹

> Post-Maccabean Judaism was riven with factionalism. There were evidently degrees of strictness in the observance of the rulings and traditions, not least regarding table-fellowship: the Pharisees 'separated' themselves from the less scrupulous . . . the Essenes were even more rigorous; Jesus himself was criticized for not being strict enough . . . As we shall see, within this intra-Jewish polemic, those who regarded themselves as 'the righteous' did not hesitate to describe other Jews as 'sinners' . . . or to castigate their Jewish opponents as acting like Gentiles (see on ii.14). *Jubilees* was itself a factional document and the Mishnah contains the traditions of the faction which subsequently was to dominate Judaism . . . the meal table was a sensitive issue, and some group would eye the practice of another group with suspicion to see what level of observance they maintained.³²

Accordingly, Dunn provides a more accurate explanation of the conflict in Galatians 2:11-14:

> Peter and the other Jewish believers were sharing table-fellowship with Gentile believers on less clearly defined Jewish terms . . . without asking too many questions (cf. 1 Cor. x.27), though presumably on the assumption that the Gentile believers would have been mindful of the basic food rules. The James' people, having come to Antioch to visit primarily the Jewish believers (cf. ii.9), would then have been shocked at the degree of laxness being shown by these Jewish believers and criticized them accordingly . . . It is unlikely that *all* the Jewish Christians would have abandoned so completely their whole religious heritage on this crucial point, so important in their history and for their identity; or that having done so, it could have failed to cause considerable comment, not to say uproar at the complete defection of so many Jews in a strong Jewish colony, long before this . . . assuming that many or most, if not all of the early Gentile converts in Antioch came from the ranks of proselytes and God-fearing Gentiles, it would have been unnecessary for the Jewish-Christians to abandon the food laws so completely . . . The talk

---

30. Keener, *Galatians*, 155.
31. Keener, *Galatians*, 155n662.
32. Dunn, *Galatians*, 120.

of 'Gentile sinners' and 'living like Gentiles' was probably the language of intra-Jewish polemic—more scrupulous Jews condemning those who were relatively less scrupulous as unfaithful to their common heritage . . . Here also may lie the significance of Paul's description of Peter's conduct in terms of 'separating himself', since this was precisely what Pharisees and Essenes did in their table-fellowship—separated themselves from others, in order that they might maintain a greater purity and fidelity to the covenant than the others, despite the fact that the latter also understood themselves to be members of the covenant.[33]

Unfortunately, most commentators seem to misunderstand Galatians 2:14. Moo, for example, writes, "Paul's claim that Peter is 'living like a Gentile' in verse 14 appears to suggest that Peter had gone farther and had begun to give up Jewish scruples about food in general. . . . Peter would have been acting on the basis of the vision he had received in Acts 10, where God showed him that there were no truly 'impure' foods."[34]

In contrast, there is another way to understand Peter's sheet vision in Acts 10 in which God is not changing his mind about clean and unclean animals. When the sheet comes down in front of Peter, "there were in it all *kinds of* four-footed animals and crawling creatures of the earth and birds of the air" (Acts 10:12). The phrase "all *kinds of* four-footed animals" would include clean and unclean animals. The fact that this sheet was coming down from the sky, "lowered by four corners to the ground" (Acts 10:11) indicates that all of the animals, both clean and unclean, were forced towards the center of the sheet, coming into close contact with each other.

Pharisaic purity laws deemed any clean animal that came into contact with an unclean animal as unclean itself. This was similar to the hand-washing controversy in Mark 7, where the Pharisees taught that all Jews must wash their hands before eating in case they had come into contact with a gentile or anything unclean. The term κοινός is used in Mark 7:1 to refer to the disciples' dirty hands because it was believed that dirt defiled their

---

33. Dunn, *Galatians*, 121–22; similarly, Keener: "it seems highly unlikely that all Jews present would have compromised their traditional food laws; most Diaspora Jews observed food laws. Presumably, most of them abhorred unclean foods. Perhaps Antioch simply determined to ask fewer questions, trusting gentile hosts' sensitivity to their concerns (cf. 1 Cor. 10:27). Perhaps the issue was treating uncircumcised gentiles as spiritual peers, as if they were full proselytes (and thus essentially Israelites) rather than merely God-fearers or righteous gentiles. Some Pharisees had joined the Jerusalem movement (Acts 15:5) and undoubtedly exerted disproportionate influence on account of their status, and pure table fellowship was a primary defining characteristic for them" (*Galatians*, 150).

34. Moo, *Galatians*, 146.

hands, and that this defilement would transfer to the individual if a person ate or drank with dirty ("common") hands. This, in turn, would make the person κοινός or "defiled, impure."

So for a Jew like Peter who kept both the Torah and Jewish purity laws, the sheet with both clean and unclean animals in close contact would have been very disturbing. Although there were clean animals on the sheet, Peter refused to eat any of them because they had come into contact with unclean animals and were thus considered κοινός according to Jewish purity laws. This explains the repeated heavenly command for Peter to "kill and eat" (Acts 10:13) and Peter's adamant protest, "By no means, Lord, for I have never eaten anything unholy (κοινὸν) and unclean (ἀκάθαρτον)" (Acts 10:14). From a Jewish perspective, the command to "kill and eat," if referring to unclean animals forbidden by Torah, would be a command to sin, something impossible for God to command. Therefore, when the voice from heaven explains, "What God has cleansed, no *longer* consider unholy [κοίνου][35]" in Acts 10:15, the point is not that God is rescinding the OT dietary laws,[36] but that whatever God cleanses (i.e., the gentiles Peter will soon come into contact with[37]) is not to be considered κοινός per Jewish purity laws.

The voice from heaven does not correct Peter's use of the word ἀκάθαρτος, as if God now contradicts himself by considering "unclean" animals "clean." The point of concern in Acts 10:15 is what Jewish purity law would consider κοινός—coming into contact with gentiles or anything considered unclean—which would prevent Peter from eventually meeting with Cornelius and hinder the advance of the gospel among gentiles. In effect, Acts 10:15 functions as a rebuke against Peter for opposing the will of God by following the religious traditions of men.

According to David Stern, Acts 10–11 does not teach that "the laws of *kashrut* had been abrogated," but that "keeping *kosher* became a less

---

35. Cf. "ritually unclean" (NET), "impure" (NIV), "common" (ESV).

36. The NASB interpretation "no *longer* consider unholy" can be misleading because it implies the reversal of something that was formerly true when this is not required in the Greek text: Ἃ ὁ θεὸς ἐκαθάρισεν, σὺ μὴ κοίνου.

37. The *three* occurrences of the sheet vision (Acts 10:16) seem to correspond with Peter's reluctance to receive *three* gentile messengers (Acts 10:19), explaining Peter's bewilderment in Acts 10:17: "Now while Peter was greatly perplexed in mind as to what the vision which he had seen might be, behold, the men who had been sent by Cornelius, having asked directions for Simon's house, appeared at the gate." According to Jewish purity laws in Peter's time, many products and practices of gentiles were regarded as κοινός and could transfer the state of being κοινός to Jews. This explains Peter's unwillingness to enter the house of Cornelius. Just as Pharisaic purity traditions prevented Peter from eating food considered κοινός, they also prevented him from meeting with κοινός people (gentiles), entering their homes, and even sharing meals with gentiles (cf. Gal 2:11–12) for fear of contracting the condition of being κοινός.

important *mitzvah*" than Jewish-gentile fellowship.[38] It seems inaccurate, however, to apply the Jewish laws of *kashrut* and the practice of "keeping kosher" to Acts 10–11. The details and practical applications of *kashrut* are spelled out in Jewish oral law, as codified in the Mishnah (ca. AD 200) and Talmud and elaborated upon in later rabbinical literature. Elements of Jewish *kashrut* rules, such as those involving the mixture of meat and dairy products, *shechita* animal slaughtering procedures, and elaborate food preparation and certification, are not required by any biblical commandments.[39] The reality is that a believer can adhere to the biblical dietary regulations without the Jewish laws of *kashrut* and "keeping *kosher*" in a Jewish *halakhic* sense.

Moreover, to claim that Peter was concerned with the laws of *kashrut* in Acts 10–11 may suffer from anachronism if the contemporary *kashrut* laws that Stern has in mind are not identical to the Jewish dietary laws that Peter abided by in Acts 10–11. What Stern fails to acknowledge is that obeying modern Jewish *kashrut* laws is not identical to the faithful observance of biblical dietary commandments. Indeed, Stern himself affirms this sentiment when he writes, "The flaw is in assuming that the *Torah* as set forth by non-Messianic Judaism is the standard by which to judge a Jew's Jewishness . . . it was the legalizers who had a distorted view of *Torah*, while the Jewish believers observed 'the *Torah*'s true meaning, which the Messiah upholds' ([Gal] 6:2)."[40]

In contrast to Moo's traditional understanding of Galatians 2:14, Dunn rightly detects the language of intra-Jewish polemic in this verse. His observations are very important and worthy of reproduction:

> It is important to recognize here that these are relative terms: 'to live like a Gentile' does *not* necessarily mean that they had wholly abandoned everything that would normally mark out a Jew ('Cephas' total emancipation from Judaism'—Betz 112); the contrast is primarily with 'live like a Jew' and is determined by what 'live like a Jew' was understood to mean in that context. In fact, we should probably recognize here the tones of *intra-Jewish polemic*, of Jewish factionalism (as already suggested on ii.12). In the factionalism of the Maccabean and post-Maccabean period there were those who saw themselves as 'righteous'

---

38. Stern, *Jewish New Testament Commentary*, 528–29.

39. For example, it is highly debated whether the biblical prohibition not to "boil a young goat in the milk of its mother" (Exod 23:19; 34:26; Deut 14:21) is a legitimate basis for all of the Jewish *kashrut* laws concerning the mixture of meat and dairy products that developed over time.

40. Stern, *Jewish New Testament Commentary*, 529.

and other Jews as 'sinners'; that is to say, they regarded themselves as alone faithful to the covenant obligations laid on Israel, and dismissed other Jews (or at least their Jewish opponents) as effectively outside the covenant ('sinners' equivalent in effect to 'Gentile sinners') (see on ii.15). Thus *Jubilees* condemns not only the sons of Israel who failed to circumcise their sons as 'making themselves like the Gentiles', and who thus had left the covenant and for whom there was no pardon (xv.33-4). But it also condemns those Jews who used a different calendar to calculate the feast days as 'forgetting the feasts of the covenant and walking in the feasts of the gentiles, after their errors and after their ignorance' (vi.35). And the *Psalms of Solomon* condemn in even stronger terms their (probably Sadducean) opponents: 'Their lawless actions surpassed the gentiles before them' (i.8); 'there was no sin they left undone in which they did not surpass the gentiles' (viii.13).[41]

Therefore, in Galatians 2:11-14 Paul strongly opposed Peter's vacillating behavior since it seemed to legitimize the purity rules of Pharisaic Judaism in the presence of gentile believers. Peter did not want to offend the more traditional Pharisaic perspective that the (physically) uncircumcised, no matter how devout or faithful, were still considered "sinners" unless they underwent proselyte conversion into Judaism (circumcision) and adhered to the standards of Pharisaic purity (cf. Acts 15:1, 5). As Dunn explains, "what Paul objected to so vehemently was that an element of compulsion on gentiles to adopt distinctive Jewish laws and customs as a *necessary* part of the gospel, which Paul thought had been ruled out at Jerusalem, was now once again being reasserted in defiance of the spirit of that agreement."[42]

[15] Ἡμεῖς φύσει Ἰουδαῖοι καὶ οὐκ ἐξ ἐθνῶν ἁμαρτωλοί· [16] εἰδότες [δὲ] ὅτι οὐ δικαιοῦται ἄνθρωπος ἐξ ἔργων νόμου ἐὰν μὴ διὰ πίστεως Ἰησοῦ Χριστοῦ, καὶ ἡμεῖς εἰς Χριστὸν Ἰησοῦν ἐπιστεύσαμεν, ἵνα δικαιωθῶμεν ἐκ πίστεως Χριστοῦ καὶ οὐκ ἐξ ἔργων νόμου, ὅτι ἐξ ἔργων νόμου οὐ δικαιωθήσεται πᾶσα σάρξ.
[15] "We *are* Jews by nature and not sinners from among the Gentiles; [16] nevertheless knowing that a man is not justified by the works of the Law but through faith in Christ Jesus, even we have believed in Christ Jesus, so that we may be justified by faith in

---

41. Dunn, *Galatians*, 127-28; emphasis original. So Keener (*Galatians*, 159): "Jewish teachers often condemned Jewish hypocrisy [e.g., 'Abot R. Nat. 48, §132B], so the charge was also frequent in intra-Jewish polemic"; "Living like gentiles was common Jewish polemic against less strict Jewish sects" (163).

42. Dunn, *Galatians*, 129-30; emphasis original; similarly, Zetterholm, *Approaches to Paul*, 25, 27.

Christ and not by the works of the Law; since by the works of the Law no flesh will be justified."

The NASB is the only translation that clearly accounts for the separation marker ἐκ (*from, out of, away from*) in 2:15, "sinners from among the Gentiles" (ἐξ ἐθνῶν ἁμαρτωλοί). This clarification is important because this spatial distinction lends support to the idea that the "sinners" Paul is addressing here are secularized/Hellenized diaspora Jews/Israelites. Although non-Israelite gentiles would naturally be included in this category, Paul is chiefly concerned with irreligious diaspora Israelites who are living no differently than pagan gentiles.

Dunn lends credence to this reading when he explains the intra-Jewish polemical usage of descriptions like ἐξ ἐθνῶν ἁμαρτωλοί.

> [T]he same epithet was often used in intra-Jewish polemic, by one faction, who claimed to be 'righteous', against another faction, whom they regarded as 'sinners', because the latter failed to conform to their (sectarian) definition of 'righteousness' (e.g. 1 Macc. i.34; ii.44, 48; 1 *Enoch* v.4–7; 82.4–5; 1QH ii.8–12; 1QpHab v.4–8; *Pss. Sol.* iv.8; xiii.6–12)—a usage which, of course, makes perfect sense of the criticism of Jesus that he 'ate with sinners' (Mark ii.16) . . . he was using the language of typical Jewish factionalism, which was ready to condemn those Jews who disagreed with the sect's interpretation of what the law required as 'sinners'—outside their sectarian understanding of the covenant, which meant, of course, from the sectarian viewpoint, outside the covenant. In fact, Paul was probably echoing the language used by the 'individuals from James'.[43]

Keener confirms Dunn's cross-reference to "sinners" in Mark 2:16: "Even more likely, Paul probably evokes scenes that Peter would have known firsthand: Pharisaic scribes challenged Jesus's disciples because Jesus ate with sinners" (cf. Matt 11:19; Luke 7:34).[44] William Lane clarifies that "sinners" in Mark 2:16 is referring to irreligious Jews and not non-Israelite gentiles.

> This term cannot be understood in the generally accepted sense of "transgressors of the moral law of God" . . . The term is technical in this context for a class of people who were regarded by the Pharisees as inferior because they showed no interest in the scribal tradition. With the derisive epithet "the people of the land," the scribes often dismissed as inconsequential the common people who possessed neither time nor inclination to

---

43. Dunn, *Galatians*, 133.
44. Keener, *Galatians*, 170.

regulate their conduct by Pharisaic standards. They were particularly despised because they did not eat their food in a state of ceremonial cleanness and because they failed to separate the tithe. The designation "sinners" as used by the scribes is roughly equivalent to "outcasts."[45]

Lane further cites K. Rengstorf: "For the Pharisee, however, a ἁμαρτωλός is one who does not subject himself to the Pharisaic ordinances, i.e., the so-called 'am ha-ares. He is not a sinner because he violates the Law, but because he does not endorse the Pharisaic interpretation."[46]

Although in general Christian usage, the term "sinner" has taken on the sense of moral imperfection, in the original historical setting of Galatians 2:16 it carried a more specific meaning in relation to the religious authorities of that time. In intra-Jewish polemical contexts the term "sinner" was used primarily to describe irreligious Jews who did not conform to a particular set of sectarian *halakah*, and not non-Israelite gentiles in general.

2:16. "a man is not justified" (οὐ δικαιοῦται ἄνθρωπος): Moo rightly comments that Galatians 2:16 "is one of the most important and debated [verses] in the Letters of Paul . . . Much of the rest of Galatians is devoted to elaborating this fundamental contrast."[47] According to Moo, Paul is saying, "Although we Jews, in contrast to the Gentiles, would seem to have an inherent right to justification, even we have turned our backs on the law of Moses and have embraced faith in Christ as the means to justification."[48] However, the lawlessness of "turning our backs on the law of Moses" is explicitly condemned by the Messiah in passages like Matthew 5:19; 7:23.

The plain sense of δικαιόω in this passage is the formal or official recognition by God as "righteous"—living in faithful heart obedience to the

---

45. Lane, *Mark*, 103.

46. Lane, *Mark*, 103n39. Lane's citation of Rengstorf: *Theologisches Wörterbuch zum Neuen Testament*, vol. 1 (ed. G. Kittel and G. Friedrich; Eng. tr. 1964), 1:328.

47. Moo, *Galatians*, 157.

48. Moo, *Galatians*, 156. Further, "He is not arguing that Gentiles should be included, with Jews, in the people of God; he is arguing, rather, that Jews should be included, with Gentiles, in the mass of ordinary humanity. Jews are 'sinners' just like the Gentiles, with the radical implication that follows: their obedience to the covenant stipulations cannot put them right with God; only a total reliance on Christ, by faith, can do so" (157). Yet Moo seems to disregard his own warning: "The Reformers may have moved too quickly from this phrase ["works of the law"] to general theological conclusions about 'works'" (160). Similarly, Keener: "Regardless of varied conclusions on matters of detail, it seems clear at least that Jewish believers who kept the law recognized, no less than gentile believers, the need to depend on Christ. The law was their heritage and culture; imposing it as a spiritual requirement for gentiles, however, rejected the spiritual sufficiency of Christ" (*Galatians*, 172).

stipulations of the Sinai Covenant.⁴⁹ In the present, one is "justified" by living in faithful compliance with the law of God, thereby being counted as one of God's own people. In the eschatological judgment of God, when the lives of all men will be scrutinized (e.g., Rom 2:5–16), a person will be "justified" in the sense of being recognized by God as "righteous."⁵⁰

In evangelical Christian doctrine, the term "justification" is over-theologized because of a popular but faulty misconception. It is commonly believed that the OT law of God required lifelong flawless perfection rather than faithful heart obedience. This errant belief seems to be based largely on allegorizing purity requirements required by the physical presence of God within the context of the curse of death (Gen 3:19; cf. Isa 25:8).

Yet, contrary to this misguided doctrine of flawless perfectionism, "Noah was a righteous man, blameless in his generation" (Gen 6:9), Abraham "obeyed my voice and kept my charge, my commandments, my statutes, and my laws" (Gen 26:5), and Simeon of Jerusalem "was righteous and devout" (Luke 2:25). Since it is commonly believed that God demands flawless perfection, many theologians argue that the alien righteousness of Christ must be imputed to all sinners and that justified believers are reckoned "righteous" even if their lives do not habitually exhibit covenant faithfulness. In this logic, the act of believing that the Messiah died for one's sins is the only requirement for justification, and thus replaces the need for a life of faithful obedience to the commandments of God. Yet this clashes with NT teaching that only "doers of the law will be justified" (Rom 2:13), and that believers are to pursue "the sanctification without which no one will see the Lord" (Heb 12:14).

Dunn helps untangle much of the confusion around the phrase "works of the law" in Paul's writings in modern biblical scholarship:

> This has traditionally been understood as a denial that human beings, even the most religious of individuals, can achieve salvation by their own 'works'; they cannot 'work' their passage to heaven; they cannot earn salvation by their own efforts. Valid as that is as a theological insight of tremendous importance, it is

---

49. Cf. Dunn, *Galatians*, 134–35.

50. Moo comments, "the rhetorical situation of Galatians provides good reason to think that Paul implies some kind of future aspect to justification. The agitators probably adopted the usual Jewish view that justification was tied to the last judgment, and in that judgment God's positive verdict would take into account the degree to which one had done 'the works of the law'" (*Galatians*, 162). Stern's attempt to distinguish between "forensic" and "behavioral" righteousness is actually categorizing future and present aspects of the same reality: "In the present verse [Gal 2:16] and the next, all four instances of '*dikaioo*' refer to forensic righteousness. But in v.21, the related word '*dikaiosune*' refers to behavioral righteousness" (*Jewish New Testament Commentary*, 535).

doubtful whether it quite catches Paul's meaning here. Paul was evidently objecting to a current Jewish conviction.[51]

Simply stated, "works of the law" in Galatians 2:16 refers to the Pharisaic purity *halakah* that the Messiah opposed in passages like Mark 7:1-13. The "law" in this phrase refers, of course, to the biblical commandments of the OT Torah, but the "works" represents the extrabiblical religious applications and traditions that calcified into a system of rules. In the Pharisaic mindset these "works of the law" were naturally "deeds or actions which the law requires" *according to their interpretations* of Scripture. The problem and point of confusion for modern interpreters is when this *Jewish* law of Judaism ("works of the law") is equated to and identified as the biblical law of God recorded in Scripture.

Dunn further explains,

> [S]econd-Temple Judaism was split into various factions, each claiming to have the proper understanding of the law and of its obligations . . . 'Works of the law', then, would probably reflect this factionalism and the common concern within second-Temple Judaism to draw the lines of demarcation round covenant righteousness as clearly as possible. This is confirmed by what is a close parallel to the phrase within one of the most prominent of these factions—the Essene community at Qumran. In the DSS it was precisely the covenanter's 'deeds of the law' which had to be tested in order to check whether his membership of the community could be sustained (1QS v.21, 23; vi.18); the implication of 4QFlor. i.7 is that only at Qumran were 'the works of the law' able properly to be performed; the Qumran document known as "Some of the Deeds of the Law" (whose contents have only recently been made public) contains a series of distinctive Qumran rulings on disputed points of law (4QMMT). In other words, at Qumran 'works of the law' denoted a sectarian understanding of the law, denoted, indeed, the sect's distinctive understanding and practice of the law—that understanding and practice of the law which marked it out from others, including other Jews.[52]

---

51. Dunn, *Galatians*, 135.

52. Dunn, *Galatians*, 136. Elsewhere, Dunn writes, "As in MMT, the phrase seems to be first used (in Gal. 2.16) as a summary reference to a series of legal/halakhic rulings/practices which have been at the centre of the previous paragraphs" regarding "table-fellowship with Gentiles" (*New Perspective on Paul*, 343). Similarly, N. T. Wright: "The (sectarian) code of MMT is designed to say, 'Do *these* particular "works of Torah," and they will mark you out in the present as the true covenant people.' These 'works' in question in MMT were not sabbath, food laws and circumcision . . . Rather,

In its historical context, ἔργων νόμου in Galatians 2:16 corresponds well with the recurring phrase מעשי התורה in the Dead Sea Scroll document 4QMMT.⁵³ In 4QMMT, מעשי התורה defined the rules for inclusion among the Qumran community. Similarly, "works of the law" in Paul's writings correspond to religious characteristics and regulations that were distinctively Pharisaic. Thus, "works of the law" in Paul is likely the apostle's equivalent phrase for מעשי התורה found in 4QMMT—the Qumran community's distinct religious regulations primarily concerning ritual purity and sectarian membership. For Peter and the other Jewish believers rebuked in Antioch, their "works of law" included Pharisaic requirements of ritual proselyte circumcision to be included as a part of true Israel and table-fellowship purity. Accordingly, in Galatians 2:16 Paul is not decrying faithful obedience to the law of God, but the errant belief that observance of Pharisaic *halakah* was genuine righteousness that would vindicate a person before God in the final judgment.

Avi ben Mordechai agrees that, in its original context, ἔργων νόμου in Galatians 2:16 should be understood as a false system of justification, namely a Pharisaic system of decrees and oral traditions erected as a fence around the biblical commandments of God.⁵⁴

> With this, the Pharisees built up their authority in accordance with their widespread teachings on ritual hyper-purity and religious separation from the Gentiles and the *am haaretz* (the common people of the land). *Works of the law*, as it was understood in the first century, produced a torah of false "righteousness" replete with its many reforms developed by using the Law of Moses as a source text. *Works of the law* had become another torah added to the written Torah of Moses.⁵⁵

---

the particular and very specific codes in MMT include various aspects of ritual performance (the calendar, regulations about water, marriage laws and so on), some of which were markers against Gentiles, but most of which were markers designed to demonstrate membership of the particular sect, the people that believed itself to be the inauguration of God's new covenant people. What the author is saying is: these 'works of Torah' will bring upon you God's reckoning of righteousness here and now, and that verdict will be repeated 'on the last day'" (*Justification*, 146; emphasis original).

53. Martin Abegg contends that when Paul spoke of ἔργων νόμου, he was not speaking of keeping Torah in general, but rather of the type of sectarian rulings found in 4QMMT ("'Works of the law' and MMT," 11–12). In other words, "works of the law" is not a general expression for obeying the Torah; it refers to Pharisaic *halakah* requirements concerning purity that were presumed to be proper applications of biblical law.

54. ben Mordechai, *Galatians*, 216.

55. ben Mordechai, *Galatians*, 216; emphasis original.

Stern understands ἔργων νόμου in Galatians 2:16 as "legalism": "One of the best-kept secrets about the New Testament is that when Sha'ul writes '*nomos*' he frequently does not mean 'law' but 'legalism'... Even when he uses *erga* by itself, the implied meaning is frequently 'legalistic works' (5:19; Ro 4:2, 6; 9:11; 11:6; Ep 2:9; 2 Ti 1:9; Ti 3:5), although he uses it 17 times in a neutral way."[56]

> I submit that in every instance "*erga nomou*" means not deeds done in virtue of following the *Torah* in the way God intended, but deeds done in consequence of perverting the *Torah* into a set of rules which, it is presumed, can be obeyed mechanically, automatically, *legalistically*, without having faith, without having trust in God, without having love for God or man, and without being empowered by the Holy Spirit. "*Erga nomou*," therefore, is a technical term coined by Sha'ul.... it speaks of legalism, not Law. But because Sha'ul's subject is misunderstanding and perverting *Torah* into something it was never meant to be, *erga nomou* are, specifically, in context, "works of legalism in relation to the *Torah*".... Hence my rendering, *legalistic observance of Torah commands*. Likewise, the term "*upo nomon*" ("under law"), which appears five times in this letter, never means simply "under the *Torah*," in the sense of "subject to its provisions," "living within its framework." Rather, with one easily explainable variation, it is Sha'ul's shorthand for "living under the oppression caused by being enslaved to the social system or the mindset that results when the *Torah* is perverted into legalism."[57]

Therefore, it would be incorrect to equate "works of the law" in Galatians 2:16 to the biblical commandments of God or the idea of "good works" in general. Paul is not criticizing the OT law of God but sectarian traditions extrapolated from the OT commandments that distinguish Pharisaic Judaism from other (less religious) Jews. Another complication is that Paul seems to use "law" elsewhere in the NT to refer not only to the OT commandments but also to the Jewish oral law and rabbinic traditions that were also embraced by Jews as "Torah" from God. As ben Mordechai explains, the key is to recognize that "works of the law" in Galatians 2:16 does not refer to the biblical law of God alone but "a Pharisaic system of decrees and oral traditions erected as a fence around the written commandments."[58]

---

56. Stern, *Jewish New Testament Commentary*, 536–37.
57. Stern, *Jewish New Testament Commentary*, 537; emphasis original.
58. ben Mordechai, *Galatians*, 216.

Dunn makes another important point when he explains that circumcision and food laws in particular had become "make or break" issues for Jewish identity and covenant faithfulness since the Maccabean crisis.[59] A historically accurate interpretation of Galatians, and the NT in general, must account for the threat of Hellenization and the emergence of the Pharisees during the Maccabean revolt.

The Pharisees (*parushi*, "separatist") formed from a group of scribes and sages during John Hyrcanus's priestly Hasmonean dynasty in 152 BC. Their name refers to their separation from irreligious Jews who were favorable toward Hellenization during the Maccabean crisis.[60] According to Josephus,

> The Pharisees handed down to the people certain regulations from the ancestral succession and not recorded in the laws of Moses, for which reason they are rejected by the Saducean group, who hold that only those regulations should be considered valid which were written (in Scripture), and that those which had been handed down by the fathers need not be observed. And concerning these matters the two parties came to have controversies and serious differences.[61]

The Sadducees' rejection of the Pharisaic doctrine of an Oral Torah resulted in two Jewish understandings of the Torah or "law" of God. As Cohen explains,

> By the first century of our era, the Pharisees were priests and laypeople who believed that the ancestral tradition was as binding as the written Torah of Moses. The ancestral tradition included observance of the purity laws (that is, priestly piety transferred to the laity), tithing (another matter of interest to priests), and numerous details in the laws of oaths, Sabbath, and marriage.[62]

Therefore, from a Pharisaic perspective, the "works of the law" in particular, and the Torah/"law" of God in general, would undoubtedly have included the "Oral Torah" of their ancestral traditions and applications. In fact, this Oral Torah prescribed specific requirements for circumcision and food purity that are not found in Scripture, and the required adherence to this Pharisaic standard of "righteousness" is what Paul opposes in Galatians 2:16.

---

59. Dunn, *Galatians*, 136.

60. Cohen, *Maccabees to the Mishnah*, 154–57.

61. Josephus, *Ant.* 13.10.6, §297–98 as cited in Cohen, *Maccabees to the Mishnah*, 140–41.

62. Cohen, *Maccabees to the Mishnah*, 155. What Cohen means by the phrase "priestly piety transferred to the laity" is the Pharisaic conviction that all Jews had to observe the purity laws (which applied to the temple service) outside the temple.

2:16. "but through faith in Christ Jesus" (ἐὰν μὴ διὰ πίστεως Ἰησοῦ Χριστοῦ): Dunn is the only commentator to note that the linking conjunction ἐὰν μὴ in 2:16 is exceptive and not adversative. "It is not simply equivalent to 'but', but to 'but only'. . . . Which means that 'works of the law' and 'faith in Jesus Christ' are not necessarily being posed here as mutually exclusive antitheses."[63]

Although all contemporary English versions translate ἐὰν μὴ in Galatians 2:16 as "but," the other 51 occurrences in the NT introduce a limitation, giving the sense of "unless" or "except." J. Louw and E. Nida define εἰ μή as "a marker of contrast by designating an exception—'except that, but, however, instead, but only.'"[64] In two examples that Louw and Nida provide (Gal 1:7 and Matt 12:4), the sense of limitation or exception is dominant, and according to Louw-Nida, εἰ μή has this same semantic meaning in Galatians 1:7, 19; 2:16; 6:14. Thus in Galatians 2:16 Paul indicates that a person is not justified by works of Torah observance unless those works of Torah obedience are in accordance with the faithfulness of the Messiah (i.e., his teaching and life example). From this perspective, Torah obedience and the "faithfulness of Jesus Christ" are not in opposition, but the latter specifies the former.

Schreiner claims that this limitation or exception understanding of ἐὰν μὴ in Galatians 2:16 undermines Paul's main argument.

> The translation adopted above ("but") is unusual, for typically the phrase means "unless" or "if not." If the Greek phrase (ἐὰν μή) is translated as "unless," it seems that Paul argues that a person may be justified by works of law as long as they also have faith in Jesus Christ. But such a view cannot be sustained from the remainder of 2:16 or from elsewhere in Galatians (3:2, 5, 10). Paul emphatically concludes 2:16 by saying that "by works of law no flesh shall be justified." So too, in 3:10 he says that "as many as are of works of law" are cursed. Therefore, it violates clear statements from Paul to say that one can be justified by works of law as long as one also has faith in Christ (cf. also Rom 3:20, 28).[65]

Similarly, every Christian interpreter this author could find prefers to translate ἐὰν μὴ in Galatians 2:16 as "but" instead of "unless" or "except." Context is the decisive criterion in interpretation, it is argued, and a strong contrastive/adversative reading has been the rendering of Christian Greek grammarians throughout church history. After all, Paul could not possibly

---

63. Dunn, *Galatians*, 137.
64. Louw and Nida, *Greek-English Lexicon*, 794.
65. Schreiner, *Galatians*, 162.

have changed his mind mid-verse and espoused some type of works-plus-faith position.

However, a normal, plain-sense grammatical rendering of ἐὰν μὴ in Galatians 2:16 is "if not" or "unless/except," and this reading does not necessarily contradict the rest of Paul's arguments in Galatians. If ἐὰν μὴ is translated in Galatians 2:16 with its normal sense of limitation or qualification ("unless, except") instead of contrast ("but"), then Paul is indicating that a person is not justified by "works of the law" unless those works are διὰ πίστεως Ἰησοῦ Χριστοῦ. Accordingly, "works of law" and "faithfulness of Jesus Christ" are not in opposition, but the latter specifies or defines the former. A fine line exists between context and theological presupposition, with all sorts of errors resulting from a predetermination of what Paul "must" have meant in any particular passage. To put it differently, prior theological commitments must yield to a normal reading of the text.

2:16. πίστεως Ἰησοῦ Χριστοῦ: The term πίστις regularly translates the Hebrew word אֱמוּנָה in the LXX.[66] The verb אָמַן means "to confirm, support, uphold" (*Qal*), "to be established, be faithful" (*Niphal*), or "to be certain, i.e. to be faithful toward" (*Hiphil*).[67] The basic root idea is firmness or certainty, as in אֱמוּנָה which denotes *firmness, steadfastness, fidelity*.[68]

The KJV and NET translations rightly understand πίστεως Ἰησοῦ Χριστοῦ in 2:16 as a subjective genitive. Matthew Easter has summarized the main arguments in the subjective-objective genitive debate concerning πίστις Χριστοῦ.[69] Easter provides the following arguments supporting the subjective genitive position: (1) an objective genitive creates redundancies, (2) *pistis* followed by a genitive of a person never refers to faith in that person, (3) it is questionable how human faith reveals the righteousness of God in Romans 3:21–22, (4) a subjective genitive better explains the use of Habakkuk 2:4 in Galatians 3:11 and Romans 1:17, and (5) the arrival of a singular, external *pistis* in Galatians 3:23 also supports the subjective genitive position.

Keener concedes that the faithfulness of God in Romans 3:3, the faithfulness of Abraham in Romans 4:16, and the faithfulness of Christ in Galatians 2:20 are strong arguments in support of the subjective genitive position.[70] George Howard observed that the Peshitta Syriac always translates the phrase *pistis christou Iesou* with the meaning of "the faith of the Messiah"

---

66. T. F. Torrance equates πίστις to אֱמוּנָה and אֱמֶת (*Royal Priesthood*, 2) while C. H. Dodd contends that אֱמוּנָה and אֱמֶת are synonyms (*Bible and the Greeks*, 68–70).

67. Scott, "1:51 ", אָמַן.

68. Brown et al., *Hebrew and English Lexicon*, 53.

69. Easter, "*Pistis Christou* Debate," 33–47.

70. Keener, *Galatians*, 179.

(especially is this clear in its rendition of Galatians 2:16 and Ephesians 3:12), showing how the ancient Syrian Church understood the construction.[71]

Proponents of the objective genitive position offer two main arguments. First, the occurrence of noun-verb cognates in Galatians 2:16 (πίστις/πιστεύω) and elsewhere (Gal 3:6–9, 22; Rom 4) supports the objective genitive position since Christ's "believing" does not occur in the NT.[72] The cognates should have the same sense of "belief/to believe in" when used together. Second, it is argued that Paul's use of Genesis 15:6 in Galatians 3:6 and Romans 4:3 supports the objective genitive position.[73] In Genesis 15:6 the emphasis is upon Abraham's trust in what God had promised he would do, and not on Abraham's faithfulness/obedience.

The argument concerning the noun-verb cognate (πίστις/πιστεύω) in Galatians 2:16 is correct in that both words should carry parallel meanings. However, this argument supports the subjective genitive position just as well. Moo actually supports this perspective with his comments on the "directional" εἰς in the phrase ἡμεῖς εἰς Χριστὸν Ἰησοῦν ἐπιστεύσαμεν in 2:16:

> [T]he faith Paul has in view is faith that is directed toward Christ... the language of believing "into Christ" shows that it is much more, involving both trust and commitment. "*Pisteuo* (or *pistis*) *eis Christon* depicts the committal of one's self to the person of Christ, something more than an intellectual acceptance of the message of the gospel or a recognition of the truth about Christ" (Harris 2012: 236–37).[74]

Yet if we simply replace Moo's "faith/belief" understanding of πίστις/πιστεύω with "faithfulness," then the meaning of the phrase ἡμεῖς εἰς Χριστὸν Ἰησοῦν ἐπιστεύσαμεν in Galatians 2:16 is that Paul and his fellow Jewish believers have also *become faithful toward* the Messiah Jesus. According to Matthew Bates, "so we also *have given allegiance* to the Christ" or "we have *given pistis* unto the Christ."[75] Thus the parallel meaning in the noun-verb cognate argument supports the subjective genitive reading equally well.[76]

---

71. Howard, "Romans 3:21–31," 229.

72. Dunn, *Galatians*, 139; Moo, *Galatians*, 160; Keener, *Galatians*, 180.

73. Dunn, *Galatians*, 139; Moo, *Galatians*, 160.

74. Moo, *Galatians*, 163; Dunn (*Galatians*, 139) also equates "believing into Christ" with "commitment to Christ" and notes the limited occurrence of the phrase in only two other passages (Rom 10:14; Phil 1:29).

75. Bates, *Salvation by Allegiance Alone*, 81, 84; emphasis original.

76. Paul's use of Genesis 15:6 in Galatians 3:6 will be explained in the commentary for that passage.

Interpreters are unclear on the precise meaning of πίστις Χριστοῦ in Galatians 2:16 as a subjective genitive. Dunn suggests "Christ's faithfulness in going the way of the cross" or "Jesus' own faith in God."[77] However, if πίστις is understood as "faithfulness" in the sense of heart obedience to the law or covenant loyalty, then Paul is contrasting "works of the law" with the Messiah's heart obedience to the law of God and faithfulness toward God. In other words, the contrast is between Jewish sectarian traditions and the Messiah's teaching and life obedience to the written commandments of God, a πίστις that is defined by Christ.

2:16. "since by the works of the Law no flesh will be justified" (ὅτι ἐξ ἔργων νόμου οὐ δικαιωθήσεται πᾶσα σάρξ): Paul seems to be citing Psalm 143:2: "for in Your sight no man living is righteous" (כִּי לֹא־יִצְדַּק לְפָנֶיךָ כָל־חָי). That no man could claim to be sinless before God is found throughout the OT like in 1 Kings 8:46 where Solomon prays, "there is no man who does not sin" while dedicating the Temple. Dunn explains, "The sentiment was thoroughly Jewish—that no one could claim to be sinless before God, worthy of (final) acquittal by reason of the quality of his life (e.g. Job ix.2; Ps. xiv.1–3; Isa. lix.2ff.; 1 *Enoch* lxxxi.5; 1QH ix.14–15)."[78]

Pharisaic Judaism, however, developed a religious system in which self-justification festered. In Luke 10:29 a "lawyer" (νομικός) eagerly questions the Messiah, "desiring to justify himself" (θέλων δικαιῶσαι ἑαυτὸν). In Luke 16:15 the Lord condemns scoffing Pharisees, "You are those who justify yourselves in the sight of men but God knows your hearts; for that which is highly esteemed among men is detestable in the sight of God." In Luke 18:9 the Messiah teaches the parable of the Pharisee and the publican to "some people who trusted in themselves that they were righteous and viewed others with contempt."

Therefore, Paul's argument that "by the works of the law no flesh will be justified" in Galatians 2:16 is not an abrogation of the OT commandments of God or a criticism of faithful heart obedience to the Mosaic Law. The apostle is arguing that the sectarian *halakah* of Pharisaic Judaism ("works of the law") will not render one "righteous" in the end-time judgment of God, in full agreement with the Messiah in Matthew 5:20: "unless your righteousness surpasses *that* of the scribes and Pharisees, you will not enter the kingdom of heaven."

[17] εἰ δὲ ζητοῦντες δικαιωθῆναι ἐν Χριστῷ εὑρέθημεν καὶ αὐτοὶ ἁμαρτωλοί, ἆρα Χριστὸς ἁμαρτίας διάκονος; μὴ γένοιτο.

---

77. Dunn, *Galatians*, 138.
78. Dunn, *Galatians*, 140.

¹⁷ But if, while seeking to be justified in Christ, we ourselves have also been found sinners, is Christ then a minister of sin? May it never be!

Evangelical interpreters explain the phrase ζητοῦντες δικαιωθῆναι ἐν Χριστῷ ("seeking to be justified in Christ") as a reference to immediate forensic justification for believers who are united to Christ by faith. Yet the plain sense of ζητέω here indicates that "'Justification' here is thought of more as a future hope—in the final judgment."[79] This hoped-for future justification is also corporate in nature (cf. plural εὑρέθημεν καὶ αὐτοὶ ἁμαρτωλοί). Throughout the OT, צְדָקָה is used to describe Israel's ideal covenant status as "righteous" before God. Therefore, the end-time decree of "righteous" that is hoped for by the believing community *is also corporate* and not just individualistic.

Accordingly, when Paul writes "seeking to be justified in Christ" in 2:17, he is describing believers who have left traditional Pharisaic Judaism to pursue Torah obedience as taught and lived out by the Messiah (ἐν Χριστῷ).[80] By transferring their loyalty to Christ, Jewish believers have abandoned the Pharisaic purity traditions as the standard for righteousness. The biblical commandments of God remain the same but what changes is their interpretation and application, from Pharisaic Judaism to the covenant faithfulness embodied by the Messiah. Thus, "seeking to be justified in Christ" describes the lifelong process of Torah obedience as a disciple of the Messiah, and "justification" in 2:17 occurs at the end-time judgment.

εἰ . . . εὑρέθημεν καὶ αὐτοὶ ἁμαρτωλοί ("if . . . we ourselves have also been found sinners"): Paul may be responding to a charge that abandoning Pharisaic Judaism and seeking to be justified in Christ amounted to sinfulness. The phrase καὶ αὐτοί ("also ourselves") in connection with ἁμαρτωλοί ("sinners") recalls ἐξ ἐθνῶν ἁμαρτωλοί in v. 15. The opponents' accusation may have been that if believers did not live according to the Pharisaic "works of the law" then they were no different than gentile sinners. The verb εὑρίσκω ("find") suggests a surprising discovery: Jewish believers' eating with gentile believers caused the former to be regarded as "sinners" even by their fellow Jewish believers.[81] Paul's opponents insisted that, unless gentile believers underwent proselyte conversion, they were still "sinners,"

---

79. Dunn, *Galatians*, 141.

80. The phrase ἐν Χριστῷ appears frequently in Paul's letters to signal the sphere within which the believer lives (cf. 1:22; 2:4; 3:14, 26, 28; 5:6, 10), and parallels the expressions διὰ πίστεως Ἰησοῦ Χριστοῦ and ἐκ πίστεως Χριστοῦ of 2:16.

81. Dunn, *Galatians*, 141.

and those Jewish believers like Paul who disregarded Pharisaic traditions by eating with gentile believers were equally "sinners."

ἄρα Χριστὸς ἁμαρτίας διάκονος; ("is Christ then a minister of sin?"): ἁμαρτίας διάκονος describes Christ as an agent of sin who promotes lawlessness. If followers of the Messiah have abandoned Pharisaic purity traditions and are thus accused of being no better than gentile "sinners," does this mean that the Messiah promoted lawlessness by leading others to commit sin? By leading believers away from Pharisaic Judaism did Christ increase lawlessness? Paul was doubtless aware of the Messiah's frequent meals and interactions with tax collectors and sinners.[82] Thus when disciples of the Messiah followed his example by disregarding sectarian purity rules and dining with gentile believers, the accusation could be made that Christ led his followers to sin. The conflict centered on the authority to define sin between the Jewish religious leaders and the Messiah.

μὴ γένοιτο ("May it never be!"): Paul's emphatic response to the notion that the Messiah could possibly be a ἁμαρτίας διάκονος, one who promotes lawlessness, is a strong indication that the apostle is addressing Jewish purity *halakah* in Galatians 2:17-18 and not the written commandments of God. If justification through faith in the Messiah meant that believers were no longer bound to the law of God, then the Messiah would indeed be a ἁμαρτίας διάκονος.

> [18] εἰ γὰρ ἃ κατέλυσα ταῦτα πάλιν οἰκοδομῶ, παραβάτην ἐμαυτὸν συνιστάνω.
> [18] For if I rebuild what I have *once* destroyed, I prove myself to be a transgressor.

Paul insists that to go back to Pharisaic *halakah* after having followed the Messiah validates Pharisaic traditions and demonstrates that one is truly a lawbreaker.[83] If Jewish believers rebuild the wall of Pharisaic purity laws that they formerly demolished by renouncing Pharisaic Judaism and embracing the Messiah, then they are acknowledging the sinfulness of the Messiah's doctrine. If Pharisaic Judaism is right, then the Messiah was wrong and thus an agent of sin. If Pharisaism was in fact the standard of true righteousness, then those who aligned themselves to the teaching and example of the Messiah had actually become transgressors of the law.

---

82. Dunn, *Galatians*, 141-42.

83. The term παραβάτης ("violator of the law," "lawbreaker") is used here to make a distinction from the pejorative use of ἁμαρτωλός ("sinner") in the preceding context. According to Longenecker, "It has to do with not just breaking a specific statute of the law but with setting aside the law's real intent (cf. Rom 2:25, 27; Jas 2:9, 11; Josephus, *Ant.* 3.318; 5.112; 8.129)" (*Galatians*, 91).

Tim Hegg sees a close parallel between the phrase "rebuild what I have *once* destroyed" in 2:18 and Ephesians 2:14-16, where the apostle describes a wall of religious ordinances that formerly separated Jew and gentile but had been torn down through the death of the Messiah.[84] Hegg observes that in the phrase τὸν νόμον τῶν ἐντολῶν ἐν δόγμασιν in Ephesians 2:15, the word δόγμασιν is always used to refer to the decrees and laws of men, not the biblical law given by God.

> Thus, in Ephesians, Paul speaks of a dividing wall that consisted of man-made decrees and ordinances, a wall that kept Jew and Gentile separated. In Messiah Yeshua, however, the authority of these man-made *halachot* had lost their power, and a return to the written word of God, as demonstrated in the life and words of Yeshua, had united believer to believer, regardless of their racial identification. It would appear that the group from Jerusalem was trying their best to rebuild the wall of separation—to put into place among the congregations of Galatia those man-made rules by which a Jew and Gentile were separated. And it would likewise appear that they were pressuring Paul to agree to just such a rebuilding.[85]

The shift from first-person plural to singular in Galatians 2:18 may be significant. According to Dunn, "the sharpness of the contrast evoked (destruction/reconstruction) was true of [Paul] in a way that was not so true of Peter."[86] Paul's tearing down of his "former manner of life in Judaism" (1:13), his Pharisaic zeal that he used to prize (Phil 3:5-7), was an essential part of his newfound allegiance to the Messiah. The apostle's previous commitment to Pharisaic Judaism was wholly at odds with the faithfulness taught and lived out by the Messiah. For Paul, a former Pharisee, to reestablish those sectarian purity traditions would be to admit their validity and prove his own lawlessness as a deliberate transgressor of God's commandments.

[19] ἐγὼ γὰρ διὰ νόμου νόμῳ ἀπέθανον, ἵνα θεῷ ζήσω. Χριστῷ συνεσταύρωμαι·

[19] For through the Law I died to the Law, so that I might live to God. [20] I have been crucified with Christ

In Galatians 2:19-21, the apostle explains the transfer of his loyalty from the oral traditions of Pharisaic Judaism to the teaching and example of

---

84. Hegg, *Galatians*, 92. Keener (*Galatians*, 192n954) also notes this language used for the Jewish concept of building a fence around the law: m. 'Abot 1:1; 3:14; Sipre Deut. 48.1.5; 'Abot R. Nat. 2; 3A; the principle in m. Ber. 1:1; m. Sanh. 11:4.

85. Hegg, *Galatians*, 92-93.

86. Dunn, *Galatians*, 142.

the Messiah. The explanatory γάρ introduces the reason why Paul does not rebuild the Pharisaic ordinances referred to in the previous verse. Grammatically, then, the preceding referent of διὰ νόμου in 2:19 is ἃ κατέλυσα ταῦτα in 2:18. Thus, νόμος in 2:19 does not refer to the biblical commandments of God alone, but to the *Pharisaic* law as enforced by the religious leaders of Paul's time (cf. 1 Cor 9:20–21).

As in Semitic thought, Paul's usage of "to die to" something carries the sense of "separation from," "to cease having any further relation to" (cf. Rom 6:2, 10–11; 7:2–6). Conversely, "to live to" someone means "to be united to," "to have a personal relationship with" (cf. Rom 6:10–11; 14:7–8; 2 Cor 5:15). In passages like Luke 20:38; 4 Maccabees 7:19; 16:25, the idea of "living to God" (ζῆν τῷ θεῷ) bears the sense of resurrection after death or martyrdom.[87] At first, Paul's statement of dying to the law in order to live to God in 2:19 seems paradoxical since the law of God is the source of life in the OT (Deut 30:15–20). This apparent contradiction is resolved, however, if one understands that in Paul's mind, Pharisaic regulations were no longer equivalent to the biblical commandments of God. Paul is no longer shut off from God by legalistic misinterpretations and misapplications of the biblical law.

On account of the *Jewish* law Paul "died to the law, so that I might live to God," a declaration the apostle explains more fully in the following phrase: "I have been crucified with Christ" (Χριστῷ συνεσταύρωμαι). Although modern English translations locate this phrase at the beginning of 2:20, critical Greek editions are almost unanimous in placing it at the end of v.19.[88] Thus Paul's argument is: (1) the Messiah was crucified on account of Pharisaic traditions; (2) the Messiah's death released him from the jurisdiction of Pharisaic Judaism and its laws; and (3) in Paul's union to and identification with the Messiah, he too has been released from the jurisdiction of Pharisaic Judaism so that he is now free to "live to God" by obeying the biblical commandments of God. Similarly, in Romans 7:6 Paul asserts, "But now we have been released from the law, having died to that by which we were bound, so that we serve in newness of the Spirit and not in oldness of the letter."

---

87. Cf. ζῆν τῷ θεῷ in 4 Macc 7:19: "since they [the devout who are willing to endure martyrdom for their faith] believe that they, like our patriarchs Abraham and Isaac and Jacob, do not die to God, but live to God"; 16:24–25: "By these words the mother of the seven encouraged and persuaded each of her sons to die rather than violate God's commandment. They knew also that those who die for the sake of God live to God, as do Abraham and Isaac and Jacob and all the patriarchs." Luke 20:38: "Now He is not the God of the dead but of the living; for all live to Him (ζῶσιν αὐτῷ)."

88. Longenecker, *Galatians*, 92.

²⁰ ζῶ δὲ οὐκέτι ἐγώ, ζῇ δὲ ἐν ἐμοὶ Χριστός· ὃ δὲ νῦν ζῶ ἐν σαρκί, ἐν πίστει ζῶ τῇ τοῦ υἱοῦ τοῦ θεοῦ τοῦ ἀγαπήσαντός με καὶ παραδόντος ἑαυτὸν ὑπὲρ ἐμοῦ.
²⁰ and it is no longer I who live, but Christ lives in me; and the *life* which I now live in the flesh I live by faith in the Son of God, who loved me and gave Himself up for me.

Although Paul's statement "it is no longer I who live, but Christ lives in me" is easily over-spiritualized, it actually serves two primary functions: (1) to strengthen the apostle's identification with and allegiance to the Messiah in the preceding phrase (Χριστῷ συνεσταύρωμαι), and (2) to reaffirm the apostle's rejection of Pharisaic traditions and his appropriation of "the faithfulness of the Son of God" (πίστει... τῇ τοῦ υἱοῦ τοῦ θεοῦ) in the following clause. "It is no longer I who live" in the sense that the former Pharisee, "zealous for my ancestral traditions" (1:14), has decisively embraced the teaching and example of the Messiah—"Christ lives in me."

ὃ δὲ νῦν ζῶ ἐν σαρκί ("and the *life* which I now live in the flesh"): The postpositive particle δέ ("and") here is continuative (like δέ at the beginning of v.20), clarifying what Paul meant by "Christ lives in me." ἐν σαρκί ("in the flesh") here may be polemical (cf. 6:12, "those who desire to make a good showing in the flesh"). Following Paul's identification with the Messiah, the apostle no longer values the outward superficiality of Pharisaic traditions but lives in accordance with "the faithfulness" lived out by the Messiah, the Son of God.

Paul's description of the Son of God as the one "who loved me and gave himself up for me" combines the OT motifs of God's covenant love for the people of Israel and the substitutionary atonement prophesied in Isaiah 52:13—52:12.[89] As the mediatorial ruler on behalf of God, the Messiah embodies and manifests the covenant love that God has for his people by dying in their place as a substitutionary sacrifice to atone for their sins.[90]

---

89. Dunn (*Galatians*, 147): "The talk of Jesus' love (cf. Eph. v.2) reflects the familiar Jewish thought of God's love both of Israel as a people (as in Deut. vii.8, 13; 1 Kings x.9; Ps. xlvii.4; Isa. xliii.4; Jer. xxxi.3; Hos. iii.1; *Pss. Sol.* ix.8) and of individuals within Israel (as in Deut. iv.37; 2 Sam. xii.24; Ps. cxlvi.8; Prov. iii.9; Sir. iv.14; Wisd. Sol. iv.10; more sectarian in 1QS iii.26 and CD viii.17)"; similarly, Keener, *Galatians*, 199 (God's love for his people corporately [Deut 7:7, 13; 10:15; 23:5; 33:3; Isa 43:4; 63:9; Hos 11:1; *Tob* 13:10 [in some MSS]; *Bar* 3:36; CD 8.17; *Jub* 31:15, 20; *Pss Sol* 9:8; *4 Ezra* 5:27; Rom 11:28; *Sipre Deut* 24.3.1; 344.1.1; 344.3.1; 344.5.1; *'Abot R. Nat.* 36, §94B], individuals [*Sir* 45:1; 46:13; Philo, *Abraham* 50; *T. Ab.* 7:1; 8:11 A; *T. Jos* 1:2; *3 En* 1:8], and the righteous in general [*Wis* 4:10; 7:28; *Pss Sol* 13:9; *T. Jos.* 11:1]).

90. The language of "gave himself for me" (παραδόντος ἑαυτὸν ὑπὲρ ἐμοῦ) in Gal 2:20 seems based on LXX Isaiah 53:6, where it is said of the Servant that κύριος παρέδωκεν αὐτὸν ταῖς ἁμαρτίαις ἡμῶν, and 53:12, παρεδόθη εἰς θάνατον ἡ ψυχὴ αὐτοῦ.

As in Galatians 2:16, the subjective genitive interpretation of the phrase ἐν πίστει ζῶ τῇ τοῦ υἱοῦ τοῦ θεοῦ ("I live in the faithfulness of the Son of God") in 2:20 is likely (as in KJV, NET). The NET commentary note on 2:16 explains,

> Though traditionally translated "faith in Jesus Christ," an increasing number of NT scholars are arguing that πίστις Χριστοῦ (pistis Christou) and similar phrases in Paul (here and in v.20; Rom 3:22, 26; Gal 3:22; Eph 3:12; Phil 3:9) involve a *subjective* genitive and mean "Christ's faith" or "Christ's faithfulness" (cf., e.g., G. Howard, "The 'Faith of Christ,'" *ExpTim* 85 [1974]: 212–15; R. B. Hays, *The Faith of Jesus Christ* [SBLDS]; Morna D. Hooker, "Πίστις Χριστοῦ," *NTS* 35 [1989]: 321–42). Noteworthy among the arguments for the subjective genitive view is that when πίστις takes a personal genitive it is almost never an objective genitive (cf. Matt 9:2, 22, 29; Mark 2:5; 5:34; 10:52; Luke 5:20; 7:50; 8:25, 48; 17:19; 18:42; 22:32; Rom 1:8, 12; 3:3; 4:5, 12, 16; 1 Cor 2:5; 15:14, 17; 2 Cor 10:15; Phil 2:17; Col 1:4; 2:5; 1 Thess 1:8; 3:2, 5, 10; 2 Thess 1:3; Titus 1:1; Phlm 6; 1 Pet 1:9, 21; 2 Pet 1:5).

²¹ οὐκ ἀθετῶ τὴν χάριν τοῦ θεοῦ· εἰ γὰρ διὰ νόμου δικαιοσύνη, ἄρα Χριστὸς δωρεὰν ἀπέθανεν.
²¹ I do not nullify the grace of God, for if righteousness *comes* through the Law, then Christ died needlessly.

οὐκ ἀθετῶ τὴν χάριν τοῦ θεοῦ: whoever pleads the validity of the Pharisaic traditions after the substitutionary sacrifice of Christ nullifies the grace of God. By continuing to live under the Pharisaic traditions of the Jewish law, the opponents were denying the grace of God by acting as if the substitutionary death of the Messiah made no difference (cf. 5:4).

εἰ γὰρ διὰ νόμου δικαιοσύνη, ἄρα Χριστὸς δωρεὰν ἀπέθανεν. The γάρ explains the preceding phrase about nullifying the grace of God. The death of Christ occurred to secure his people's justification before God (cf. 3:10–14; Rom 3:21–26); had the Pharisaic works of the law been sufficient to achieve this end, the death of Christ was superfluous. Paul's argument is based on his firm conviction that Christ did not die in vain; therefore true righteousness is not attained through the religious traditions of Pharisaism, but through the faithfulness taught and lived out by the Messiah (cf. 3:21).

The phrase "through the law" (διὰ νόμου) is to be equated with "the works of the law" in vv. 16–17, which are in opposition to "the faithfulness of Christ." Thus "the law" in this context refers to the Jewish Law of Pharisaic Judaism and not just the biblical commandments recorded in the

OT. The noun "righteousness" (δικαιοσύνη) picks up the sense of the verb "justify" (δικαιόω) in vv. 15–16. The Jewish law of Pharisaic Judaism does not yield true righteousness. If Pharisaic Judaism did produce genuine righteousness then "Christ died for no purpose" (Χριστὸς δωρεὰν ἀπέθανεν) in that he would not have clashed with the religious authorities of his time. If the way in which one attains righteousness is through the oral traditions of Pharisaism then the Messiah's death was pointless.[91]

A key interpretive principle found in this passage is that νόμος is not used throughout the NT in a single monolithic sense to refer exclusively to the biblical commandments recorded in the OT alone. The term νόμος must be understood in the way Paul, a former Pharisee, and other Jews would have understood "the law" or "Torah". Therefore in Paul's usage, νόμος would certainly have included Jewish oral law and religious traditions. This understanding of νόμος as not just biblical law but the broader Jewish law means that Paul is not referring to the OT commandments in Galatians 2:19–21, but to the religious legal system of Judaism in general. This perspective also clarifies how Paul "died to the law" in Galatians 2:19. When the apostle declares, "I have been crucified with Christ; and it is no longer I who live, but Christ lives in me" in 2:20, he declares that, just as the Messiah was crucified on account of the Pharisaic traditions and decrees of Jewish law, he is now dead to that Jewish law because of his identification with the Messiah, and it is no longer the observant former Pharisee who lives, but one who now pursues Torah obedience in accordance with the teachings and example of the Messiah. Thus, when Paul writes, "the *life* which I now live in the flesh I live by faith in the Son of God" (Gal 2:20), he is explaining that his new life as a Jewish believer is governed by πίστει ... τῇ τοῦ υἱοῦ τοῦ θεοῦ—the faithfulness of the Son of God as expressed through Messiah's Torah obedience. In other words, Paul now pursues Torah obedience in the way Messiah did.

---

91. ben Mordechai explains, "As Yeshua was crucified for his resistant stand against the traditions of the elders and their polluted authority, while supporting only the written commandments, so too Paul was always ready to agree with the structure of Yeshua's ideology. Any compromise (for Paul or for us today) will be construed by the Holy One Himself as the equivalent of frustrating the grace of Elohim ... The truth is, righteousness cannot be obtained or maintained by walking in Pharisaic tradition and law" (*Galatians*, 225).

4

Commentary on Galatians 3

> ³:¹ Ὦ ἀνόητοι Γαλάται, τίς ὑμᾶς ἐβάσκανεν, οἷς κατ' ὀφθαλμοὺς Ἰησοῦς Χριστὸς προεγράφη ἐσταυρωμένος;
> ³:¹ You foolish Galatians, who has bewitched you, before whose eyes Jesus Christ was publicly portrayed *as* crucified?

As F. F. Bruce points out, the normal sense of προγράφω is "to write in advance" (cf. Rom 15:4; Eph 3:3; Jude 4).[1] Paul seems to be describing a time when he vividly explained the Messiah's crucifixion "before the eyes" (κατ' ὀφθαλμοὺς) of the Galatians from a passage of OT prophecy like Isaiah 52:13—53:12 (cf. Acts 18:4–5; Rom 1:1–4; 10:16; 1 Cor 1:13, 17–18, 23; 2:2, 8; 15:3; 2 Cor 13:4; Gal 5:11; 6:12, 14; Phil 2:8; 3:18; Col 1:20; 2:14–15).

> ² τοῦτο μόνον θέλω μαθεῖν ἀφ' ὑμῶν· ἐξ ἔργων νόμου τὸ πνεῦμα ἐλάβετε ἢ ἐξ ἀκοῆς πίστεως;
> ² This is the only thing I want to find out from you: did you receive the Spirit by the works of the Law, or by hearing with faith?

The apostle presses the heart of the matter. The Galatians' reception of the Holy Spirit was apparently accompanied by miracles (δυνάμεις, v. 5) and thus undeniable (cf. Acts 2; 10:44–48; 1 Cor 12:6, 11).

τὸ πνεῦμα ἐλάβετε ("did you receive the Spirit"): Paul states in 3:14 that the Galatians received "the promised Holy Spirit" (ESV, NLT; τὴν

---

1. Bruce, *Galatians*, 148. On προγράφω here, Keener notes, "in the context Scripture does foresee; Gal. 3:8" (*Galatians*, 213).

ἐπαγγελίαν τοῦ πνεύματος). That this receiving of the Holy Spirit was not the end-time fulfillment of passages like Isaiah 32:15; 44:3; Ezekiel 36:27; 37:1–14; Joel 2:28–29; and Zechariah 12:10 is clarified in Ephesians 1:13–14 where "the promised Holy Spirit" (NRSV, ESV, NIV, NET) was given to the Ephesians "as a pledge of our inheritance, with a view to the redemption of *God's own* possession." Thus, by receiving the Holy Spirit, the Galatian believers were being joined to the eschatological people of God who will partake in the future restoration of the nation of Israel.

Richard Longenecker helpfully explains ἐξ ἔργων νόμου as,

> Paul's catch phrase to signal the whole legalistic complex of ideas having to do with winning God's favor by a merit-amassing observance of Torah. That Paul places ἐξ ἔργων νόμου first (for emphasis) in the sentence—before the subject, verb, and object of the sentence and separated from its coordinate predicate phrase ἐξ ἀκοῆς πίστεως—highlights the fact that his major concern in vv.1–5 (as well as thereafter through v.18) is with countering legalism.[2]

As in 2:16, what Paul has in mind in the phrase ἔργων νόμου in 3:2 is sectarian purity *halakah*. Although most Christian interpreters see a contrast between the Spirit of God and the law of God in this passage, this misunderstanding is due to an imprecise interpretation of the phrase "works of the law." According to Ezekiel 36:27, the purpose of giving the Spirit of God is to enable his people to live in obedience to his commandments: "I will put My Spirit within you and cause you to walk in My statutes, and you will be careful to observe My ordinances" (cf. Ezek 11:19–20).[3]

Since the same phrase ἐξ ἔργων νόμου was contrasted earlier in 2:16 with διὰ πίστεως Ἰησοῦ Χριστοῦ, the phrase ἐξ ἀκοῆς πίστεως in 3:2 must be related to the "faithfulness of the Messiah" in Paul's mind. Moo is correct to associate ἀκοή in Galatians 3:2 with "the disposition to obey" in its Hebrew equivalent שָׁמַע (e.g., Exod 15:26; 19:5; 23:22; Deut 11:13, 27; 15:5; 28:1–2; 2 Sam 22:45; Jer 17:24; and LXX 1 Sam 15:22 ["To hear [ἀκοή] is better than sacrifice"]).[4] Therefore, ἀκοῆς πίστεως in Galatians 3:2 should be understood in the Semitic sense of "obeying," "acting upon what one hears."[5] Paul's

---

2. Longenecker, *Galatians*, 102.

3. So Keener (*Galatians*, 216), ironically: "Paul's opponents probably envisioned biblical prophecy differently: the Spirit should enable God's people to keep the law, as in Ezek. 11:19–20; 36:26–27."

4. Moo, *Galatians*, 183.

5. Contra Matthew Harmon who, after an extended discussion on the difficulty of the phrase, decides on "hearing with faith" like most Christian interpreters (*Paul's*

point here is not that the Galatians merely heard a message and mentally affirmed its content, but that they responded with the hearing/obedience of faithfulness. ἀκοῆς πίστεως in Galatians 3:2 seems to be synonymous with the ὑπακοὴν πίστεως ("obedience of faithfulness") of "all nations/Gentiles" described by Paul in Romans 1:5; 16:26.

> ³ οὕτως ἀνόητοί ἐστε, ἐναρξάμενοι πνεύματι νῦν σαρκὶ ἐπιτελεῖσθε; ⁴ τοσαῦτα ἐπάθετε εἰκῇ; εἴ γε καὶ εἰκῇ. ⁵ ὁ οὖν ἐπιχορηγῶν ὑμῖν τὸ πνεῦμα καὶ ἐνεργῶν δυνάμεις ἐν ὑμῖν, ἐξ ἔργων νόμου ἢ ἐξ ἀκοῆς πίστεως;
>
> ³ Are you so foolish? Having begun by the Spirit, are you now being perfected by the flesh? ⁴ Did you suffer so many things in vain—if indeed it was in vain? ⁵ So then, does He who provides you with the Spirit and works miracles among you, do it by the works of the Law, or by hearing with faith?

The contrast between ἔργων νόμου and πίστεως Ἰησοῦ Χριστοῦ in 2:16, and between ἔργων νόμου and ἀκοῆς πίστεως in 3:2 is now presented in 3:3 as a contrast between Spirit (πνεύματι) and flesh (σαρκὶ). The connection Paul seems to be making is that "the faithfulness of the Messiah" (2:16), the example of his heart obedience to the law of God, is the "hearing/obedience of faithfulness" (3:2) that God accepts as truly righteous. This heart faithfulness to the law of God is what the Holy Spirit enables in his indwelling of believers. In sharp contrast, Paul uses "works of the law" and "flesh" to describe the man-made stipulations of Pharisaic Judaism that fail to result in genuine righteousness. The phrase "being perfected by the flesh" (σαρκὶ ἐπιτελεῖσθε) or "ending with the flesh" (NRSV) in 3:3 probably refers to the official ritual of circumcision as a part of proselyte conversion under Pharisaic authority in Paul's time. The apostle focuses on this antithesis between Pharisaic Judaism and "the faithfulness of the Messiah" (2:16) throughout 3:1–18 and continues the Spirit versus flesh motif in 5:16–26.

Although the specific reasons for the Galatians' suffering (v.4) are not explained, it is likely that they faced persecution for their belief in the Messiah and identification with him.[6] Thus, their suffering because of the Messiah would be "in vain" if they acknowledged the validity of Pharisaic authority and yielded to the pressure to undergo the authorized rite of circumcision as a part of proselyte conversion.

Isaianic Gospel in Galatians, 131, 133).

6. On πάσχω as "suffer" in Gal 3:4, Longenecker explains that the term "always in the LXX and elsewhere in the NT (some forty-one times in addition to Gal 3:4) is used in the unfavorable sense of 'experience suffering' (e.g., Luke 22:15; 24:46; Acts 1:3; 3:18; 17:3; 1 Cor 12:26; Heb 2:18; 9:26; 1 Peter 2:20, 23; 3:17)" (*Galatians*, 104); so Michaelis, "πάσχω," 5:905–23.

⁶ καθὼς Ἀβραὰμ ἐπίστευσεν τῷ θεῷ, καὶ ἐλογίσθη αὐτῷ εἰς δικαιοσύνην.

⁶ Even so Abraham believed God, and it was reckoned to him as righteousness.

The comparative conjunction καθὼς at the beginning of 3:6 associates Abraham's faithfulness in Genesis 15:6 with the "hearing/obedience of faithfulness" (ἀκοῆς πίστεως) at the end of Galatians 3:5. The Galatians' ἀκοῆς πίστεως, through which they received the Holy Spirit, is likened to the faithfulness of Abraham in Genesis 15:6.

The patriarch Abraham is rightly esteemed as an exemplar of faithfulness in Jewish literature.[7] Yet Paul tempers Jewish merit theology concerning the account of Abraham in Genesis 15:6: "Now to the one who works, his wage is not credited as a favor, but as what is due. But to the one who does not work, but believes in Him who justifies the ungodly, his faith is credited as righteousness" (Rom 4:4-5). At the same time, James 2:23 cites Genesis 15:6 to prove that "faith/faithfulness was working with [Abraham's] works, and as a result of the works, faith/faithfulness was perfected" (Jas 2:22) and "a man is justified by works and not by faith/faithfulness alone" (2:24). Abraham's exemplary faithfulness and God's grace in justifying imperfect sinners are not mutually exclusive.

Longenecker explains why Paul included Abraham in Genesis 15:6 in his argument at this point in the epistle.

> No doubt the Judaizers were citing Abraham as the great example of faith plus circumcision (even keeping the Mosaic law before it was actually given), probably using Gen 17:4-14 in support . . . It would have been difficult to refute the Judaizers on the basis of an exegesis of Gen 17:4-14, for vv.10-14 are particularly plain as to the necessity of being circumcised in order to be accepted by God and remain in covenant relation with him. . . . Jews of Paul's day also, of course, used Gen 15:6 when speaking about Abraham. In many Jewish references, however, Abraham's faith is set in the context of his righteous deeds, with the result that the faith of Abraham in Gen 15:6 becomes the faith of one already righteous before God because of his previous works of righteousness. The Aramaic Targums, for example, which represent interpretive readings of Scripture that were

---

7. Cf. 1 Macc 2:52; *Jub.* 23:10; *Sir.* 44:19-21; CD 3.2; Keener also lists 2 Bar. 57:2; T. Ab. 1:3, 18; 2:3; 4:6-7; 7:8; 9:2; 13:2; 15:6, 9; 16:7, 11; 17:10; 18:1; 20:3, 11A; 4:10; 13:5B; m. Qidd. 4:14; 'Abot R. Nat. 36, §94B (*Galatians*, 226n201). See Longenecker, "Excursus: Abraham's Faith and Faithfulness in Jewish Writings and in Paul" (*Galatians*, 110-12); Keener, "A Closer Look: Righteous Abraham in Jewish Tradition" (*Galatians*, 226-27).

prevalent in the synagogues of Palestine during (roughly) Paul's day, speak of Gen 15:6 in the context of Abraham's merits before God in rescuing Lot and his family from the four northern kings in Gen 14 (see *Tg. Ps.-J.*, *Tg. Neof.*, Tg. Onq.).[8]

The nuance that seems to escape most commentators today, however, is that Paul's opponents in Galatians were likely citing Abraham and Genesis 17 to argue for their required rite of circumcision as a part of official proselyte conversion under Pharisaic authority. As Dunn explains, "as one who had himself abandoned idols at the call of God, [Abraham] was remembered as in effect the first proselyte and type of true conversion (*Jub.* xii; *Apoc. Ab.* i-viii; Philo, *Abr.* 60-88; Josephus, *Ant.* i.155). Abraham, therefore was the classic test case for what acceptance by God involved."[9] In other words, Paul's opponents were using Abraham to mandate their sectarian traditions while the apostle was clarifying the true nature of the patriarch's right-standing before God. Paul's problem was not with the biblical command of circumcision recorded in Genesis 17, but with the forced requirement for new Gentile believers to undergo proselyte conversion under Pharisaic authority to be considered in right-standing before God.

David Stern explains,

> Legalistically oriented Jews thought of Avraham as the archetypical legalist. They even tried to show that he obeyed the Oral Law—which didn't yet exist! For example, efforts are still made to prove that Avraham followed the rabbinic prohibition against serving milk with meat, even though Avraham, displaying lavish hospitality much like the Bedouins of 4,000 years later, served his three guests butter, milk and a dressed calf (Genesis 18:8). Rabbi Hertz's commentary on the Pentateuch explains it thus: "The verse may be understood as meaning that the guests

---

8. Longenecker, *Galatians*, 112-13. Similarly, Dunn provides a helpful Jewish perspective on Abraham's faithfulness: "as 1 Macc. ii.52 and James ii.23 show, it was customary in Jewish understanding of Abraham to link Gen. xv.6 with the other promise-to-Abraham passages in Genesis, particularly Gen. xxii, climaxing as it does in xxii.17-18. That is to say, it was customary to interpret 'Abraham believed God' in the light of Abraham's subsequent faithfulness under trial, so that it was by virtue of Abraham's faith, that is faithfulness, that 'he was reckoned righteous' and given the promise (Sir. xliv.19-21; 1 Macc. ii.52; *Jub.* xvii.15-18; *m.* Abot v.3); to rephrase such language in terms of 'meritorious achievement' (Fung 135), however, is to transform it into a later issue (cf. Philo, *Heres* 94; *Abr.* 262 . . .). Not least of interest is the fact that the same formula, 'it was reckoned to him for righteousness', was used within the tradition of the faithful zealot, like Phinehas, and Simeon and Levi (Ps. cvi.31; *Jub.* xxx.17-19), since Paul had previously counted himself as belonging to that tradition (see on i.14)" (*Galatians*, 161).

9. Dunn, *Galatians*, 160.

were given curd and milk to slake their thirst and refresh them (cf. Judges 4:19), and then followed the meal proper, which consisted of the calf. This procedure would be quite in accord with the dietary laws" of the Oral *Torah*, which allow dairy foods to be served before meat but not with or after it.[10]

Similarly, ben Mordechai notes how Jewish interpreters utilized Genesis 26:5 to argue that Abraham adhered to Jewish oral traditions.

> Literally in Hebrew, this verse [Gen 26:5] says that Avraham "protected my protections, my mitzvot, my statutes, and my teachings." Because the Rabbinites are bent on seeing their oral tradition in everything, they therefore perform what is called biblical *eisegesis*, meaning they must read their predetermined views into texts like this verse, teaching that Avraham made fences around YHWH's commandments, since it says in Hebrew that Avraham, "protected my protections." The Rabbinites also find an authoritative second revelation oral law revealed in the Hebrew word תורתי (*torotai*, "my laws") because it appears plural and thus, it is supposedly referring to the oral law *and* the written law.[11]

According to Marion Soards, in much of the Jewish literature contemporary with Paul,

> Abraham is consistently remembered and cited as the paragon of faithfulness to God in and through obedience and Law observance. First Maccabees 2:52 is typical of the Jewish regard for Abraham, stating, "Was not Abraham found faithful when tested, and it was reckoned to him as righteousness?" Similarly see Sirach 44:19–21; Philo, *Heir* 90–95; *Abraham* 262, 273–74; *Jubilees* 23.10; and James 2:20–24 (?). For such Jewish (and Christian?) authors, the Law was given at Sinai after the lifetime of Abraham, but many authors contended that he knew and kept the unwritten law beforehand.[12]

Therefore, Paul's argument in Galatians 3:6 is to contrast Abraham-like "hearing/obedience of faithfulness," as described in Genesis 15:6, with sectarian "works of the law" and Pharisaic oral traditions that his opponents claimed Abraham adhered to. Paul focuses on Abraham in this section because religious Jews of this time portrayed Abraham as a keeper of Jewish

---

10. Stern, *Jewish New Testament Commentary*, 543–44.
11. ben Mordechai, *Galatians*, 249.
12. Soards and Pursiful, *Galatians*, 128.

oral law. Thus, Paul's concern in this section, and throughout the epistle, is with the man-made religious stipulations, not the actual OT commandments of God. When the apostle contrasts ἔργων νόμου with ἀκοῆς πίστεως in Galatians 3:2, 5, he is emphasizing the difference between sectarian rules of Jewish oral law and the simple "hearing/obedience of faithfulness" exemplified by Abraham. For Paul, there is no conflict between ἀκοῆς πίστεως in Galatians 3:2, 5 and the biblical law of God.

Some commentators may argue that Paul's citation of Genesis 15:6 in Galatians 3:6 proves that ἀκοῆς πίστεως in Galatians 3:2 refers solely to the Galatians' *hearing* of the gospel message *in faith*. Max Rogland, however, has contended that the *weqatal* form of וְהֶאֱמִן in Genesis 15:6 expresses "repeated activity (i.e., an 'imperfective' situation) and . . . would be more accurately translated as 'and he *kept believing*' rather than 'and he believed.'"[13]

> By taking note of the aspectual value of והאמן, it emerges that Abram's "believing" in the Lord is not to be viewed as a single "moment of trust" that took place in Gen 15 but rather as something that occurred repeatedly. Abram has been responding in faith and obedience to the Lord from the start of the narrative cycle (Gen 12:1–4; cf. Heb 11:8), indicating that Gen 15 does not intend to present Abram as "coming to faith" for the first time. The literary function of v.6 is not to provide one more link in the narrative chain of events; rather, the author "is editorializing on the events reported, not including Abram's faith in the chain of events as a consequence of the theophanic message."[14] As such, the verse is to be understood as a summarizing, evaluative statement on the part of the narrator.[15]

Accordingly, the contrast between ἐξ ἀκοῆς πίστεως and ἐξ ἔργων νόμου in Galatians 3:2 is not between a one-time hearing of the gospel message and law observance. Paul is contrasting the "obedience of faithfulness," as modeled by Abraham prior to the stipulations of circumcision (Gen 17) and the Sinai covenant (Exod 20), with the "works of the law" as defined by the Pharisaic authorities of Paul's time. This Abraham-like "obedience of faithfulness" certainly includes believing in the gospel message about the person and work of the Messiah and ongoing trust in Christ, but it is not restricted only to these traditional Christian conceptions in Galatians 3:2.

The phrase ἐλογίσθη αὐτῷ εἰς δικαιοσύνην ("it was reckoned to him as righteousness") in Galatians 3:6 translates the Hebrew וַיַּחְשְׁבֶהָ לּוֹ צְדָקָה of

---

13. Rogland, "Abram's Persistent Faith," 239.
14. Rogland cites Matthews, *Genesis 11:27—50:26*, 166.
15. Rogland, "Abram's Persistent Faith," 243.

Genesis 15:6: "and he reckoned it to him as righteousness." It is synonymous with δικαιόω ("justify") in 2:16, denoting "a relationship of acceptance by God, that status or character of a life which God regarded as acceptable."[16]

> [7] Γινώσκετε ἄρα ὅτι οἱ ἐκ πίστεως, οὗτοι υἱοί εἰσιν Ἀβραάμ.
> [7] Therefore, be sure that it is those who are of faith who are sons of Abraham.

It is easy to misinterpret this verse without carefully considering the flow of Paul's preceding argument. The apostle continues to focus on the rhetorical antithesis between Pharisaic Judaism and the faithfulness taught and lived out by the Messiah (2:16). God established the Abrahamic covenant between himself and Abraham and Abraham's descendants (Gen 12:7; 13:5; 15:5; 17:7–9). Since covenant membership and blessing were limited to Abraham's descendants, the debate Paul addresses in Galatians 3:7 is how to acquire status as a descendant of Abraham. For Paul's opponents, the means of covenant inclusion were physical lineage (birth) or proselyte conversion.[17] For Paul, the only requirement to become an offspring of Abraham was to possess Abraham-like faithfulness to God.

As Dunn observes, Abraham "was naturally regarded as the father of the Jewish people, the founder of the Jewish race (Gen. xii–xxiv; Isa. li.2; Matt. iii.9; *TDNT* v.976). Israel naturally thought of itself as 'the seed of Abraham' (as in Ps. cv.6; Isa. xli.8) and counted descent from him a matter of pride (as in *Pss. Sol.* ix.17; *3 Macc.* vi.3)."[18] Keener notes that Jewish people regularly spoke of "our father Abraham"[19] and of themselves as his children.[20]

Consequently, Paul's opponents likely argued that in order for new gentile believers to experience the full blessings of God, they needed to be attached to Abraham and his descendants (Gen 12:3) through circumcision (Gen 17:10–13; Lev 12:3).[21] Moreover, in order to be considered righteous like Abraham (Gen 15:6), a true "son of Abraham" must obey the oral law

---

16. Dunn, *Galatians*, 161.

17. Cf. Lancaster who understands "sons of Abraham" in Galatians 3:7 as a technical phrase referring to gentile proselytes (*Galatians*, 124).

18. Dunn, *Galatians*, 160.

19. Keener (*Galatians*, 226) cites 4 Macc. 16:20; Sipre Deut. 311.1.1; 313.1.3;'Abot R. Nat. 23, §46B; 36, §94; cf. Josephus, *Ant.* 14.255 (*Galatians*, 226n190).

20. E.g., Ps 105:6; 3 Macc. 6:3; 4 Macc. 6:17, 22; 18:1; Pss. Sol. 18:3 (*Galatians*, 226n191).

21. Longenecker: "The expression υἱοὶ Ἀβραάμ . . . is probably to be seen as polemically based. The Judaizers' message undoubtedly focused on being rightly related to Abraham and God's covenant with Israel" (*Galatians*, 114).

like Abraham (Gen 26:5). Thus, according to Paul's opponents, true Abraham-like righteousness was tied to the requirements of Pharisaic Judaism.

In response, Paul argues in Galatians 3:7, "be sure that it is those who are of faithfulness who are sons of Abraham." The true sons of Abraham are those who exhibit Abraham's "hearing/obedience of faithfulness" (Gal 3:2), the same heart loyalty manifested in "the faithfulness of the Messiah" (2:16). Rather than the religious system of Pharisaic Judaism, it is the heart faithfulness modeled by the Messiah and Abraham that God acknowledges as righteous.

> ⁸ προϊδοῦσα δὲ ἡ γραφὴ ὅτι ἐκ πίστεως δικαιοῖ τὰ ἔθνη ὁ θεός, προευηγγελίσατο τῷ Ἀβραὰμ ὅτι Ἐνευλογηθήσονται ἐν σοὶ πάντα τὰ ἔθνη· ⁹ ὥστε οἱ ἐκ πίστεως εὐλογοῦνται σὺν τῷ πιστῷ Ἀβραάμ.
> ⁸ The Scripture, foreseeing that God would justify the Gentiles by faith, preached the gospel beforehand to Abraham, *saying*, "All the nations will be blessed in you." ⁹ So then those who are of faith are blessed with Abraham, the believer.

Paul's language of "gospel" (εὐαγγέλιον) is based on the "good news" (בְּשׂרָה) of Israel's ultimate restoration in Isaiah 40:9: "Get yourself up on a high mountain, O Zion, bearer of good news, lift up your voice mightily, O Jerusalem, bearer of good news; lift *it* up, do not fear. Say to the cities of Judah, 'Here is your God!'" Therefore, the sense of προευαγγελίζομαι ("proclaim good news beforehand") in Galatians 3:8 is that gentiles would experience the full blessings of God in his ultimate kingdom through their union with Abraham by their Abraham-like faithfulness to God: "All the nations will be blessed in you." Paul extends the gracious principle of righteousness by heart faithfulness, apart from religious systems of merit or legalistic effort, from Abraham to new gentile believers.

D. Thomas Lancaster draws on Mishnaic Hebrew to offer an interesting observation on the phrase "preached the gospel beforehand to Abraham" in Galatians 3:8. Lancaster observes that in Genesis 12:3, the verb וְנִבְרְכוּ ("shall be blessed") in the phrase "In you all the families of the earth shall be blessed" is in the unusual *Niphal* form. "When the Hebrew verb *barach* ('to bless') appears in the *niphal* form, it appears as *nivrach*, and in this case, as *nivrechu*. Apparently, this looks a lot like the Mishnaic Hebrew word *mavrich*, based on the same *barach* root, and it means to 'graft' or 'engraft' a vine or a shoot."[22]

> With that Apostolic Age reading of the Hebrew text, Genesis 12:3 could be translated to read: "In you all the families of the

---

22. Lancaster, *Galatians*, 133.

earth shall be engrafted." The context of the passage makes this translation impossible . . . However, the sages are seldom accused of being responsible translators. And this is why we read in the Talmud, commenting on Genesis 12:3, as follows: Rabbi Elazar expounded, "What is meant by the verse, 'And all peoples on earth will be blessed through you'? The Holy One, blessed be he, said to Abraham, 'I have two goodly shoots (*berachot*) to engraft (*lehivrich*) on you: Ruth the Moabitess and Naamah the Ammonitess.' All the families of the earth, even the other families who live on the earth are blessed only for Israel's sake. All the nations of the earth, even the ships that go from Gaul to Spain are blessed only for Israel's sake." (b.*Yevamot* 63a)[23]

Rabbi Elazar uses Genesis 12:3 to explain how two gentile women came to be regarded as part of Israel and even mothers of the Davidic kings. These gentile women were no longer to be considered Moabite and Ammonite but had been grafted into Abraham through this blessing that God announced beforehand in Genesis 12:3: "In you all the families of the earth shall be engrafted."

In Lancaster's view, the grafting parable is Paul's, but the concept that "all peoples on earth will be grafted into you" is not Paul's invention. Instead, it represents an intentional misreading of the Hebrew of Genesis 12:3. "Paul and Rabbi Elazar were virtually contemporaries . . . Either Paul found the inspiration for his olive tree parable in the same misreading of Genesis 12:3, or both Paul and Rabbi Elazar shared a common source."[24] At any rate, Rabbi Elazar's imagery is consistent with Paul's theology, and may have expressed a prevalent Jewish teaching in Paul's time. As Lancaster shows, the verse that Rabbi Elazar intentionally misread in order to arrive at the engrafting metaphor is the same verse Paul quoted in Galatians 3:8, the same verse he referred to as "the gospel" that was announced "beforehand to Abraham." "According to Paul's theology, the gospel as it was preached to Abraham was: 'In you shall all the families of the earth be blessed by being grafted into your faith.'"[25]

Accordingly, σὺν τῷ πιστῷ Ἀβραάμ at the end of 3:9 is best translated "with faithful Abraham."[26] Those who are "of faithfulness" (οἱ ἐκ πίστεως), who possess Abraham-like faithfulness, are genuine "sons of Abraham"

---

23. Lancaster, *Galatians*, 134.
24. Lancaster, *Galatians*, 134.
25. Lancaster, *Galatians*, 135–36.
26. Nearly every other NT occurrence of singular πιστός with the article describes "faithfulness" (e.g. Matt 24:45; Luke 12:42; 16:10; Col 4:9; 1 Pet 5:12; Rev 1:5; 2:13; 3:14).

despite the claims of Paul's opponents, and will share in the patriarch's covenant blessings in the future kingdom of God.

> ¹⁰ ὅσοι γὰρ ἐξ ἔργων νόμου εἰσίν, ὑπὸ κατάραν εἰσίν· γέγραπται γὰρ ὅτι Ἐπικατάρατος πᾶς ὃς οὐκ ἐμμένει πᾶσιν τοῖς γεγραμμένοις ἐν τῷ βιβλίῳ τοῦ νόμου τοῦ ποιῆσαι αὐτά.
> ¹⁰ For as many as are of the works of the Law are under a curse; for it is written, "Cursed is everyone who does not abide by all things written in the book of the law, to perform them."

The explanatory γάρ clarifies why it is οἱ ἐκ πίστεως ("those who are of faithfulness," 3:9), and not those who rely upon "works of the law," who will be "blessed with faithful Abraham" (3:9). Those who are ἐξ ἔργων νόμου are actually "under a curse" (3:10).

Tim Hegg explains the need for precision when interpreting "works of the law" in Galatians 3:10.

> It is clear that in the 1st Century the Oral Torah (the rulings of the Sages that had taken on *halachic* authority) had found its place alongside of the Written Torah. In some cases it was viewed as secondary to the Written Torah, but in practical measures it was received as equal or even superior. The prevailing view was that the Oral Torah gave the proper manner in which the Written Torah was to be obeyed. We must remember, then, that when we encounter the word 'Law' (*nomos*) in the Apostolic Scriptures, we cannot simply presume that the Books of Moses are its referent. Such a monolithic approach to the word ignores the historical setting. We must, in every case, at least give way to the possibility that Written and Oral Torah are viewed as a unified whole (to one degree or another) in the use of the word "Law."[27]

With Dunn, Hegg emphasizes the importance of the Dead Sea Scroll document 4QMMT in understanding Paul's use of the terms "law" and "righteousness" in Galatians.

> The fact that both the phrases ("works of the Torah" and "counted as righteousness") are found in this document [4QMMT] is incredibly important for understanding the same phrases in Paul. What we now see is that the phrase "works of the Law/Torah" was used in Paul's day to refer to specific sets of rules or *halachah* which a given group required in terms of its self-definition. Simply put, such a list of "works of the Torah" constituted the entrance requirements into the group. Since the group

---

27. Hegg, *Galatians*, 125.

would no doubt consider its own interpretations of the Written Torah to be the correct interpretation, they would also have held that only those who adhere to their *halachah* would actually be obeying the Torah and living righteously. "Works of the Torah," then, refers to *halachah* required for entrance into the covenant community (as envisioned by each sect), not personal obedience to God's word. And since covenant membership was considered one and the same with the status of "righteous," it is not difficult to understand how adhering to a given set of *halachot* to gain membership in the community was one-and-the-same to being reckoned as righteous.[28]

For most Christian interpreters, Paul's citation of Deuteronomy 27:26 in Galatians 3:10 is to demonstrate that it is impossible to keep all of the law, and this failure renders a person under the OT covenant curses. Thomas Schreiner, for example, suggests,

> The traditional notion that Paul is maintaining that the curse is incumbent on all who do not obey the law perfectly is the most compelling interpretation. The latter view explains in the most sensible manner the import of the OT citation in Gal 3:10. Paul's claim that the OT itself curses those who do not abide by the law in its entirety is an effective statement only if one cannot obey it perfectly. The idea that Paul assumed that no one could obey the law perfectly explains why he believed that only Christ could remove the curse from humanity (Gal 3:13). Indeed, in Gal 2:21 Paul remarks that if justification were attainable by law-obedience, then Christ died for nothing.[29]

Similarly, Moo defends this traditional Christian understanding of Galatians 3:10:

> [T]he repeated mention of "all" in the Deuteronomy texts to which Paul refers provides clear warrant for Paul's inference that "perfect" or "complete" adherence to the law is necessary if the curse is to be avoided. And Paul makes clear that this is, in fact, his view in Gal. 5:3: "Again I declare to every man who lets himself be circumcised that he is obligated to obey the whole law" . . . Jews would respond that, though they certainly could not perfectly obey the law, the law itself provided the means of atonement for those failures. But arguing from this side of the cross, Paul assumes that Christ has provided the final and only

---

28. Hegg, *Galatians*, 127.
29. Schreiner, "Perfect Obedience," 159.

means of atonement... This new "either-or" situation created by the climax of salvation history now forces obedience to the law to be perfect if it is to furnish a basis for the blessing.[30]

Dunn, however, provides a needed correction.

> There is no hint in Deut. xxvii.26 or in Paul's use of it that the obedience called for is impossible. Deuteronomy certainly did not think so (Deut. xxx.11–14); and neither did Paul (Rom. viii.4; see on v.14). The mistake, once again, has been to read into the argument the idea that at this time the law would be satisfied with nothing less than sinlessness, unblemished obedience, that the law was understood as a means to achieving righteousness from scratch. But in Jewish thought to 'abide within all that was written in the law and do it' meant living within the provisions of the law, including all its provisions for sin, through repentance and atonement.[31]

Schreiner and Moo's claims concerning the requirement of flawless Torah obedience are filled with subjective inferences. OT descriptions of a "whole" or "complete" faith and undivided devotion to God are not to be confused with Christian philosophical conceptions of flawless impeccability. The former is urged, commanded, and expected in Scripture, the latter is completely absent. Scriptural ideas of "completion" or "perfection" in the sense of faithful maturity are not the same as zero-tolerance flawlessness in the performance of a checklist of regulations. This notion of flawless compliance to Torah requirements was not a teaching in the Judaism of Paul's time; nor is it found anywhere in Scripture. Schreiner's reading of Galatians 2:21 and Moo's of 5:3 are examples of theologized interpretation. Earlier, regarding the idea that the OT law provided no basis for blessing because it involved "doing"—something "humans find to be impossible"—Moo opines, "This argument, central to the Reformation soteriology, seems to be present in our text [Gal 3:10]."[32]

Christian interpreters like Schreiner and Moo, who strongly identify with the Protestant Reformation and Reformed theology, have assumed that the Judaism Paul described in his writings was a merit-based religion that promised salvation according to the "works-righteousness" that results from Torah obedience. Thus Paul's criticism of the Torah represented his rejection of merit-based religion and "works-righteousness." Most Christian

---

30. Moo, *Galatians*, 204–5.
31. Dunn, *Galatians*, 171.
32. Dunn, *Galatians*, 204.

interpreters have assumed that Paul rejected Judaism and gave up his own Torah obedience because he found belief in Christ all sufficient for Jew and Gentile alike. This was Martin Luther's interpretation of Paul, which dominated Christian theology for more than five hundred years. Paula Fredriksen summarizes Luther's view: "The Torah only tangled man in self-righteousness, inducing him to think that he could earn salvation through the accumulation of good works."[33]

Recently scholars have argued that Luther's emphasis on the faith-works dichotomy says more about his war against medieval Roman Catholic practices than about either Judaism or Paul. Jewish NT scholars have disputed this traditional or "Lutheran" approach to Paul prior to the 1970s and the rise of the "New Perspective on Paul" (NPP), but a significant shift in NT scholarship did not seem to occur until Christians themselves raised objections. In recent times, a "Radical Perspective," or as proponents call it, the "Paul Within Judaism" view, presents a thoroughly Jewish Paul, who remained Torah-observant throughout his life.[34] In this view, Paul merely wanted to extend God's covenant to all the gentiles as gentiles and not as Jewish converts. In this author's opinion, this new "Radical Perspective" on Paul fails to account for much of the apostle's sharp criticisms of Pharisaic *halakah* recorded in the NT. Some tenets of the NPP are unconvincing as well, but the newfound focus on the Jewish background of Paul and the NT that has accompanied these paradigm shifts have proven to be helpful and instructive in many ways.

Paul is not addressing obedience to the biblical commandments of God in Galatians 3:10, nor requiring flawless obedience to the law of God. In the larger context of Galatians 3, the apostle is contrasting two different systems of law: one that is man-made (based on "works of the law"—Pharisaic *halakah*) and falls under the covenant curses because of its inadequacy, and one that is based on heart obedience to the biblical commandments of God recorded in Scripture.

In contrast to traditional Christian interpreters, David Stern rightly challenges the flawless compliance reading of Galatians 3:10.

> [D]espite the contrary opinion of many Christian interpreters, his point is not that imperfect human nature is incapable of keeping all the commands of the *Torah*; for he neither says this nor proves it.[35] On the contrary, the *Torah* itself, anticipating

---

33. Fredriksen, *From Jesus to Christ*, 160.

34. E.g., Nanos and Zetterholm, *Paul Within Judaism*; a similar perspective is adopted by Amy-Jill Levine concerning Jesus Christ in *The Misunderstood Jew*.

35. Contra Arnold Fruchtenbaum: "James 2:10 teaches that unless you keep the law

> that people will fall short of complete obedience and thereby go out of fellowship with God, states what those who disobey *Torah* commands must do in order to restore such fellowship—they must repent, and sometimes they must bring a prescribed sacrifice . . . Not only does the *Torah* expect disobedience but it makes explicit provision for it, mentioning sin offerings in twenty chapters of Exodus, Leviticus and Numbers and some 120 times in the *Tanakh*.[36]

Thus, according to Stern, the apostle's point in Galatians 3:10 is not that people are unable to obey the law of God perfectly, but that "legalists in particular, merely by being legalists, violate at least one of the *Torah's* commands; and therefore, on the basis of Deuteronomy 27:26 and the other verses cited, they (1) do not attain life, (2) are not righteous, and (3) come under a curse."[37] This "curse" (Gal 3:13) is comprised of the covenant curses recorded in Deuteronomy 28:15–68.[38]

Moreover, Deuteronomy is written with the perspective that God intends Israel to obey his laws, and that she is able to do so (e.g., Paul quotes Deut 30:12, 14 in Rom 10:6, 8). Hegg asserts,

> No one in Paul's day believed that anyone could live out Torah perfectly, and no teacher would have required such a thing. To "abide" in the things of the Torah meant living within the provisions of the Torah, including its provisions for what a person was to do when he or she sinned (i.e., transgressed the Torah).[39]

Paul's modification of Deuteronomy 27:26 in Galatians 3:10 to include the phrase "things written in the book of the law" is significant. If ἔργων νόμου in Galatians 3:10 refers to the *halachic* observance of a particular Jewish sect, then Paul is clearly not opposing obedience to the biblical laws of God. In other words, to be "of the works of the law" is not equivalent to faithful heart obedience to God's law, it is apparently less than what the law of God requires. This is made clear later in Galatians 6:13 where "those who

---

perfectly—unless you keep every single commandment—you are in violation of the whole law. In fact, to break only one commandment is to incur the guilt of breaking the whole law. There is a special curse on those who do not follow and obey every precept, yet, apart from the Messiah, no one has ever kept it perfectly. All are under its curse, and the curse of the law means physical death. Therefore, those who operate in the sphere of the law *are under a curse*" (*Faith Alone*, 28; original emphasis).

36. Stern, *Jewish New Testament Commentary*, 545–46.
37. Stern, *Jewish New Testament Commentary*, 546.
38. Stern, *Jewish New Testament Commentary*, 547.
39. Hegg, *Galatians*, 128.

are circumcised do not even keep the law themselves." Thus, the apostle's point in 3:10 seems to be that the purity traditions of "the works of the law" fall short of the actual righteousness the law of God requires. Hence, those who practice these "works of the law" fall under the covenant curses of the law of God for their disobedience.

Avi ben Mordechai's reading of Galatians 3:10 is similar:

> Paul is contrasting two different systems of law: 1) man-made and 2) divine. The point that Paul drives home is that if we submit to a system of rules and regulations invented and hatched by men (those who always have a bent on not doing things according to the revealed Will of YHWH), then clearly we are NOT following the words of the Torah. If we, as all Israel, are not following the words of YHWH then we are all guilty of breaching His contract, and that means we are all justifiably under the curses found in Deuteronomy Chapters 27 and 28.[40]

> [11] ὅτι δὲ ἐν νόμῳ οὐδεὶς δικαιοῦται παρὰ τῷ θεῷ δῆλον, ὅτι Ὁ δίκαιος ἐκ πίστεως ζήσεται· [12] ὁ δὲ νόμος οὐκ ἔστιν ἐκ πίστεως, ἀλλ' Ὁ ποιήσας αὐτὰ ζήσεται ἐν αὐτοῖς.
> [11] Now that no one is justified by the Law before God is evident; for, "The righteous man shall live by faith." [12] However, the Law is not of faith; on the contrary, "He who practices them shall live by them."

At this point, a nested diagram of 3:9–14 is helpful in clarifying the structure of Paul's argumentation in this section:[41]

Premise: [9] So then (ὥστε) those who are of faithfulness are blessed with faithful Abraham

- [10] for (γὰρ) as many as are of the works of the law are under a curse for (γὰρ) it is written, "cursed is everyone who does not abide by all things written in the book of the law, to perform them" [Deut 27:26]

- [11] and (δὲ) that no one is justified by law before God is evident[42] because (ὅτι) "the righteous will live because of his faithfulness" [Hab 2:4]

---

40. ben Mordechai, *Galatians*, 250; original emphasis.

41. On the difficulty of understanding Paul in this section Terence Donaldson writes, "The path of Paul's argumentation in Gal 3.1—4.7 presents vexing problems for any who would attempt to retrace it. The terminal points are clear: he begins with 'Christ . . . crucified' (3.1; cf. 2.21) and ends with the inclusion of the uncircumcized Gentile believers among the true 'seed' of Abraham (3.26–29; 4.7). But the route by which he moves from 'cross' to 'Gentiles'—a maze of laboured exegesis, puzzling illustration, and cryptic theological shorthand—is anything but clear" ("Curse of the Law," 94).

42. Some scholars (Keener [*Galatians*, 247] citing Das, F. Thielman, B. Longenecker,

- [12] and (δὲ)[43] the law is not of/based on faithfulness but (ἀλλά) "the one doing them will live in/by [keeping] them" [Lev 18:5]

The connective phrase ὅτι δὲ at the beginning of 3:11 marks the apostle's further explanation of why "those who are of faithfulness are blessed with faithful Abraham" (3:9). Moreover, the connective phrase ὅτι δὲ indicates that ἐν νόμῳ in 3:11 encompasses the "works of the law" in 3:10 and thus the broader Jewish law that included Pharisaic "ancestral traditions" (1:14).[44]

Concerning the use of νόμος to translate תורה in Rabbinic Judaism, Walter Gutbrod recognizes,

> But in a given context Torah can also have the sense of valid teaching generally. Tradition as distinct from Scripture is תורה שבעל פה. In relation to this broadest sense the translation "law" is often not very apposite. Torah has here the more general meaning of "valid teaching," "revelation," though with particular ref. to man's action which this Torah regulates.[45]

Defining ancient Jewish law as mainly the rabbinic law from AD 70 to the mid-fifth century, Catherine Hezser explains, "Rabbinic law is based on biblical law but constitutes a further development, innovation, and expansion in accordance with the changed circumstances and the particular interests and concerns of rabbis."[46]

> The term "law" is not entirely appropriate for rabbinic teachings and instructions, since "law" is usually associated with an agreed-upon and binding system of rules. Rabbis' recommendations

---

and N. T. Wright) argue that δῆλον usually goes with the following ὅτι: "and since no one is justified by law before God, it is evident that 'the righteous will live because of his faithfulness'" (3:11).

43. Unlike most modern English translations, Lancaster rightly suggests that δὲ at the beginning of 3:12 should be translated as "and" instead of a strong adversative: "In that case, Paul simply presented two proof texts to prove the same thing. 'The righteous will live by faith' is the same as 'He who does them will live by them.' 'He who does them' is the righteous man, living by faith. The real opposites that Paul contrasted was 'living by faith' and 'the works of the Torah,' that is, 'having Jewish status.' He called Jewish status 'the law' as a shorthand reference for 'works of the law,' the term he used in the previous verse" (*Galatians*, 152).

44. So Bruce: "To the fuller phrase ἐξ ἔργων νόμου there the more concise ἐν νόμῳ corresponds here: after ἐξ ἔργων νόμου in v.10 ἐν νόμῳ suffices to express the same idea (cf. Phil. 3:6, δικαιοσύνην τὴν ἐν νόμῳ)" (*Galatians*, 161); also Longenecker, *Galatians*, 118.

45. Gutbrod, "νόμος," 4:1055.

46. Hezser, "Law, Jewish," 7:3947.

were neither unanimous nor systematic nor legally binding. Each rabbi expressed his own legal teachings and had his own set of sympathizers and disciples who followed his advice. Therefore, a wide variety of legal opinions circulated orally and were eventually transmitted in writing in rabbinic documents of Late Antiquity: the Mishnah, Tosefta, Palestinian, and Babylonian Talmuds, and Midrashim.⁴⁷

Gutbrod and Hezser both note that the English word "law" is not always the most accurate rendering for all that is encompassed in תורה. While Christian interpreters may be tempted to consistently equate νόμος to the Mosaic "law" in Paul's writings, the apostle may also use νόμος to cover the same conceptual range of תורה that includes teaching, instruction, revelation, insight, opinion, and recommendation. One can understand how Jewish *halakah* might carry the same authority of Scripture if that *halakah* is based on the accurate interpretation and proper application of God's word. Thus, the line between Scripture and its interpretation/application is easily blurred, and so one can see how Paul's use of νόμος in the NT could refer to both Scripture and the corollary teachings of Jewish *halakah*.

3:11. "and that no one is justified by law before God is evident" (ὅτι δὲ ἐν νόμῳ οὐδεὶς δικαιοῦται παρὰ τῷ θεῷ δῆλον): recalls Psalm 143:2: "in Your sight no man living is righteous" (לֹא־יִצְדַּק לְפָנֶיךָ כָל־חָי; LXX, οὐ δικαιωθήσεται ἐνώπιόν σου πᾶς ζῶν).

3:11. "for 'The righteous man shall live by faith'" (ὅτι Ὁ δίκαιος ἐκ πίστεως ζήσεται): translates the Hebrew וְצַדִּיק בֶּאֱמוּנָתוֹ יִחְיֶה of Habakkuk 2:4.⁴⁸ The NET translation understands this phrase as, "the person of integrity will live because of his faithfulness," and offers a helpful commentary note.⁴⁹

> The Hebrew word אֱמוּנָה (*'emunah*) has traditionally been translated "faith," but the term nowhere else refers to "belief" as such. When used of human character and conduct it carries the notion of "honesty, integrity, reliability, faithfulness." The antecedent of the suffix has been understood in different ways. It could refer to God's faithfulness, but in this case one would expect a first person suffix (the original form of the LXX has "my faithfulness" here). Others understand the "vision" to be

---

47. Hezser, "Law, Jewish," 7:3947.

48. Keener suggests that Habakkuk 2:4 "may supply the template for Paul's language 'from faith' (ἐκ πίστεως . . . as in the Greek text of Gal. 2:16; 3:2, 5, 7, 8, 9, 11, 12, 22, 24; 5:5)" (*Galatians*, 245).

49. The only other major English translation to clarify the causal בְּ preposition with "faithfulness" is the NLT: "the righteous will live by their faithfulness" (cf. Waltke and O'Connor, *Biblical Hebrew Syntax*, 198).

the antecedent. In this case the reliability of the prophecy is in view ... The present translation assumes that the preceding word "[the person of] integrity" is the antecedent. In this case the LORD is assuring Habakkuk that those who are truly innocent will be preserved through the coming oppression and judgment by their godly lifestyle, for God ultimately rewards this type of conduct. In contrast to these innocent people, those with impure desires (epitomized by the greedy Babylonians; see v.5) will not be able to withstand God's judgment (v.4a).[50]

Bruce sheds light on Habakkuk 2:4 from Qumran:

In the Qumran literature the Hebrew text of Hab. 2:4b is applied to 'all the doers of the law in the house of Judah, whom God will save from the place of judgment because of their toil ('āmāl) and their faith in (or 'loyalty to') the Teacher of Righteousness' (1QpHab 8:1–3). The Teacher of Righteousness was not only a spiritual leader but a figure of eschatological significance. Acceptance of his teaching, or loyalty to the path which he marked out for his followers, was the way to eternal life.[51]

Lancaster points out that a well-known passage in the Talmud (b.*Makkot* 24a) reduced and simplified the whole Torah into one principle recorded in Habakkuk 2:4: "The righteous shall live by his faithfulness."

---

50. NET Bible commentary note on Habakkuk 2:4b, https://netbible.org/bible/Habakkuk+2; cf. Moo (*Galatians*, 207) on the πίστις/אֱמוּנָה sense of "faithfulness." The NET translators' understanding of the preceding clause in Habakkuk 2:4a ("Look, the one whose desires are not upright will faint from exhaustion") supports their interpretive decisions: "The meaning of this line [Hab 2:4a] is unclear, primarily because of the uncertainty surrounding the second word, עֻפְּלָה ('uppelah). Some read this as an otherwise unattested verb עָפַל ('afal, "swell") from which are derived nouns meaning 'mound' and 'hemorrhoid.' This 'swelling' is then understood in an abstract sense, 'swell with pride.' This would yield a translation, 'As for the proud, his desires are not right within him' (cf. NASB "as for the proud one"; NIV "he is puffed up"; NRSV "Look at the proud!"). A multitude of other interpretations of this line, many of which involve emendations of the problematic form, may be found in the commentaries and periodical literature. The present translation assumes an emendation to a Pual form of the verb עָלַף ('alaf, "be faint, exhausted"). (See its use in the Pual in Isa 51:20, and in the Hitpael in Amos 8:13 and Jonah 4:8.) In the antithetical parallelism of the verse, it corresponds to חָיָה (khayah, "live"). The phrase לֹא יָשְׁרָה נַפְשׁוֹ בּוֹ (lo' yasherah nafsho bo), literally, 'not upright his desire within him,' is taken as a substantival clause that contrasts with צַדִּיק (tsaddiq, "the righteous one") and serves as the subject of the preceding verb. Here נֶפֶשׁ (nefesh) is understood in the sense of 'desire' (see BDB 660–61 s.v. נֶפֶשׁ for a list of passages where the word carries this sense)."

51. Bruce, *Galatians*, 162.

Lancaster asserts that the writers of the Talmud understood the word "live" in Habakkuk 2:4 as "live in the world to come."[52]

Thus, in Galatians 3:11, Paul cites Habakkuk 2:4b to demonstrate the OT teaching that God promises life to the righteous *on account of* their faithfulness (and not earned merit through compliance with specifically enumerated religious traditions).

As noted earlier, the connective phrase ὅτι δὲ at the beginning of 3:11 indicates that ἐν νόμῳ in 3:11 and ὁ δὲ νόμος at the beginning of 3:12 encompass the "works of the law" in 3:10 and thus the broader Jewish law that included Pharisaic "ancestral traditions" (1:14).

Commentators have offered a variety of interpretations of the phrase ὁ δὲ νόμος οὐκ ἔστιν ἐκ πίστεως ("and/but the law is not of faith" in 3:12: (1) the [Mosaic] law or law-keeping is not based on faith [belief in the gospel/Messiah]; (2) the legalistic mindset of law-keeping / merit theology contradicts the disposition of heart faithfulness; (3) the Jewish law, including its sectarian oral traditions, is at odds with true faithfulness; (4) rhetorical language contrasting oral traditions and the written/biblical law of God[53]; (5) outward law-keeping does not guarantee inward heart obedience; (6) the law/law-keeping does not produce faithfulness, faithfulness causes obedience to the law; (7) yielding to "works of the law" and proselyte conversion is not motivated by faithfulness. The most accurate interpretation of ὁ δὲ νόμος οὐκ ἔστιν ἐκ πίστεως in 3:12, based on Paul's cumulative argument thus far, is "the law is not a result of / does not come from faithfulness"; on the contrary, faithfulness results in eternal life.[54]

Longenecker provides a more Hebraic understanding of Leviticus 18:5.

> In the targumic tradition arising out of the synagogues of Palestine, Lev 18:5 is seen as having reference to the life of the age to come, which is the reward of obedience to the Torah: "And

---

52. Lancaster, *Galatians*, 150.

53. E.g., ben Mordechai paraphrases Gal 3:11-12, "that no man is justified by the law (works of the law) before Elohim is evident, for it is written, 'the righteous will live by faith' (trust in YHWH by doing exactly what He said). Thus the law (works of the law) is not made by faith (because it teaches us to trust the Rabbis and not YHWH), but whosoever will do the things that are written in it (the written Law) will live in it" (*Galatians*, 255).

54. Cf. use of Lev 18:5 in Luke 10:28 ("do this and you will live") and Rom 10:5. Bruce admits, "True, in the context of Lv. 18:5 the promise of life to those who do what God commands is a genuine promise" (*Galatians*, 163). Lancaster explains that Paul, like other Pharisaic and rabbinic interpreters, would have understood "to live" in Habakkuk 2:4 and Leviticus 18:5 as attaining to the resurrection, eternal life, and the world to come while "to die" meant to die without hope of the world to come, with only the dread of the final judgment (*Galatians*, 147-48; cf. "life," "die," and "live" in John 11:25-26).

> you shall keep my statutes and my judgments, which if a man do he shall live by them an everlasting life" (Tg. Onq.); "And you shall keep my statutes, and the order of my judgments, which if a man do he shall live in them, in the life of eternity, and his position shall be with the just" (Tg. Ps-J.). In rabbinic thought that represents more the scholastic tradition of Judaism, "The Torah," as W. Gutbrod aptly states, "may be summed up in two inwardly related principles: 1. God has revealed Himself once and for all and exclusively in the Torah; 2. man has his relationship with God only in his relationship with Torah" ("νόμος," *TDNT* 4:1055). "The aim of the Torah," as Gutbrod continues, "is to show man what he should do and not do in order that, obedient to the Torah, he may have God's approval, righteousness, life, and a share in the future world of God" (ibid., 4:1058). So in Judaism there is an emphasis not only on knowing the law but more importantly on doing the law (cf. the texts supplied by Gutbrod, ibid., 4:1058, and Str-B 4:6).[55]

Longenecker also demonstrates that Paul's general argument concerning Leviticus 18:5, and in this section of the epistle, was shared by contemporary Jewish thought.

> One tradition of talmudic lore that goes well back into the Tannaitic period lays stress on the fact that the general term "man" appears in Lev 18:5 and draws from that the conclusion that even a Gentile may be regarded in God's sight as a high priest if he observes the law. So, for example, Rabbi Meir (second generation Tannaim) is cited in *b. Sanh.* 59a as saying: Whence do we know that even a Gentile who studies the Torah is as a High Priest? From the verse "[Ye shall therefore keep my statutes and my judgments,] which if a man do, he shall live in them" [Lev 18:5]. Priests, Levites, and Israelites are not mentioned, but "men"; hence thou mayest learn that even a Gentile who studies the Torah is as a High Priest" (cf. *b. B. Qam.* 38a; *Midr. Ps.*; 1.18; *Num. Rab.* 13.15-16, where the same tradition appears).[56]

---

55. Longenecker, *Galatians*, 120. Although Longenecker concludes, "It is this emphasis that is captured in the Jewish use of Lev 18:5, 'the one who does these things shall live by them,' to which Paul objects so much" (*Galatians*, 120), the apostle's opposition in Galatians seems more focused on the legalism of Pharisaic traditions and forced proselyte conversion ("circumcision") for new Gentile believers than on general heart obedience to the biblical commandments of God.

56. Longenecker, *Galatians*, 120-21.

Dunn rightly asserts, "To dismiss Lev. xviii.5 as 'legalism' . . . also mistakes its character of covenant paraenesis . . . Nor is the thought of the unfulfillability of the law anywhere in sight here."[57]

Therefore, Paul stayed in line with mainstream Jewish interpretation by citing Leviticus 18:5 to argue that if a person keeps the biblical commandments of God, he will attain eternal life by them (cf. the Lord's quotation of Lev 18:5 in Luke 10:28).[58]

Lancaster claims that Paul's use of Leviticus 18:5 and Habakkuk 2:4 in Galatians 3:11-12 reflects a common rabbinic interpretive principle called *gezerah shavah* where a verbal analogy is made based upon a common term shared by two or more passages. In Galatians 3:11-12, this shared common term is "will live." "The rabbis quoted verbal analogies between two passages in precisely the same manner, not to contrast them but to link them together or to use one to define the other. According to that type of rabbinic interpretation, the righteous one who *lives* by faith in Habakkuk 2:4 is the same person as the fellow who does the commandments in Leviticus 18:5."[59] Thus, Paul's overarching argument in Galatians 3:11-12 is that genuine righteousness is not defined by Pharisaic "works of the law" or official proselyte conversion, but by faithful heart obedience to the word of God.

> [13] Χριστὸς ἡμᾶς ἐξηγόρασεν ἐκ τῆς κατάρας τοῦ νόμου γενόμενος ὑπὲρ ἡμῶν κατάρα, ὅτι γέγραπται, Ἐπικατάρατος πᾶς ὁ κρεμάμενος ἐπὶ ξύλου
> [13] Christ redeemed us from the curse of the Law, having become a curse for us—for it is written, "Cursed is everyone who hangs on a tree"

The Messiah's rebuke and correction of Pharisaic errors concerning the law of God and true righteousness resulted in his crucifixion. Yet it was the Messiah's clarification of the law of God and true righteousness, and his living example that liberated[60] his followers from the Jewish law and its curse.[61]

---

57. Dunn, *Galatians*, 176; cf. Moo: "'find life by [obeying] them' . . . [Lev 18:5] intends to motivate Israel to obey God's law by promising them life if they obey" (*Galatians*, 208).

58. Cf. Keener, *Galatians*, 248-49.

59. Lancaster, *Galatians*, 153.

60. Keener understands ἐξαγοράζω in Gal 3:13 and 4:5 as "securing someone's deliverance" since in 4:5 "liberation from subjection seems fairly clear" (*Galatians*, 256).

61. Keener: "As David deSilva notes, 'Israel's collective experience down to the time of Paul . . . is a testimony to the Sinaitic covenant essentially ensuring a fairly consistent state of 'curse' for Israel' . . . Abraham's descendants should be blessed (Gal. 3:8-9), but the law has introduced for them the possibility (realized repeatedly in Israel's history) of a curse" (*Galatians*, 252-53). Although Israel's sinfulness regularly brought upon

Longenecker mentions the "striking" feature of the first person plural pronoun ἡμᾶς at the beginning of 3:13, "which in Galatians often refers to Jewish Christians (see esp. 2:15; 3:23-25; 4:5) and here certainly has in mind those 'under the law,' yet refers to gentiles who as yet had not submitted to circumcision."[62] Yet Longenecker's confusion is resolved if the "deliverance" that Paul refers to in 3:13 is understood as liberation from the legalistic Jewish law of Pharisaic Judaism. It is this Pharisaic law and religion that Jewish believers have been set free from, not the biblical commandments of God. And it is this Pharisaic law and religious system that threaten to enslave new gentile believers. According to 3:10, it is this Pharisaic system ("as many as are of the works of the law") that leads to the curse of God.

The "curse of the law" (τῆς κατάρας τοῦ νόμου) here refers specifically to the curse pronounced upon the law-breaker (Deut 27:26) that Paul applies to those "of the works of the law" in 3:10.[63] As discussed earlier, since Deuteronomy 27:26 is not mandating flawless compliance but cursing deliberate rebellion, Paul's argument in 3:10 is that those "of the works of the law" are actually guilty of deliberate rebellion against the law of God. The implication is that others who adhere to these "works of the law" will also become law-breakers and thus fall under the curse of Deuteronomy 27:26. It is from this curse against deliberate law-breakers that the Messiah has liberated his people by becoming a curse for their sake.[64]

Paul cites the Hebrew phrase כִּי־קִלְלַת אֱלֹהִים תָּלוּי (lit. "for the curse of God the one hanged") in Deuteronomy 21:23.[65] The NET commentary on this phrase is helpful:

---

the covenant curses, Paul's focus in 3:12 seems to be on how the sectarian traditions of Pharisaic Judaism result in the curse upon the law-breaker in Deuteronomy 27:26. Pharisaic Judaism brings the covenant curses because it transgresses the law of God (Gal 3:10).

62. Longenecker, *Galatians*, 121.
63. Bruce, *Galatians*, 163-64.
64. Moo admits, "The preposition ὑπὲρ means basically 'on behalf of' . . . It is not that ὑπὲρ *means* 'in place of'" but suggests that a substitutionary idea may be present in Gal 3:13 because "Christ is pictured as identifying with the plight of those he redeems" in context (*Galatians*, 213; original emphasis). On the contrary, the context supports the idea that the Messiah's execution was *for the sake of* (ὑπὲρ) liberating his followers from the bondage and curse of Pharisaic Judaism.
65. Bruce offers a helpful explanation of Paul's biblical citations: "As Paul quotes Dt. 21:23, it shares a common term with Dt. 27:26 (quoted in v.10), and thus provides an instance of the exegetical principle known to the rabbis as *gezerah shawah* ('equal category'). Where two texts share a common term in this way, each may throw light on the other (cf. the common term ζήσεται in Hab. 2:4b and Lv. 18:5, quotes in vv.11f.). Paul's present use of *gezerah shawah* is based on the Greek version; there is no term common to the two texts in Hebrew. Whereas Dt. 21:23 MT says that a hanged man is

The idea behind the phrase *cursed by God* seems to be not that the person was impaled because he was cursed but that to leave him exposed there was to invite the curse of God upon the whole land. Why this would be so is not clear, though the rabbinic idea that even a criminal is created in the image of God may give some clue (thus J. H. Tigay, *Deuteronomy* [JPSTC], 198).[66]

Accordingly, the person hanged in Deuteronomy 21:23 becomes a curse in that his corpse, if left exposed overnight, would defile the purity of the land and thus invite the curse of God upon the defiled land.[67] The person is not hanged because he is cursed, but following his legal execution

---

qilelaṯ 'elōhîm (lit. 'a curse of God'), Dt. 27:26 MT calls the law-breaker 'ārûr ('cursed'). The LXX, however, uses a form of the verb (ἐπι)καταράομαι in both places—the perfect participle passive κεκατηραμένος in Dt. 21:23 and the verbal adjective ἐπικατάρατος in Dt. 27:26. (Yet Paul shows that he knew the Hebrew text of Dt. 21:23, for in his exposition he uses the noun κατάρα, corresponding to Heb. *qelālāh*.) Paul probably uses ἐπικατάρατος (in preference to the LXX κεκατηραμένος) when quoting Dt. 21:23 here by the way of assimilation to his quotation of Dt. 27:26 in v.10 (cf. M. Wilcox, "'Upon the Tree'—Deut. 21:22-23 in the NT," *JBL* 96 [1977], 85-99, especially 87)" (*Galatians*, 165).

66. NET Bible commentary note on Deuteronomy 21:23, www.netBible.org.

67. So Bruce (*Galatians*, 164): "The exposure of a criminal's corpse on a tree or pole, then, was not to be prolonged beyond sundown: such continued exposure was an affront not only to human decency but to God himself (Heb. *qilelaṯ 'elōhîm* could mean 'affront to God' rather than 'accursed by God', although the LXX chooses the latter rendering). An early instance of this is recorded in Jos. 10:26f.: when Joshua captured the Canaanite kings who were defeated in the battle of Beth-horon, he 'put them to death, and hung them on five trees. And they hung upon the trees until evening; but at the time of the going down of the sun, Joshua commanded, and they took them down from the trees, and threw them into the cave where they had hidden themselves, and they set great stones against the mouth of the cave' (cf. the treatment of the king of Ai in Jos. 8:29). So, in the Johannine passion narrative, the bodies of Jesus and the two robbers who were crucified with him were removed from their crosses before sundown, at the instance of the Jewish authorities, who were specially concerned that the sanctity of the ensuing sabbath should not be violated (Jn. 19:31; cf. Mk. 15:42f.)." Bruce also notes the propitiatory hanging of the chiefs in Numbers 25:4 and the hanging of Saul's sons in 2 Samuel 21:9 to argue that "Christ accordingly underwent the penalty prescribed for the covenant-breaker" (*Galatians*, 164; cf. Keener, *Galatians*, 254-56), but this is not explicit in Gal 3:13. Longenecker adds, "In the NT period . . . Deut 21:22-23 was applied both to the exposure of a dead corpse on a tree or pole and the impalement or crucifixion of a living person (cf. J. A. Fitzmyer, "Crucifixion in Ancient Palestine, Qumran Literature, and the NT," *CBQ* 40 [1978]: 493-513). So, for example, in 11QTemple 64.6-13 regulations are given for hanging the corpse of a man executed 'on a tree' and hanging a living man 'on a tree that he may die,' with both forms of hanging related to Deut 21:22-23 and the phrase 'cursed by God' expanded to 'cursed by God and men'" (*Galatians*, 122; cf. Dunn, *Galatians*, 178).

his dead corpse, if left exposed overnight, causes the curse of God upon the defiled land.

First Corinthians 12:3 ("no one speaking by the Spirit of God says, 'Jesus is accursed'") suggests that those who rejected the Messiah used Deuteronomy 21:23 as a proof-text. As Bruce points out, the interpretation of Deuteronomy 21:23 in the later Mishnah (*Sanhedrin* 6:4) inferred from the phrase קִלְלַת אֱלֹהִים that the hanged man had blasphemed the name of God.[68] Longenecker observes,

> For Jews, the proclamation of a crucified Messiah was scandalous (cf. 1 Cor 1:23; Gal 5:11), "a blasphemous contradiction in terms" (Bruce, *Galatians*, 166). Undoubtedly the central problem for all Jewish Christians was how to understand Jesus as God's Messiah and yet as cursed by God, with the magnitude of the problem only heightened by the pronouncement of Deut 21:23.[69]

Lancaster further explains how Deuteronomy 21:23 was used as a Jewish polemic against the early followers of Yeshua the Messiah.[70] The term תָּלוּי (*talui*, "hanged one" or "crucified one") in Deuteronomy 21:23 became a common title for Yeshua in the Judaism of Paul's time. As most of Judaism resisted the claims of Yeshua and his followers, the *Talui* moniker provided a catchy polemic. Who is Yeshua? He is *Talui*, the Crucified One. And what does the Torah say? "*Talui* is accursed of God." Lancaster suggests that in Galatians 3:13, Paul returned to his former anti-Yeshua, *Talui*-polemic and cited Deuteronomy 21:22–23 with reference to Yeshua again, but this time with a new spin.

> [14] ἵνα εἰς τὰ ἔθνη ἡ εὐλογία τοῦ Ἀβραὰμ γένηται ἐν Χριστῷ Ἰησοῦ, ἵνα τὴν ἐπαγγελίαν τοῦ πνεύματος λάβωμεν διὰ τῆς πίστεως.
>
> [14] in order that in Christ Jesus the blessing of Abraham might come to the Gentiles, so that we would receive the promise of the Spirit through faith.

The purpose of the Messiah's setting his followers free from the curse of Pharisaic Judaism was so that gentile believers could receive the blessing of Abraham in Christ, and that believers would receive the promised Holy Spirit through faithfulness.[71]

---

68. Bruce, *Galatians*, 166.
69. Longenecker, *Galatians*, 122.
70. Lancaster, *Galatians*, 161–62.
71. The article τῆς before πίστεως points back to ἐκ πίστεως in 3:7, 9, 11, 12 (Bruce, *Galatians*, 168). In 3:2 the Galatians had received the Spirit through ἀκοῆς πίστεως

Paul's arguments from Scripture in 3:6–14 conclude with two ἵνα clauses that bring to a climax the two main themes of both this section and the previous one: (1) the blessing of Abraham given to gentiles in/through the Messiah (cf. "in Christ" in 1:22; 2:4, 17; 3:26, 28; 5:6, 10), and (2) the receiving of the promised Spirit by faithfulness apart from legalistic "works of the law."

Moo observes that διὰ τῆς πίστεως in the second ἵνα clause corresponds, "by virtue of both its placement in the clause and by its meaning," to ἐν Χριστῷ Ἰησοῦ in the first ἵνα clause.[72] In their union to the Messiah, and adherence to his teachings and example, gentile believers will receive the full covenant blessings of Abraham in the future kingdom of God. And it is through faithfulness, the same faithfulness that the Messiah exemplified toward God and his law (2:16), that the nation of Israel will receive the promised eschatological outpouring of the Holy Spirit.[73]

> [15] Ἀδελφοί, κατὰ ἄνθρωπον λέγω· ὅμως ἀνθρώπου κεκυρωμένην διαθήκην οὐδεὶς ἀθετεῖ ἢ ἐπιδιατάσσεται. [16] τῷ δὲ Ἀβραὰμ ἐρρέθησαν αἱ ἐπαγγελίαι καὶ τῷ σπέρματι αὐτοῦ. οὐ λέγει, Καὶ τοῖς σπέρμασιν, ὡς ἐπὶ πολλῶν ἀλλ᾽ ὡς ἐφ᾽ ἑνός, Καὶ τῷ σπέρματί σου, ὅς ἐστιν Χριστός.
>
> [15] Brethren, I speak in terms of human relations: even though it is *only* a man's covenant, yet when it has been ratified, no one sets it aside or adds conditions to it. [16] Now the promises were spoken to Abraham and to his seed. He does not say, "And to seeds," as *referring* to many, but *rather* to one, "And to your seed," that is, Christ.

The apostle argues from the lesser to the greater: "Since even in the lesser sphere of human justice it is illegal to change the conditions of a covenant after one has sworn to it (v. 15), it is more so in the sphere of divine justice, when God unilaterally swears to bless all the gentiles through Abraham's seed (v. 17)."[74]

Most commentators seem to question Paul's grammatical argument in 3:16 concerning a Messianic understanding of a singular "seed."[75] C. John

---

("hearing/obedience of faithfulness").

72. Moo, *Galatians*, 215.

73. The OT background of the covenant fulfillment envisioned in Gal 3:14 and the parallel subjunctive verbs in the two ἵνα clauses indicate a future, eschatological perspective. Keener: "The prophets associated God's Spirit among his people with the time of restoration (Isa. 32:15; 44:3; 59:21; Ezek. 36:27; 37:14; 39:29; Joel 2:28–29; cf. Hag. 2:5)" (*Galatians*, 259).

74. Hahn, "Διαθήκη in Galatians 3:15–18," 95.

75. E.g., Bruce (*Galatians*, 172): "There is no need to make heavy weather of Paul's

Collins, however, concludes that in Galatians 3:16 Paul was referring to Genesis 22:18 which speaks of an individual offspring, and that Paul properly applied Genesis 22:18 to Jesus as a Messianic text.[76] In support of Collins' conclusion, the phrase "your seed shall possess the gate of their enemies" in Genesis 22:17b can also be translated, "your seed shall possess the gate of *his* enemies" with a singular, masculine possessive pronoun. The following phrase then repeats God's promise, "In your seed (singular) all the nations of the earth shall be blessed" (Gen 22:18a). The idea of a singular, preeminent "seed" of Abraham "possessing the gate of his enemies" portends the image of a future conquering king and has thus been interpreted Messianically by Jewish and Christian scholars alike.[77] Paul was thus expounding Genesis 22:17-18 in a straightforward manner as a Messianic passage.

> [17] τοῦτο δὲ λέγω· διαθήκην προκεκυρωμένην ὑπὸ τοῦ θεοῦ ὁ μετὰ τετρακόσια καὶ τριάκοντα ἔτη γεγονὼς νόμος οὐκ ἀκυροῖ εἰς τὸ καταργῆσαι τὴν ἐπαγγελίαν. [18] εἰ γὰρ ἐκ νόμου ἡ κληρονομία, οὐκέτι ἐξ ἐπαγγελίας· τῷ δὲ Ἀβραὰμ δι' ἐπαγγελίας κεχάρισται ὁ θεός.
>
> [17] What I am saying is this: the Law, which came four hundred and thirty years later, does not invalidate a covenant previously ratified by God, so as to nullify the promise. [18] For if the inheritance is based on law, it is no longer based on a promise; but God has granted it to Abraham by means of a promise.

The γάρ at the beginning of 3:18 is explanatory, presenting the reason for Paul's assertion in v. 17. The covenant blessing of the inheritance was granted to Abraham on the basis of God's gracious promise and not by obeying the law. Paul's argumentation continues the antithetical categories established from 2:15 to 3:18.

Paul's opponents likely argued that adherence to the Torah (both biblical law and oral purity traditions) was necessary for gentile believers to

---

insistence that the biblical text has σπέρματί (singular) and not σπέρματιν (plural)"; Longenecker (*Galatians*, 132): "the parallels they cite do not force us to believe that Paul understood 'seed' here as a specific singular rather than a generic singular."

76. Collins, "Galatians 3:16," 86. Similarly, Scott Hahn argues that the covenant in view in Gal 3:17 is the Abrahamic covenant ratified in Gen 22:15-18, and that understanding the covenant oath of Gen 22:15-18 is key to understanding Paul's theological argument in Gal 3:15-18 ("Διαθήκη in Galatians 3:15-18," 80).

77. This conquering "seed" motif in Gen 22:18 seems to reach back to the promise of a deliverer "seed" of the woman in Gen 3:15. Many biblical theologians view the promise of the Messiah in Gen 3:15 as the foundation for the Abrahamic covenant which then serves as the basis for all of the covenants that follow, including the Sinai covenant (cf. Kaiser, "Eschatological Hermeneutics," 96-99; Ronning, "Curse on the Serpent," 375-76; Ojewole, "Seed in Genesis 3:15," 350).

become "children of Abraham" and thus receive the blessings of the Abrahamic covenant. And part of the process for gentiles to become "children of Abraham" was to undergo the sanctioned rite of circumcision as a part of proselyte conversion under Pharisaic authority. In other words, the Pharisaic understanding of Jewish law, including all of their religious traditions, was the only channel through which gentiles could receive the covenant blessings promised to Abraham's descendants. Paul's argument, however, is that in Genesis 22:16–18, God put himself under a unilaterally binding oath to fulfill his covenant with Abraham, and that the blessing of "all the nations of the earth" (Gen 22:18) would be accomplished through Abraham's ultimate "seed," the Messiah. Consequently, to require compliance to the Pharisaic understanding of Jewish law for gentile believers to receive the blessings of the Abrahamic covenant would be nonsense. To suppose that God added stipulations in the form of Pharisaic *halakah* ("works of the law") to the Abrahamic covenant, long after it had been unilaterally sworn by God, would make God guilty of illegally violating a covenant promise in a manner that is not even tolerated in human contracts. Even the biblical law of God given at Mount Sinai came 430 years *after* the ratification of the Abrahamic covenant.

Paul's use of νόμος in Galatians 3:17–18 is nuanced. It is clear that νόμος in 3:17 refers to the covenant stipulations received at Sinai. Yet over time these biblical commandments developed into a religious system that the apostle refers to as his "former manner of life in Judaism" (1:13) that included a complex of extrabiblical rules Paul describes as "my ancestral traditions" (1:14). These extrabiblical traditions are also designated as "works of the law" in the epistle (2:16; 3:10). For the former Pharisee and religious Jews of his time these extrabiblical traditions were a part of the Torah (νόμος) that encompassed both biblical law and oral traditions. Therefore, it is important to keep in mind that νόμος in Paul's writings may not always refer exclusively to the biblical law of God but may also include the oral traditions of Pharisaic Judaism.

Since the technical phrase ἔργων νόμου (3:10) is understood as focusing primarily on Pharisaic *halakah*, the occurrences of νόμος in the phrases ἐν νόμῳ οὐδεὶς δικαιοῦται (3:11) and ὁ δὲ νόμος οὐκ ἔστιν ἐκ πίστεως (3:12) can serve as shorthand for ἔργων νόμου or the broader category of *Jewish* law (including oral traditions) given all of the connective particles and prepositions in this unit of discourse. The key in 3:12 is that the strong adversative ἀλλά contrasts the phrase ὁ δὲ νόμος οὐκ ἔστιν ἐκ πίστεως with the apostle's citation of Leviticus 18:5, which clearly speaks of the Mosaic law. In 3:10, τῷ βιβλίῳ τοῦ νόμου, where νόμος clearly refers to the stipulations of the Mosaic covenant, contrasts well with the preceding ἔργων νόμου. In 3:17, the prepositional phrase μετὰ τετρακόσια καὶ τριάκοντα ἔτη γεγονὼς comes between νόμος and its article, specifying precisely the particular νόμος Paul is referring to—the Sinai covenant stipulations that came 430 years after God's promise to Abraham. Given the grammatical connectors, νόμος in 3:18-19 points back to the Sinai covenant stipulations referred to in 3:17.

Some may argue that this nuanced perspective is subjective. Yet this mutifaceted use of νόμος originates from Paul whose usage is heavily governed by the immediate context of his argument. Evidently, Paul can use νόμος to refer to the entire written Torah of the OT, parts of the OT Torah, as shorthand for "works of Torah" (i.e., Jewish *halakah*), general Torah obedience, or in a broader sense to encompass the entirety of Jewish law including both biblical law and oral religious traditions.

Another example of Paul's nuanced use of νόμος is found in Romans 2:15 where he states that when Gentiles do by nature what Torah requires they show that (singular) τὸ ἔργον τοῦ νόμου (i.e., the doing or living out of Torah = what the Torah requires) is written on their hearts. Then, in Romans 3:28, Paul reiterates his thesis that δικαιοῦσθαι πίστει ἄνθρωπον χωρὶς ἔργων νόμου. To support this, he asks rhetorically, "Or is God the God of Jews only? Is he not the God of Gentiles also? Yes, of Gentiles also" (3:29). Here, ἔργων νόμου must be something characteristic of Jews as compared to gentiles. If Paul has in mind anything particular here, it would presumably be the distinctive Jewish teachings and oral traditions concerning how to live out (how to "action") the written Torah of God. The ἔργων νόμου in Romans 3:28 is evidently different from τὸ ἔργον τοῦ νόμου written upon gentile hearts (2:15) and done "by nature" (2:14).

It is easy to assume that when Paul speaks against ἔργων νόμου, he is opposing the observance of OT commandments. Some might qualify this conclusion by adding that Paul is opposing the ceremonial aspects of Torah, or those features that pertain to Jewish identity. Many believers would detach ἔργων νόμου from, for example, the Ten Commandments, or OT commandments to love God with all one's heart (Deut 6:5) or to love one's neighbor as oneself (Lev 19:18).

Once it becomes evident that ἔργων νόμου cannot refer to obeying the biblical commandments in general, some other key Pauline passages may help clarify how Paul views "the law" and ἔργων νόμου in a more nuanced way. In Colossians 2, Paul addresses the topic of false teaching, and in verse 8 he warns, "See to it that no one takes you captive through philosophy and empty deception, according to the tradition of men." Under this category, the apostle further warns, "Therefore no one is to act as your judge in regard to food or drink or in respect to a festival or a new moon or a Sabbath day" (Col 2:16). While many Christian interpreters might use Colossians 2:16 as a proof-text to argue that Christ has done away with keeping the Mosaic law, an originalist perspective would argue that the passage is focusing rather on *how*—the manner in which—these observances are carried out. Paul is not teaching the Colossians to desist from biblical food laws or the appointed times prescribed in the OT. The inclusion of "drink" in the phrase "food or drink" suggests that Paul is concerned with Jewish purity *halakah* concerning food and drink rather than clean and unclean animals for consumption (Lev 11; Deut 14). He is insisting that they do not need to subject themselves to false teachers who are requiring a specific *halakah* in which these ordinances are to be carried out, *halakah* that is apparently based on "philosophy and empty deception, according to the tradition of men" (Col 2:8). The dietary requirements in Leviticus 11 and the appointed times of Leviticus 23 are not based on philosophy, empty deception, or human tradition. Judaism's teachings on *how* to observe biblical food laws and feast days can be.

Another helpful passage in more accurately understanding Paul's view of Torah is Galatians 5:3: μαρτύρομαι δὲ πάλιν παντὶ ἀνθρώπῳ περιτεμνομένῳ ὅτι ὀφειλέτης ἐστὶν ὅλον τὸν νόμον ποιῆσαι. According to traditional Christian interpretations, Paul might appear to be promoting lawlessness, or to be minimizing "ceremonial" or "Jewish" components of the OT commandments. Yet the apostle seems to be using "circumcision" as a technical term for proselyte conversion, and his warning against "keeping the whole law" might actually refer to the entire *Jewish* law, including all of the oral Torah and traditions affixed to the written Torah that gentile proselytes would legally be bound under. From a Jewish perspective, ὅλον τὸν νόμον may have included the oral Torah and traditions of the sages.[78] This understanding of Galatians 5:3 seems to be corroborated by 1 Corinthians 9:20–21 where the apostle explicitly distinguishes between the status of

---

78. In the 1906 *Jewish Encyclopedia*, Solomon Schechter and Julius Greenstone define a *gezerah* as "A rabbinical enactment issued as . . . a guard or a fence ('geder') to a Biblical precept." Authorized rabbis "did not hesitate to enact a gezerah even when it contradicted a Biblical law (Ber. 54a; Sanh. 46a), and . . . when the reason for the gezerah no more existed, they abolished the gezerah itself." One example of an extra-biblical *gezerah* that has been accepted as "Torah" by religious Jews concerns the OT prohibition of eating or possessing yeast/leaven during Passover. Since Passover begins midday on the fourteenth day of Nisan, Jewish sages added a two-hour buffer to the OT prohibition since someone might eat leavened foods after noon on a cloudy day. Religious Jews understand Deuteronomy 17:8–11 as authorizing rabbinic *gezerot* since the written Torah does not always address modern circumstances and contemporary issues. Traditional Judaism claims that, until the end of the Talmudic Era (ca. 1500 years ago), there was a central rabbinic authority which issued *gezerot* that was accepted by all Jews.

"under the law" (understood as the entire Jewish law including oral traditions) and being under "the law of God" and "the law of Christ."

Paul's use of νόμος in Galatians 3:17-18 is as nuanced as Hebrew understandings of Torah during the Second Temple Period. Without a nuanced understanding of νόμος, Galatians 3:17-18 becomes confusing and contradictory. More specifically, Paul seems to use νόμος in this passage to refer either to (1) Jewish law (in part or in whole) or (2) the stipulations of the Mosaic law (in part or in whole). This nuanced approach to Paul's use of νόμος also finds support in other Pauline passages about the law such as Romans 2:14-15; 3:28-29; Colossians 2:8, 16; Galatians 5:3; and 1 Corinthians 9:20-21.

Longenecker offers a traditional Christian understanding of "the inheritance" (ἡ κληρονομία) in Galatians 3:18.

> "Inheritance" is introduced by Paul into the discussion here for the first time, though subsequently it plays a major role (κληρονομία, "inheritance," here; κληρονόμος, "heir," at 3:29; 4:1, 7; κληρονομέω, "inherit," at 4:30; 5:21; with the idea being prominent in the illustration of 4:1-7, the allegory of 4:21-31, and the blessing of 6:16). It stems, of course, from references to the promise(s) contained in the Abrahamic covenant of vv.16-17. The inheritance promised in the Abrahamic covenant had principally to do with territorial, material possessions (cf. Gen 13:14-17; 15:7, 18-21; 17:3-8), but since these were expressions of God's favor they easily became spiritualized as well (cf. 2 Chr 6:27; *Pss. Sol.* 7:2; 9:2; 14:3; 17:26). The territorial and material features of the Abrahamic inheritance are not mentioned here by Paul, for in Christian thought "inheritance" had become thoroughly spiritualized (cf. 5:21; also Acts 20:32; 1 Cor 6:9-10; Eph 5:5; Col 3:24) and Paul's opponents would undoubtedly have thought along such lines as well.[79]

Unfortunately, Longenecker's spiritualization of "inheritance" in 3:18 has more to do with Platonic dualism and Gnosticism (material world is inherently flawed or evil) than the OT. An originalist approach to interpreting the NT would carry the original OT understanding of "inheritance" (Promised Land, territorial and material blessings) in the Abrahamic covenant (Gen 13:14-17; 15:7, 18-21; 17:3-8) into the NT passages that allegedly "spiritualize" the OT meaning of the Abrahamic "inheritance" (according to Longenecker, Acts 20:32; 1 Cor 6:9-10; Gal 5:21; Eph 5:5; Col 3:24). The inheritance that Paul has in mind in Galatians 3:18 is the same material

---

79. Longenecker, *Galatians*, 134.

inheritance that was promised repeatedly to Abraham and his descendants throughout the OT.

> ¹⁹ Τί οὖν ὁ νόμος; τῶν παραβάσεων χάριν προσετέθη, ἄχρις οὗ ἔλθῃ τὸ σπέρμα ᾧ ἐπήγγελται, διαταγεὶς δι' ἀγγέλων ἐν χειρὶ μεσίτου. ²⁰ ὁ δὲ μεσίτης ἑνὸς οὐκ ἔστιν, ὁ δὲ θεὸς εἷς ἐστιν.
> ¹⁹ Why the Law then? It was added because of transgressions, having been ordained through angels by the agency of a mediator, until the seed would come to whom the promise had been made. ²⁰ Now a mediator is not for one *party only*; whereas God is *only* one.

Paul explains the purpose of the law since the inheritance is not based on law but promise (3:18). A significant text-critical issue arises at the beginning of 3:19. Jason Staples has demonstrated that the manuscript tradition of Galatians 3:19a reflects three sets of readings: (1) τῶν παραβάσεων χάριν προσετέθη / ἐτέθη; (2) τῶν παραδόσεων χάριν ἐτέθη; and (3) τῶν πράξεων ([χάριν] ἐτέθη).[80] Staples argues that while the first reading enjoys the majority of manuscript support and the second reading may be a transcriptional error due to visual similarity, the third reading (τῶν πράξεων) is "an orthodox corruption to exclude Marcionite and other demiurgic interpretations and . . . an important example of an early Latin harmonization impacting the readings of P46 and other early Greek manuscripts."[81] The combination of P46 + Western manuscripts gives the third τῶν πράξεων reading stronger attestation than is generally recognized.[82] Moreover, the combined witness of P46 (ca. second century AD) and Irenaeus' application of the τῶν πράξεων reading in *Adversus Haereses* 3.7.2 (ca. 180 AD) suggests quite an early date for τῶν πράξεων.[83]

At least five reasons indicate that ὁ νόμος at the beginning of 3:19 does not refer to the biblical law of God but also includes the purity traditions ("works of the law") of Pharisaic Judaism.

---

80. Staples, "'Law of Deeds' in Gal 3,19a," 126.
81. Staples, "'Law of Deeds' in Gal 3,19a," 127.
82. Staples, "'Law of Deeds' in Gal 3,19a," 128.
83. Staples, "'Law of Deeds' in Gal 3,19a," 128. Staples cites Carlson, "Text of Galatians," 252n37. "*Legem factorum positam donec veniret semen cui promissum est*" (Irenaeus, *Adv. Haer.* 5.21.1; "This is the seed of which the apostle says in his letter to the Galatians, 'the Law of works was established until the seed came to whom the promise was made'") cited in Staples, "'Law of Deeds' in Gal 3,19a," 131n21. This same phrase (*lex factorum*) "matches closely to the Latin of Rom 3,27, where διὰ ποίου νόμου; τῶν ἔργων; οὐχί, ἀλλὰ διὰ νόμου πίστεως is rendered *est per quam legem factorum non sed per legem fidei*, contrasting the 'Law of works' (*legem factorum*) with the 'Law of fidelity' (*legem fidei*)" ("'Law of Deeds' in Gal 3,19a," 132–33; original emphasis).

1. V. 17 records ὁ μετὰ τετρακόσια καὶ τριάκοντα ἔτη γεγονὼς νόμος ("the law, which came four hundred and thirty years later"). With the first attributive position of the adjectival phrase between the article and noun (μετὰ τετρακόσια καὶ τριάκοντα ἔτη γεγονὼς), the adjectival phrase receives greater emphasis than its substantive (ὁ νόμος) which it "modifies or qualifies . . . in some way."[84] In other words, Paul is not addressing the biblical law of God in general, but specifying the portion of the law of God that was given at Mount Sinai as a part of that covenant. Thus, if Paul then refers to ὁ νόμος τῶν πράξεων ("the law of deeds") in 3:19 (as in P46, Western manuscripts, and Irenaeus), he is most likely referring to a different legal code that includes "the works of the law" (3:10) and not the one given at Sinai 430 years after God's promise to Abraham (3:17).[85]

2. The verb προστίθημι ("add to") in 3:19 contradicts the argument "no one sets it aside or adds conditions to it" in 3:15 if Paul is referring to the biblical law of God in 3:19.[86] It is difficult to explain how the decalogue of the Sinai covenant can be characterized as a mere addition.[87] If, however, Paul is shifting attention in 3:19 to a Pharisaic "law of deeds" that includes "works of the law" (3:10) and oral traditions, then the apostle accurately describes their illegitimate addition to the biblical law of God. The imagery of the law being "added" in some manuscript traditions of 3:19a recalls Romans 5:20 where "the law came in (παρεισῆλθεν, "slipping in, coming in as a side issue"[88]) so that the transgression would increase." Quite significantly, the only other NT occurrence of the same verb παρεισέρχομαι occurs in Galatians 2:4 to describe Paul's opponents: "But *it was* because of the false

---

84. Wallace, *Exegetical Syntax*, 306, 308. The adjectival emphasis of the phrase would resemble something like "the *coming-after-430 years* law."

85. Dunn recognizes Paul's nuanced use of ὁ νόμος in 3:19 when he asserts, "Paul's critique is directed against a 'works of the law' attitude, against an identity determined 'from (works of) the law' (see on iii.10 and 18) . . . Gal. v.14 shows Paul still to retain a highly positive view of the law for Christians as well" (*Galatians*, 189).

86. Keener points out that Paul's use of διατάσσω in 3:19 recalls the cognate ἐπιδιατάσσομαι in 3:15 (*Galatians*, 281). Since it is obviously unjust to "add to" (ἐπιδιατάσσομαι) a ratified contract in 3:15, it is difficult to explain how the law of God can justly be "added to" and "arranged/ordered" (διατάσσω) by messengers in 3:19 unless the latter is without the sanction of God (i.e. the addition of Pharisaic purity regulations, Jewish oral law).

87. Cf. Longenecker: "The fact that the augmented προστίθημι ("add" to something already present) appears in the text and not the simple verb τίθημι ("place", "set up") signals a nuance of disparagement and suggests that the law was not of the essence of God's redemptive activity with humankind, which undoubtedly is why D G Irenaeus (in Latin) and Ambrosiaster seem to have felt uncomfortable with προσετέθη and so read ἐτέθη" (*Galatians*, 138).

88. Wallace, "Galatians 3:19–20," 235.

brethren secretly brought in, who had sneaked in (παρεισῆλθον) to spy out our liberty which we have in Christ Jesus, in order to bring us into bondage." This action of "sneaking in" cannot possibly refer to the giving of the law of God in Romans 5:20. The supplementary nature of "the law" in Romans 5:20 and Galatians 3:19 suggests that Paul was referring to the extrabiblical purity traditions of the oral law in these passages and not the biblical law of God.

3. All three sets of variant readings in the manuscript tradition of Galatians 3:19a (τῶν πράξεων [(χάριν) ἐτέθη]; τῶν παραδόσεων χάριν ἐτέθη; τῶν παραβάσεων χάριν προσετέθη / ἐτέθη) are easily explained if Paul is addressing the broader Jewish law of his time (including its addition of Pharisaic oral traditions).[89] The opening question Τί οὖν ὁ νόμος; of 3:19 would be nonsensical if Paul was referring to the biblical law of God, regardless of the apostle's rhetorical aims.[90]

- Τί οὖν ὁ νόμος τῶν πράξεων; ἄχρις οὗ ἔλθῃ τὸ σπέρμα ᾧ ἐπήγγελται διαταγεὶς δι' ἀγγέλων ἐν χειρὶ μεσίτου.

  What is/why the law of deeds/works then? [*It functioned*] until the seed would come to whom the promise had been made, having been ordered/arranged through messengers by the hand of an intermediary.

- Τί οὖν ὁ νόμος τῶν πράξεων; ἐτέθη ἄχρις οὗ ἔλθῃ τὸ σπέρμα ᾧ ἐπήγγελται διαταγεὶς δι' ἀγγέλων ἐν χειρὶ μεσίτου.

  What is/why the law of deeds then? It was established until the seed would come to whom the promise had been made, having been ordered through messengers by the hand of an intermediary.

- Τί οὖν ὁ νόμος; τῶν πράξεων χάριν ἐτέθη ἄχρις οὗ ἔλθῃ τὸ σπέρμα ᾧ ἐπήγγελται διαταγεὶς δι' ἀγγέλων ἐν χειρὶ μεσίτου.

---

89. Cf. Bruce: "The alteration of παραβάσεων to παραδόσεων made the purpose of the law the creation of traditions (presumably in the sense of 1:14); its replacement by πράξεων yielded a reference to the 'law of works'" (*Galatians*, 176).

90. Concerning the traditional Christian interpretation of Gal 3:19 that the law was only temporary until the coming of Messiah, Longenecker admits, "Paul's view here, of course, deviates widely from that of Judaism. Wis 18:4, for example, speaks of the 'imperishable light of the law'; Josephus states that if not their wealth and their cities, at least the law given the Jews remains immortal (*Ag. Ap.* 2.277); and Philo echoes this sentiment in speaking of the changelessness of the law for as long as sun, moon, heavens, and the earth continue to exist (*Vit. Mos.* 2.14). The apocalyptic writings also emphasize the eternal and immutable character of the law (e.g., *Jub.* 1.27; 3.31; 6.17). It would, in fact, be difficult to find any Jew who thought otherwise" (*Galatians*, 139; similarly Moo, *Galatians*, 232-33). This traditional understanding of Gal 3:19 would contradict the Messiah's explicit teaching on the perpetuity of the law in Matt 5:17-19.

What is/why the law then? It was established for the purpose of [good] deeds until the seed would come to whom the promise had been made, having been ordered through messengers by the hand of an intermediary.

- Τί οὖν ὁ νόμος; τῶν παραδόσεων χάριν ἐτέθη ἄχρις οὗ ἔλθῃ τὸ σπέρμα ᾧ ἐπήγγελται διαταγεὶς δι' ἀγγέλων ἐν χειρὶ μεσίτου.

What is/why the law then? It was established for the purpose of traditions/commandments until the seed would come to whom the promise had been made, having been ordered through messengers by the hand of an intermediary.

- Τί οὖν ὁ νόμος; τῶν παραβάσεων χάριν προσετέθη ἄχρις οὗ ἔλθῃ τὸ σπέρμα ᾧ ἐπήγγελται διαταγεὶς δι' ἀγγέλων ἐν χειρὶ μεσίτου.

What is/why the [Jewish] law then? It was added for [dealing with, defining, and/or preventing] the transgressions until the seed would come to whom the promise had been made, having been ordered through messengers by the hand of an intermediary.

4. It is difficult to explain the phrase διαταγεὶς δι' ἀγγέλων in 3:19 in relation to the law of God. The verb διατάσσω means "to put into a proper order or relationship, make arrangements, to give (detailed) instructions as to what must be done, order,"[91] and has been translated differently.[92] The sense of διαταγεὶς δι' ἀγγέλων in 3:19 seems to be "having been arranged/ordered through messengers/angels." Yet as Bruce asserts, "The angelic administration of the law finds no place in the OT."[93] Although some commentators may argue for the presence of angels at Mount Sinai during the giving of the law, the verb διατάσσω in 3:19 indicates manipulation of the law by these agents.[94] As Longenecker explains, "it is almost impossible to read 'ordained

---

91. Arndt, Danker, Bauer, and Gingrich, "διατάσσω," 237.

92. Cf. "administered" (NET), "put into effect" (NIV), "put in place" (ESV), "appointed" (NKJV), "ordained" (NASB).

93. Bruce, *Galatians*, 176. Similarly, Moo: "The idea that angels were involved in the giving of the law is not taught anywhere in the OT" (*Galatians*, 235).

94. Cf. Longenecker: "And it was such an understanding of angels as being present at the giving of the Mosaic law that seems to have been the dominant tradition in Paul's day, as in *Jub.* 1.27–29; Acts 7:38, 53; Heb 2:2; Philo, *Somn.* 1.140–44; and Josephus, *Ant.* 15.136" (*Galatians*, 140). The presence of the angels and their alleged "arranging/ordering" of the law are different realities. Moo concedes, "The verb διατάσσω... is an unusual choice to describe the giving of the law. It means 'arrange' (e.g., Acts 20:13) or 'command' (1 Cor. 7:17; Titus 1:5) and is never used elsewhere in Biblical Greek to refer to the giving of the law" (*Galatians*, 235).

through angels' in any other way than with the intent 'to depreciate the law as not given directly by God' (so Burton, *Galatians*, 189; and so the vast majority of scholars, whether they agree with Paul or not)."[95]

5. Another difficulty with interpreting 3:19 as referring to the biblical law of God is the phrase ἐν χειρὶ μεσίτου ("by the hand of an intermediary/mediator"). Since Exodus 31:18 and Deuteronomy 9:10 explicitly record the giving of the law at Sinai "by the finger of God," some commentators may suggest that the μεσίτης of 3:19–20 refers to the angel/messenger of YHWH through whom the law of God was mediated at Sinai. This reading encounters a theological problem in 3:20 where this intermediary is clearly said to *not* be "(of) one" (ὁ δὲ μεσίτης ἑνὸς οὐκ ἔστιν) in contrast to the oneness of God in the following clause as recorded in Deuteronomy 6:4.[96]

Therefore, since the inheritance is not based on Jewish law but on promise (3:18), the apostle's point in 3:19 is that the purpose of the Jewish law (ὁ νόμος τῶν πράξεων, "the law of deeds") was to function temporarily until the arrival of the Messiah. The temporary nature of this "law of deeds" is evident in the fact that it was organized and put into practice by human messengers and intermediaries, the religious leaders who helped establish the Pharisaic Judaism of Paul's time.

The article at the beginning of 3:20 (ὁ δὲ μεσίτης ἑνὸς οὐκ ἔστιν, "and the intermediary is not of one") points back to the same intermediary in the preceding phrase, ἐν χειρὶ μεσίτου (3:19).[97] Since the following phrase (ὁ δὲ θεὸς εἷς ἐστιν) is clearly a reference to the oneness of God recorded in Deuteronomy 6:4, Paul's main point seems to be that the human intermediary through whom "the law of deeds" (3:19) was received does not possess the same level of authority as God. While "God is one," the human intermediary is not, and thus "the law of deeds" received from human intermediaries does not possess the same authority as the word/law of God.

> [21] Ὁ οὖν νόμος κατὰ τῶν ἐπαγγελιῶν [τοῦ θεοῦ]; μὴ γένοιτο. εἰ γὰρ ἐδόθη νόμος ὁ δυνάμενος ζῳοποιῆσαι, ὄντως ἐκ νόμου ἂν ἦν ἡ δικαιοσύνη· [22] ἀλλὰ συνέκλεισεν ἡ γραφὴ τὰ πάντα ὑπὸ ἁμαρτίαν, ἵνα ἡ ἐπαγγελία ἐκ πίστεως Ἰησοῦ Χριστοῦ δοθῇ τοῖς πιστεύουσιν.

---

95. Longenecker, *Galatians*, 140.

96. Longenecker (*Galatians*, 142–43) cites Jewish literature like 'Abot R. Nat. 1, §2B ("Moses received Torah from Sinai. Not from the mouth of an angel, and not from the mouth of the Seraph, but from the mouth of the King over the king of kings, the Holy One, blessed be He") to demonstrate how some "in early Judaism saw mediation of any kind as being inferior and stressed God's direct dealing with his people."

97. Moo notes that the article can indicate generic reference so that μεσίτης in 3:19–20 refers to a human intermediary/mediator in general (*Galatians*, 236).

> ²¹ Is the Law then contrary to the promises of God? May it never be! For if a law had been given which was able to impart life, then righteousness would indeed have been based on law. ²² But the Scripture has shut up everyone under sin, so that the promise by faith in Jesus Christ might be given to those who believe.

In contrast to the Pharisaic "law of deeds" (ὁ νόμος τῶν πράξεων in P46, Western manuscripts, and Irenaeus) in 3:19, Paul seems to revert back to the biblical law given at Sinai (3:17) at the start of 3:21.[98] "Is the biblical law given at Sinai contrary to the promises of God? May it never be!"

The following phrase (εἰ γὰρ ἐδόθη νόμος ὁ δυνάμενος ζῳοποιῆσαι) has confused many commentators. Dunn explains, "This line of argument has caused commentators difficulty, since it seems to deny the established Jewish association between the Torah and life, to which Paul has already referred (iii.12; e.g. Lev. xviii.5; Deut. vi.24; Prov. iii.1-2; vi.23; Sir. xvii.11—'the law of life'; Bar. iii.9; iv.1; *Pss. Sol.* xiv.2)."[99] The point of tension is that the phrase εἰ γὰρ ἐδόθη νόμος ὁ δυνάμενος ζῳοποιῆσαι in 3:21 appears to contradict the apostle's citation of Leviticus 18:5 in Galatians 3:12: "the law is not of faithfulness; on the contrary, 'he who practices them shall live by them.'" In other words, for some interpreters, the apostle seems to be accusing God of giving a faulty or deficient law.

In 3:21a, Paul is emphatically declaring that the stipulations of the Sinai Covenant are *not* opposed to God's promises to Abraham (μὴ γένοιτο). Yet in 3:21b, according to traditional interpretations, these covenant stipulations were never able to "impart life" and could never lead to righteousness. In what sense, then, were these God-given covenant stipulations supportive of (or minimally not a hindrance against) God's original promises to Abraham? The conventional response from verse 22 is that ἡ γραφὴ (understood in apposition to νόμος in v. 21) has verified human depravity and man's inability to obey the law of God so that the promise given to Abraham is only attainable by believing in Jesus Christ.[100] However, from this perspective v. 22 is demonstrating the utter incompatibility between the Sinai Covenant stipulations and the Abrahamic promises. The former is serving as an insurmountable obstruction to the latter. From this perspective, the apostle's

---

98. This shift from the Pharisaic "law of deeds" in 3:19 back to the biblical law of God at the start of 3:21 is the disconnect Bruce feels when he asserts, "The direction of the argument thus might prepare us for an affirmative answer, rather than for Paul's emphatic μὴ γένοιτο" (*Galatians*, 180).

99. Dunn, *Galatians*, 192; similarly, Moo: "how are we to square Paul's reference to the typically Jewish view that 'the one who does [the commandments of the law] will find life by them' [Lev 18:5] with his claim here that no law can make alive?" (*Galatians*, 238).

100. E.g., Bruce, *Galatians*, 180.

argument becomes convoluted and his emphatic μὴ γένοιτο, which should be obvious to all, makes no sense at all. If ὁ νόμος was not contrary to the Abrahamic promises, then the law of God would have indeed promoted "life" and "righteousness."[101]

However, if we trace the apostle's argument thus far and allow for his nuanced Judaic understanding of ὁ νόμος, the main point in v.21 becomes clear. In the larger context of Galatians 3, Paul is contrasting heart obedience to the biblical commandments of God (as Christ exhibited) against the Jewish law that included oral traditions, rules for proselyte conversion, and ἔργων νόμου (sectarian *halakah*). Accordingly, the first occurrence of νόμος in 3:21 refers to the biblical law given at Sinai while the second and third occurrences refer to the broader Jewish law of his time. Then, ἡ γραφὴ at the beginning of verse 22 reverts back to the biblical law. Paul is using shorthand terms to continue his contrast between the biblical law of God, clarified and lived out by the Messiah, and "the man-made teachings of the Pharisees and corrupted rulings of the chief priests in his day, a system that could not offer life to a massive influx of new Gentile converts desiring to enter the Hebrew faith."[102]

Thus the following seems to be a more accurate outline of Paul's argument in 3:21–22:

> *Question*: Is the [written] Torah then contrary to the promises of God [given to Abraham]?
> *Answer*: May it never be!
> *Reason*: For (γὰρ) if [oral] Torah had been given which was able to impart life, then righteousness would have indeed been based on [oral] Torah
> But (ἀλλὰ) the Scripture [written Torah] has shut up everyone under sin so that the promise, by the faithfulness of Jesus Christ, might be given to those who are faithful," i.e., *to God through written Torah like the faithfulness of the Messiah*]

At least four arguments support Paul's nuanced used of νόμος in 3:21. First, the connective γὰρ before the second νόμος does not absolutely require the first and second νόμος to have the same referent. γὰρ can be used as a "marker of cause or reason, *for* . . . marker of clarification, *for, you see* . . . marker of inference, *certainly, by all means, so, then*."[103] So, Paul's point could be, "The biblical law is by no means contrary to the promises of God

---

101. In Romans 7:10 Paul describes the law as ἡ ἐντολὴ ἡ εἰς ζωήν, "the commandment which was for/unto life."
102. ben Mordechai, *Galatians*, 280.
103. Danker et al., "γὰρ," 189–90.

for/because if the given Jewish law was able to impart life, then righteousness would indeed have been based on Jewish law." The *Jewish* law, with its oral traditions, does not facilitate life or righteousness, but the biblical law does (Lev 18:5).

A second argument is that νόμος must be used with multiple referents in Galatians 3:21 in order for Paul's premise in 3:21a to make sense. Paul's multifaceted use of νόμος is evident elsewhere in Galatians and throughout his other NT writings. Third, the second occurrence of νόμος is qualified by ἐδόθη and the participial phrase ὁ δυνάμενος ζῳοποιῆσαι. The verb here (δίδωμι) seems to parallel προστίθημι in 3:19 (the law was "added"), indicating that both passages are describing the illegitimate implementation of Pharisaic purity requirements. Moreover, from a Hebrew perspective, the idea of the biblical law of God giving life saturates the entire OT (Lev 18:5; Deut 30:16; Ps 1:2-3). The second and third occurrences of νόμος in Galatians 3:21, which are unable to give life and lead to righteousness, are purposely described in this manner by the apostle to forcefully contrast them with the biblical law of God which is meant to provide life and righteousness.

A fourth argument is Paul's usage of ἡ γραφὴ at the beginning of 3:22, right after the third occurrence of νόμος in 3:21, a νόμος that is incapable of leading to true righteousness. While Christian interpreters view this third occurrence of νόμος as Paul's theological lesson on man's inability to (flawlessly) obey the law of God, a likelier reading discerns the apostle's blatant characterization of an impostor νόμος since in the OT, "all Your commandments are righteousness" (Ps 119:172; cf. Isa 51:7—"Listen to Me, you who know righteousness, a people in whose heart is My law"). Thus, the apostle's otherwise unexplainable shift in using ἡ γραφὴ at the beginning of 3:22 refocuses his audience's attention back to the written law of God, in contradistinction to the impotent νόμος that does not give life, nor lead to righteousness, thereby standing as an immense obstacle to the promises given to Abraham. The Scripture (esp. Deut 27:26 in Gal 3:10) has proven that everyone—especially the religious leaders of Paul's time with their impostor νόμος—is incapable of obtaining the promise except through the Torah-faithfulness taught and lived out by the Messiah. The biblical law of God is by no means contrary to the promises given to Abraham and, contrary to the Pharisaic law that does not give life nor lead to righteousness, the Messiah's faithfulness to the true meaning of the law of God is the only means by which believers may obtain the original promise. This approach finds support from the observation that τοῖς πιστεύουσιν in 3:22 is superfluous if ἐκ πίστεως Ἰησοῦ Χριστοῦ is taken as an objective genitive. As in 2:16, the phrase ἐκ πίστεως Ἰησοῦ Χριστοῦ in 3:22 should be understood as a subjective genitive; Paul is continuing his contrast between the Messiah's faithfulness to the biblical law of God versus the ἔργων νόμου of Pharisaic purity requirements.[104]

The phrase ὑπὸ ἁμαρτίαν in 3:22 recalls ὑπὸ κατάραν ("under a curse") in 3:10 and continues a series of ὑπό phrases in the following context (cf. ὑπὸ νόμον, v.23; 4:4-5; ὑπὸ παιδαγωγόν, v.25; ὑπὸ ἐπιτρόπους καὶ οἰκονόμους, 4:2; ὑπὸ τὰ στοιχεῖα τοῦ κόσμου, 4:3).[105] This suggests that all of these ὑπό phrases are related to being under subjection to the Jewish law of Paul's time, including its extrabiblical Pharisaic purity requirements.[106] If ὑπὸ ἁμαρτίαν in 3:22 parallels ὑπὸ κατάραν in 3:10 (assuming ἡ γραφὴ in 3:22 is primarily referring to Deut 27:26), Paul is arguing that the Jewish law with its Pharisaic additions brought "everyone" (τὰ πάντα),[107] including Paul's opponents and the religious Jews of his time, under the curse of the biblical law.

> ²³ Πρὸ τοῦ δὲ ἐλθεῖν τὴν πίστιν ὑπὸ νόμον ἐφρουρούμεθα συγκλειόμενοι εἰς τὴν μέλλουσαν πίστιν ἀποκαλυφθῆναι
> ²³ But before faith came, we were kept in custody under the law, being shut up to the faith which was later to be revealed.

The connective conjunction δὲ indicates, "The sense of v.22 is here repeated in different terms."[108] The "coming of faithfulness" (τοῦ δὲ ἐλθεῖν τὴν πίστιν) explains the "faithfulness of Jesus Christ" (πίστεως Ἰησοῦ Χριστοῦ) in the preceding verse—the faithfulness to the law of God that was taught and lived out by the Messiah during his first advent. Moreover, the confinement

---

104. Stern: "Yeshua's faithfulness is described as applying only to those who, by being united with Yeshua, have acquired the same trusting faithfulness as his" (*Jewish New Testament Commentary*, 551).

105. Bruce, *Galatians*, 181.

106. ben Mordechai (*Galatians*, 282) offers the following paraphrase of 3:22 with his personal commentary in italics: "but the Scripture has encircled all things, and put them under sin (*the written Torah will stand in judgment over a keeper of the oral torah because with the oral torah, you will come up short when the written Torah judges you*), that the promise (*spoken to Avraham concerning himself and his posterity*) in the faith of Y'shua the Messiah (*who established the written Torah of Moses*) might be given to those who are faithful."

107. Longenecker, "The neuter τὰ πάντα (lit.: "all things") used of people has the effect of obliterating every distinction and referring to all humanity as an entity (so "all people" or perhaps better "everyone without distinction"; cf. Eph 1:10; Col 1:20" (*Galatians*, 144). Similarly, Dunn: "The point, in other words, is that . . . Jew as well as Greek, Israel as well as the nations, is 'under the power of sin' . . . Israel was *not* in a privileged position, as though protected under the guardianship of the law given 'through angels'" (*Galatians*, 194; original emphasis). Keener: "the neuter plural [τὰ πάντα] could also evoke Paul's only other use of this form in Galatians: 'all peoples' (NRSV: "the Gentiles") in 3:8 (cf. Rom. 1:5; 15:11; 16:26)" (*Galatians*, 288).

108. Bruce, *Galatians*, 181.

"under law" (ὑπὸ νόμον) in 3:23 mirrors the confinement described in v.22.[109] Those who observe the Jewish law violate Deuteronomy 27:26 (ἡ γραφὴ in 3:22 recalling Deut 27:26 cited in 3:10) and are thus confined "under sin" (ὑπὸ ἁμαρτίαν, 3:22). Similarly, the apostle explains in 3:23 that "we" (all those who practiced the Jewish law) were confined "under (Jewish) law" (ὑπὸ νόμον), blocked off from the true faithfulness to the law of God that would be revealed through the Messiah.

> ²⁴ ὥστε ὁ νόμος παιδαγωγὸς ἡμῶν γέγονεν εἰς Χριστόν, ἵνα ἐκ πίστεως δικαιωθῶμεν· ²⁵ ἐλθούσης δὲ τῆς πίστεως οὐκέτι ὑπὸ παιδαγωγόν ἐσμεν.
> ²⁴ Therefore the law has become our guardian[110] until Christ, so that we may be justified by faithfulness. ²⁵ And now that faithfulness has come, we are no longer under a guardian.

Bruce explains the temporal force of εἰς Χριστόν in 3:24: "As the slave-attendant kept the boy under his control until he came of age, so the [Jewish] law[111] kept the people of God in leading-strings until, with the coming of [true faithfulness], they attained their spiritual majority in Christ."[112] The phrase ἵνα ἐκ πίστεως δικαιωθῶμεν points to the justification that will result for believers who imitate the same faithfulness taught and lived out by the Messiah. Now that true "faithfulness" has been defined and clarified with

---

109. In Galatians 4, the condition of being ὑπὸ νόμον is described as slavery: "were held in bondage" (4:3); "he might redeem those who were under the law" (4:5); "therefore you are no longer a slave" (4:7); "how is it that you turn back again to the weak and worthless elemental things, to which you desire to be enslaved all over again?" (4:9); "one *proceeding* from Mount Sinai bearing children who are to be slaves" (4:24); "so then, brethren, we are not children of a bondwoman, but of the free woman" (4:31).

110. Cf. "disciplinarian" (NRSV).

111. Stern (*Jewish New Testament Commentary*, 552–53) rightly rejects the usual Christian interpretation of Galatians 3:23 as Paul declaring that Jews were imprisoned by the Mosaic law until Christ came, but are now free from it. Rather, the Jewish people were kept in subjection "to the system which results from perverting the *Torah*—specifically, its legal parts . . . into legalism." Stern notes that Paul used ὑπὸ νόμον ten times in the NT (Gal 3:23; 4:4, 5, 21; 5:18; Rom 6:14, 15; and 1 Cor 9:20 [3x]) as a technical phrase which he coined to analyze an aspect of Pharisaic legalism. Regarding παιδαγωγὸς in 3:24, Stern avers, "The *paidagogos* actually would have been a harsh disciplinarian, hired to do a job, with the boy required to obey him. Thus the *Torah*, because it was perverted into legalism, served in the role of harsh disciplinarian for the Jewish people, providing some protection but generally making the Jewish person aware of many transgression" (*Jewish New Testament Commentary*, 553). Two important aspects of the role of ancient pedagogues in 3:24–25 are its temporariness and restrictive guarding of the boy (Keener, *Galatians*, 292, citing Young, "PAIDAGOGOS," 170–75).

112. Bruce, *Galatians*, 183; adaptations added in brackets. Bruce rightly compares the temporal force of εἰς Χριστόν in 3:24 to ἄχρις οὗ ἔλθῃ τό σπέρμα ᾧ ἐπήγγελται in 3:19.

the arrival of the Messiah, believers are no longer subject to the disciplinary oversight of the Jewish law (v. 25).¹¹³

> ²⁶ Πάντες γὰρ υἱοὶ θεοῦ ἐστε διὰ τῆς πίστεως ἐν Χριστῷ Ἰησοῦ·
> ²⁷ ὅσοι γὰρ εἰς Χριστὸν ἐβαπτίσθητε, Χριστὸν ἐνεδύσασθε.
> ²⁶ For you are all sons of God through faith in Christ Jesus. ²⁷ For all of you who were baptized into Christ have clothed yourselves with Christ.

3:26. πάντες γὰρ υἱοὶ θεοῦ ἐστε: In 3:7 those who are ἐκ πίστεως are "sons of Abraham"; here they are "sons of God" through τῆς πίστεως ἐν Χριστῷ Ἰησοῦ. Just as the Messiah is the ultimate son of God and representative head over the covenant nation of Israel, those who exercise the same faithfulness to God that was embodied in the Messiah are also "sons of God" through their Messiah-like faithfulness. As "sons of God" even gentile believers are part of the covenant people of Israel as God's firstborn son (Exod 4:22) and thus share in all of the covenant promises and responsibilities granted to God's chosen people.

Moo explains,

> The language of sonship is applied to Israel in the OT. God names Israel his "son" (e.g., Exod. 4:22; Jer. 31:9), and the people of Israel are "sons of God" (in LXX, NASB, e.g., Deut. 14:1–2; Hosea 1:10). This language was appropriated by Jews in Paul's day and often focused on the eschatological gathering of God's people (Jub. 1.24–25; Sir. 36:17; 3 Macc. 6:28; 2 Esd. [4 Ezra] 6:55–59; Pss. Sol. 17.26–27 . . .). To claim that all believers—and especially, of course, Gentile believers such as the Galatians—are "sons of God" is to claim that they enjoy the full status of God's people.¹¹⁴

Similarly, Dunn contends,

> Paul here no doubt was speaking from a monotheistic Jewish standpoint—'sons of (the one) God' (cf. iii.20). And no doubt too he had in mind the more specifically Jewish claim to divine sonship: that Israel was God's son (Exod. iv.22–3; Jer. xxxi.9; Hos. xi.1) or God's sons (e.g. Deut. xiv.1; Isa. xliii.6; Hos. i.10;

---

113. Again, that Paul is speaking of the broader Jewish law in 3:24–25 that included Pharisaic oral traditions and not just the biblical law of God is affirmed in Longenecker's confused observation, "The depiction of the ancient pedagogue as a grim and ugly character is, indeed, a caricature, and must not be imported into Paul's analogy here. Yet, on the other hand, it is difficult to interpret vv.24–25 as assigning a positive preliminary or preparatory role to the law" (*Galatians*, 148).

114. Moo, *Galatians*, 250.

Jub. i.24-5; *Pss. Sol.* xvii.30), or the righteous within Israel in particular (Sir. iv.10; li.10; Wisd. Sol. ii.13-18; v.5; 2 Macc. vii.34; *Pss. Sol.* xiii.8) (*TDNT* viii.351-5, 359-60). The point of the emphasis, 'all of you', thus becomes clearer. Paul says in effect: 'all you Gentiles are already sons of God' (elsewhere in Paul particularly Rom. viii.14, 19). That is to say, they already shared fully in the closeness of relationship with God which Israel, or 'the righteous' among the Jewish people, usually saw as confined to themselves, as indeed their heritage from Abraham (cf. Gen. xvii.7; Hos. i.10; and the catena of verses cited in 2 Cor. vi.16-18)—and did so in contrast to most Jews still living 'under the law' (iv.1-7).[115]

3:27. ὅσοι γὰρ εἰς Χριστὸν ἐβαπτίσθητε, Χριστὸν ἐνεδύσασθε: To be "baptized into Christ" is to be publicly identified with the Messiah through *mikveh* washing in his name (cf. 1 Cor 1:13).[116] As with the baptism of John, this baptism into the Messiah signified repentance/remission of sins, but also identification with the person and teachings of Jesus the Messiah.

Tim Hegg explains the Hebraic cultural context of the phrase "baptized into Christ" in 3:27.

> The Torah requires immersion in water as the conclusion of purification for various kinds of ritual impurity (cf. Lev. 11:32, 36; 14:8; 15:8, 13; 17:15; Num. 8:7; 19:12, 18-19; 31:23). Moreover, in the Judaisms of the 1st Century, a *mikveh* had become part of the ritual for the proselyte.... In general, the *mikveh* of 1st Century Judaisms marked a change of status, primarily from the state of ritual impurity to that of ritual purity. Thus, the name "*mikveh*" is derived from the word meaning "hope" (*tikvah*), the waters of purification being that place of "hope" where one intended to acquire the status of ritually pure. This primary meaning, a change of status, worked perfectly for demonstrating metaphorically the change of status for those who placed their faith in Yeshua . . . "baptism" in the Apostolic Scriptures combines both the ritual act (the actual immersion into water) with the metaphoric and spiritual reality, the change of status from guilty to not guilty, from unrighteous to righteous.[117]

---

115. Dunn, *Galatians*, 202.

116. εἰς here as "with reference to" paralleling the Hebrew לשם ("with reference to the name").

117. Hegg, *Galatians*, 159.

To "put on/clothe oneself with the Messiah" is to abide by his teaching and example, and to live out the same faithfulness toward God he embodied (cf. 2 Chr 6:41; Job 29:14; Ps 132:9, 16, 18; Isa 61:10; 64:6; Zech 3:3-5).

²⁸ οὐκ ἔνι Ἰουδαῖος οὐδὲ Ἕλλην, οὐκ ἔνι δοῦλος οὐδὲ ἐλεύθερος, οὐκ ἔνι ἄρσεν καὶ θῆλυ· πάντες γὰρ ὑμεῖς εἷς ἐστε ἐν Χριστῷ Ἰησοῦ. ²⁹ εἰ δὲ ὑμεῖς Χριστοῦ, ἄρα τοῦ Ἀβραὰμ σπέρμα ἐστέ, κατ' ἐπαγγελίαν κληρονόμοι.

²⁸ There is neither Jew nor Greek, there is neither slave nor free man, there is neither male nor female; for you are all one in Christ Jesus. ²⁹ And if you belong to Christ, then you are Abraham's descendants, heirs according to promise.

Bruce helpfully explains the Jewish cultural context undergirding the three antithetical classifications in this passage.

> [T]he breaking down of the middle wall of partition between [Jew and Greek] was fundamental to Paul's gospel (Eph. 2:14f.). By similarly excluding the religious distinction between slaves and the freeborn, and between male and female, Paul makes a threefold affirmation which corresponds to a number of Jewish formulas in which the threefold distinction is maintained, as in the morning prayer in which the male Jew thanks God that he was not made a Gentile, a slave or a woman . . . This threefold thanksgiving can be traced back as far as R Judah b. Elai, c. AD 150 (*t. Ber.* 7.18), or his contemporary R Me'ir (*b. Men.* 43b)— both with 'brutish man' [*bôr*] instead of 'slave'. The reason for the threefold thanksgiving was not any positive disparagement of Gentiles, slaves or women as persons but the fact that they were disqualified from several religious privileges which were open to free Jewish males . . . It is not unlikely that Paul himself had been brought up to thank God that he was born a Jew and not a Gentile, a freeman and not a slave, a man and not a woman. If so, he takes up each of these three distinctions which had considerable importance in Judaism and affirms that in Christ they are all irrelevant.[118]

---

118. Bruce, *Galatians*, 187. Similarly, Hegg on the three *berakot* ("blessings," "benedictions") at the beginning of the Jewish cycle of morning prayers for Jewish free men: "It is not certain how old these 'blessings' are, but it is remarkable that Paul puts his list in exactly the same order. The Yerushalmi (*y.Berchot* 7.18) has this threefold blessing ascribed to R. Y'hudah b. Elai while the Bavli credits it to R. Me'ir (cf. *b.Menachot* 43b). Since both of these rabbis were Tannaim of the mid-second Century, we may presume the blessing was well in place as a liturgical element by 150 CE. Given this fact, it is likely that the inferior status of non-Jews, slaves, and women was a teaching in the earlier decades, and therefore formed a convenient list for Paul as he made his theological

The unity emphasized in the explanatory phrase πάντες γὰρ ὑμεῖς εἷς ἐστε ἐν Χριστῷ Ἰησοῦ at the end of 3:28 echoes the unity in Messiah emphasized in the preceding phrases "for you are all sons of God through the faithfulness in Christ Jesus" (3:26) and "for all of you who were baptized into Christ have clothed yourselves with Christ" (3:27). The different socio-religious classes that existed within the Pharisaic Judaism of Paul's time are no longer relevant for believers who are united to the Messiah and clothed with his righteousness by living out his faithfulness to the biblical law of God. Against the Pharisaic Judaism of his time, the apostle declares that in the Messiah God has abolished such presumptive distinctions of religious status with sweeping finality.

Paul reaffirms the theology of 3:7–9 in 3:29. If believers are identified with the Messiah and live out the faithfulness he embodied and taught, then they are the true descendants of faithful Abraham and heirs of the covenant blessings promised to the patriarch. In Paul's time, to be able to affirm "Abraham is my father" (cf. Rom 4:16) was also to claim that one is a full covenant member of the nation of Israel with all of the blessings and responsibilities enjoined by the covenant. Based on evidence from rabbinic *halakah* for proselytes,[119] it seems that Paul was opposing the Pharisaic conventions of his time by arguing that gentile believers could legitimately claim Abraham as their father, with all the rights and privileges that accompanied this status, without undergoing proselyte conversion into the official Judaism of that period.[120]

On the future inheritance of the Messianic kingdom addressed in Galatians 3:29, ben Mordechai explains, "regardless of whether one is of the house of Yehudah (the 'Jews'), or one is of Israel's ten tribes (the 'Ephraimites'), all descendants of Jacob (Israel) were given promised inheritance rights in the future resurrection, which will one day blossom through life in the physical land of Israel and in the teachings of the written Torah. Gentiles must come in with trusting faith in YHWH, obeying the written

---

point" (*Galatians*, 162).

119. E.g., *m. Bikkurim* 1:4: "These [people] bring [firstfruits] but do not recite: a proselyte brings but does not recite, because he is not able to say, '[I have come into the land] which the Lord swore to our fathers to give us,' (Deut 26:3). But if his mother was an Israelite, he brings and recites. And when he [the proselyte] prays in private, he says, 'God of the fathers [instead of 'God of our fathers']. And when he prays in the synagogue, he says, 'God of your fathers.' [But] if his mother was an Israelite, he says, 'God of our fathers'" (as cited in Hegg, *Galatians*, 165–166).

120. Hegg notes, "Rambam sides with Paul on this one, teaching that anyone who does the commandments is a part of Israel and may refer to Abraham, Isaac, and Jacob as 'our fathers.' . . . Rambam's teaching, that proselytes are one and the same with the native born Jew, may be found in *Letter to Obadiah the Proselyte*" (*Galatians*, 166).

commandments just like Jews; there is no difference in how one approaches YHWH."[121]

---

121. ben Mordechai, *Galatians*, 294.

5

Commentary on Galatians 4

⁴:¹ Λέγω δέ, ἐφ' ὅσον χρόνον ὁ κληρονόμος νήπιός ἐστιν, οὐδὲν διαφέρει δούλου κύριος πάντων ὤν, ² ἀλλὰ ὑπὸ ἐπιτρόπους ἐστὶν καὶ οἰκονόμους ἄχρι τῆς προθεσμίας τοῦ πατρός. ³ οὕτως καὶ ἡμεῖς, ὅτε ἦμεν νήπιοι, ὑπὸ τὰ στοιχεῖα τοῦ κόσμου ἤμεθα δεδουλωμένοι·
⁴:¹ Now I say, as long as the heir is a child, he does not differ at all from a slave although he is owner of everything, ² but he is under guardians and managers until the date set by the father. ³ So also we, while we were children, were held in bondage under the elemental things of the world.

Longenecker's commentary is helpful:

> With the resumptive λέγω δέ ... Paul sets out an analogy meant to illustrate what he said in 3:23–25 about living "under the law" and in 3:26–29 about new relationships "in Christ." The picture he draws is of a boy in a home of wealth and standing who is legally the heir (ὁ κληρονόμος) and so the "young master" (κύριος, lit. "lord" or "owner") of the family estate, but who is still a minor (νήπιος) and so lives under rules very much like a slave (δοῦλος).[1]

---

1. Longenecker, *Galatians*, 162. Concerning the opening λέγω δέ in 4:1 as further elaboration, Moo explains, "The connection is especially with the *paidagogos* (guardian) imagery in 3:24–25. As the child is 'under' the *paidagogos* until a certain age, so an heir is 'under' legal guardians until the time stipulated for the inheritance to be received. Both situations illustrate the position of Israel (and by extension, the Galatians)

The mention of ὁ κληρονόμος in 4:1 develops the phrase κατ' ἐπαγγελίαν κληρονόμοι ("heirs according to promise") at the end of 3:29. As Bruce notes, "The [Jewish] law has been compared to a prison-warden and as a slave-attendant; now its role is compared to that of the guardians and trustees appointed to take care of a minor and his property."[2] The phrase ὑπὸ ἐπιτρόπους . . . καὶ οἰκονόμους ("under guardians and managers") in 4:2 echoes the former confinement described "under sin" (ὑπὸ ἁμαρτίαν) in 3:22 and "under law" (ὑπὸ νόμον) in 3:23 (cf. οὐδὲν διαφέρει δούλου, "he does not differ at all from a slave" in 4:1). This sense of being confined under heavy rules and regulations is continued in 4:3: "we . . . were held in bondage under the elemental things of the world" (ἡμεῖς . . . ὑπὸ τὰ στοιχεῖα τοῦ κόσμου ἤμεθα δεδουλωμένοι).

In 4:2 the ἐπίτροποι and οἰκονόμοι, guardians and stewards or trustees, recall the παιδαγωγός in 3:24, and like the παιδαγωγός they represent the broader Jewish law with its restrictive purity *halakah*.

The phrase καὶ ἡμεῖς ("even we") in 4:3 is emphatic and in 4:3-5 the first person plural pronoun stresses the apostle's concern with Jewish believers (cf. "we/you" in 2:15-16; 3:13-14, 23-25).

The expression ὑπὸ τὰ στοιχεῖα τοῦ κόσμου in 4:3 is clearly associated with being "under the law" in 3:23,[3] "under a supervisory custodian" in 3:24-25, and "under guardians and administrators" in 4:1-2. Neil Martin translates τὰ στοιχεῖα τοῦ κόσμου in 4:3 as "worldly religious principles."[4]

---

before Christ, when they were 'under the law'" (*Galatians*, 258).

2. Bruce, *Galatians*, 192; adaptation in brackets added.

3. So Bruce: "Whatever else may be said of these στοιχεῖα, they plainly include the law, in the sense of 3:23 (which refers to the same situation): 'Before faith came, we were guarded ὑπὸ νόμον' . . . in the immediate context existence ὑπὸ τὰ στοιχεῖα τοῦ κόσμου is equated with existence ὑπὸ νόμον (vv.4f.)" (*Galatians*, 193-94).

4. Martin, "*stoicheia tou kosmou*," 450. "The context in which στοιχεῖα appears [in Galatians 4] has nothing to do with science, philosophy or apologetics. The context is a discussion about maturation from the pre-Christian state to the Christian state. And so it seems highly probable that Paul chooses the term στοιχεῖα here to refer to *the fundamental components of pre-Christian living* as it contrasts to fullness of life in Christ. He is not necessarily claiming that these components are *rudimentary*, only that they are fundamental and irreducible. Why does Paul add the genitive modifier τοῦ κόσμου? The answer, I think, lies in Gal. 4.9, where he uses στοιχεῖα terminology once again to tie Jewish and Gentile pre-Christian experience *together*. In 4.3 Paul seems to have Jews primarily in mind when he says, 'we were enslaved to the στοιχεῖα τοῦ κόσμου'. In 4.9, however, his attention is focused on his Galatian readers who are returning again to the patterns of their past—patterns that he classifies almost identically as enslavement to 'the weak and poor στοιχεῖα'. The reason for the addition of τοῦ κόσμου in 4.3, then, is simply to spread the net wide enough to include these distinctively Gentile experiences when he reaches that part of his argument" ("*stoicheia tou kosmou*," 449; original emphasis). Similarly, Bundrick: "the elementary or rudimentary religious teachings,

When applied to Jewish believers, as in Galatians 4:3, τὰ στοιχεῖα refers primarily to the fundamental religious principles of Pharisaic Judaism (cf. τὰ στοιχεῖα τοῦ κόσμου in Col 2:8, 20).[5]

> [4] ὅτε δὲ ἦλθεν τὸ πλήρωμα τοῦ χρόνου, ἐξαπέστειλεν ὁ θεὸς τὸν υἱὸν αὐτοῦ, γενόμενον ἐκ γυναικός, γενόμενον ὑπὸ νόμον, [5] ἵνα τοὺς ὑπὸ νόμον ἐξαγοράσῃ, ἵνα τὴν υἱοθεσίαν ἀπολάβωμεν. [6] Ὅτι δέ ἐστε υἱοί, ἐξαπέστειλεν ὁ θεὸς τὸ πνεῦμα τοῦ υἱοῦ αὐτοῦ εἰς τὰς καρδίας ἡμῶν κρᾶζον, Αββα ὁ πατήρ. [7] ὥστε οὐκέτι εἶ δοῦλος ἀλλὰ υἱός· εἰ δὲ υἱός, καὶ κληρονόμος διὰ θεοῦ.

> [4] But when the fullness of the time came, God sent forth His Son, born of a woman, born under the Law, [5] so that He might redeem those who were under the Law, that we might receive the adoption as sons. [6] Because you are sons, God has sent forth the Spirit of His Son into our hearts, crying, "Abba! Father!" [7] Therefore you are no longer a slave, but a son; and if a son, then an heir through God.

Longenecker explains γενόμενον ὑπὸ νόμον ("born under law") in 4:4:

> In early rabbinic (Tannaitic) writings, the expressions "the yoke of the Torah" (עוֹל תּוֹרָה, *ôl tôrâ*), "the yoke of the kingdom of heaven" (עוֹל מַלְכוּת שָׁמַיִם, *'ôl malkût sāmayim*), and "the yoke of the commandments" (עוֹל מִצְוֹת, *'ôl miṣwot*) are synonyms for the idea of being in submission to the will of God as revealed through Moses (cf. Str-B, 1:608–10; K. H. Rengstorf, "ζυγός," *TDNT* 2:900–901). It was essential for Jews to be under "the yoke of the Torah"—in fact, being under "the yoke of the Torah" comprised the very meaning of existence for Jews. For Jews generally, this yoke was not felt to be a burden but a privilege. Jewish believers in Jesus, however, looking back from the perspective of their new relationship with Christ and having experienced

---

possessed by the whole human race, to which both Jew and Gentile were enslaved prior to experiencing freedom by faith in Christ" ("*TA STOICHEIA TOU KOSMOU*," 364).

5. Hegg detects pagan elements within Judaism in the phrase: "If indeed a pre-Gnosticism was already extant in the Judaisms of Paul's day, he could well speak of being under the 'elemental principles of the world' when he considered the manner in which the rabbinic interpretations of his day had combined Hellenistic thought with the study of Torah. But for Paul, the Hellenistic concept of the *stoicheia* was not merely an errant form of philosophy—it was pagan and the realm of demons. Not unlike the kabbalism that would captivate Judaism in the middle-ages, the nascent Jewish Gnosticism in Paul's day was a mixing of things that essentially differ. Before coming to faith in Yeshua, Paul had fully espoused the rabbinic theology of his day, with its increasing anti-Gentile bias, and its security in man-made rituals" (*Galatians*, 172–73).

Christ's "yoke," saw living under "the yoke of the Torah" to be both condemnatory and oppressive (cf. Matt 11:28–30).[6]

What Longenecker fails to clarify, however, is that "the yoke of the Torah" for Judeans of Paul's time undoubtedly included the extrabiblical "ancestral traditions" (1:14) of oral law and Pharisaic *halakah* that the Messiah opposed (cf. Mark 7:1–13).

The expression "so that he might redeem those who were under the law" (ἵνα τοὺς ὑπὸ νόμον ἐξαγοράσῃ) in 4:5 recalls the similar expression "Christ redeemed us from the curse of the law" (Χριστὸς ἡμᾶς ἐξηγόρασεν ἐκ τῆς κατάρας τοῦ νόμου) in 3:13, and speaks of the Messiah's liberation of his people from the Jewish law—the enslaving religious system of Pharisaic Judaism. The purpose/result clause "that we might receive the adoption as sons" (ἵνα τὴν υἱοθεσίαν ἀπολάβωμεν) points back to the phrase "until the date set by the father" (ἄχρι τῆς προθεσμίας τοῦ πατρός) in 4:2 and describes the heir's freedom of release from the bondage of the Jewish law.

4:5. ἵνα τὴν υἱοθεσίαν ἀπολάβωμεν: The term υἱοθεσία ("adoption," "sonship") refers to the special status/designation of the nation of Israel (Rom 9:4) as the firstborn son of God (Exod 4:22).[7] The article τήν specifies the particular hope of Israel for the eschatological culmination of God's covenant promises in the inheritance of the future Messianic kingdom. The subjunctive of ἀπολαμβάνω following the ἵνα looks ahead to the future hope of the Messianic kingdom when believers will finally receive their inheritance as sons of God.[8]

4:6. ἐξαπέστειλεν ὁ θεὸς τὸ πνεῦμα τοῦ υἱοῦ αὐτοῦ εἰς τὰς καρδίας ἡμῶν ("God has sent forth the Spirit of His Son into our hearts"): the promised Spirit of God (Ezek 36:26–27) is not experienced through the Pharisaic purity traditions of the Jewish law but through the faithfulness of the Messiah now lived out by his followers. The phrase εἰς τὰς καρδίας ἡμῶν ("into our hearts") corresponds to the language of Ezekiel 36:26: "I will give you a new heart and put a new spirit within you and I will remove the heart of stone from your flesh and give you a heart of flesh" (וְנָתַתִּי לָכֶם לֵב חָדָשׁ וְרוּחַ חֲדָשָׁה אֶתֵּן בְּקִרְבְּכֶם וַהֲסִרֹתִי אֶת־לֵב הָאֶבֶן מִבְּשַׂרְכֶם וְנָתַתִּי לָכֶם לֵב בָּשָׂר).

---

6. Longenecker, *Galatians*, 171.

7. Moo is misleading when he writes, "In claiming that Christians enjoy υἱοθεσία, then, Paul is claiming not only that we believers become his adopted children, with all the rights and privileges pertaining to that status, but also that we have become his own people, inheriting the status and blessings promised to his people Israel" (*Galatians*, 268). The "Christian church" does not replace national Israel; gentile believers are grafted into the believing remnant of Israel (cf. Rom 9:24–29; 11:24).

8. Keener, "Many Judeans anticipated in some sense Israel's eschatological adoption" (*Galatians*, 339).

4:6. κρᾶζον Αββα ὁ πατήρ ("crying, 'Abba! Father!'"): The fact that followers of the Messiah call God "Abba" using the same term the Messiah used (Mark 14:36) is evidence that they are indwelt by the same Spirit who indwelt Christ. According to Bruce,

> Jesus addressed God as Abba: in one place (Mk. 14:36) the term is taken over as a loanword in the Greek gospel narrative: ἀββὰ ὁ πατήρ (in Mt. 26:39 πάτερ μου correctly translates ʾabbā). It is reasonably certain that Abba lies behind the vocative Πάτερ with which the Lord's Prayer opens (Lk. 11:2 . . .). Jesus also spoke of God to others as Abba, thus expressing his sense of loving nearness to God and his implicit trust in him. In addition, he taught his disciples similarly to call God Abba and to look to him with the same trustful expectation as children show when they look to their fathers to provide them with food and clothes.[9]

> [8] Ἀλλὰ τότε μὲν οὐκ εἰδότες θεὸν ἐδουλεύσατε τοῖς φύσει μὴ οὖσιν θεοῖς· [9] νῦν δὲ γνόντες θεόν, μᾶλλον δὲ γνωσθέντες ὑπὸ θεοῦ, πῶς ἐπιστρέφετε πάλιν ἐπὶ τὰ ἀσθενῆ καὶ πτωχὰ στοιχεῖα οἷς πάλιν ἄνωθεν δουλεύειν θέλετε; [10] ἡμέρας παρατηρεῖσθε καὶ μῆνας καὶ καιροὺς καὶ ἐνιαυτούς, [11] φοβοῦμαι ὑμᾶς μή πως εἰκῇ κεκοπίακα εἰς ὑμᾶς.
> [8] However at that time, when you did not know God, you were slaves to those which by nature are no gods. [9] But now that you have come to know God, or rather to be known by God, how is it that you turn back again to the weak and worthless elemental things, to which you desire to be enslaved all over again? [10] You observe days and months and seasons and years. [11] I fear for you, that perhaps I have labored over you in vain.

4:8. Ἀλλὰ τότε μὲν οὐκ εἰδότες θεόν. Dunn explains the OT background behind "knowing God" well:

> 'Knowledge of God' was a characteristically Jewish theme. It included the idea of acquaintance with (Israel's own experience

---

9. Bruce, *Galatians*, 199. Keener: "The *Abba* prayer might therefore recall Gethsemane and Jesus's cries of anguish as he prepared to face the world's hostility, a usage relevant for its recurrence in Rom. 8:15 (cf. 8:17-23, 26, 35-39). It should not be lost on us that the Spirit inspiring the 'Abba' cry here is the Spirit of God's Son, so that we as God's children utter the very term of love and intimacy that Jesus expressed to his Father, including in settings like Gethsemane. It is a prayer in a sense moved by 'Christ in us' (Gal. 2:20), as we share in Jesus's relationship with his Father (cf. John 10:14-15)" (*Galatians*, 347).

of God's dealings) and acknowledgment of (hence of obedience due to God). This was Israel's privilege (Deut. iv.39; 1 Sam. iii.7; Pss. ix.10; xlvi.10; Isa. xliii.10; Hos. viii.2; Mic. vi.5; Wisd. Sol. ii.13)—that which they should cherish and to which they should aspire (Prov. ii.5; ix.10; Jer. xxxi.34; Dan. xi.32), that for failure in regard to which they were rebuked (Judg. ii.10; Isa. i.3; Jer. xxii.16; Hos. iv.6; v.4; vi.6). The converse was the equally characteristic Jewish claim that the other nations did *not* 'know God' (Ps. lxxix.6; Jer. x.25; Judith ix.7; 2 Macc. i.27): that is, the Gentiles had had no experience of his covenantal grace, and did not realize that he was the only God—hence the gods they actually worshipped were 'no gods' (2 Chron. xiii.9; Isa. xxxvii.19; Jer. ii.11; v.7; xvi.20; Wisd. Sol. xii.27 ...).[10]

Although most commentators understand Paul as addressing his gentile converts more particularly, it is possible that he is also addressing secularized Israelites who had assimilated into Hellenism and were thus no different than non-Israelite gentiles. If the apostle is addressing formerly secularized Israelites/Jews in 4:8-10, then v. 8 seems to be describing their previous participation in the Roman imperial cult while vv. 9-10 are describing their return to religious bondage by submitting to the Pharisaic ritual of proselyte conversion. Paul is warning against pagan cult worship and Pharisaic Judaism in this passage, not heart obedience to the biblical law of God.

4:8. ἐδουλεύσατε τοῖς φύσει μὴ οὖσιν θεοῖς ("you were slaves to those which by nature are no gods"): Bruce explains how the language of "those which . . . are no gods" (τοῖς . . . μὴ οὖσιν θεοῖς) recalls passages like Deuteronomy 32:17, 21 and was common in Jewish polemic (cf. Isa 37:19; Jer 2:11; 5:7; 16:20; Ep Jer 6:24, 28, 49-53, 64, 68, 71).[11] Thus, "The application of such language to Israel in Dt. 32:17, 21 warns us against assuming in advance that it could not embrace Jews as well as Gentiles here."[12]

4:9. μᾶλλον δὲ γνωσθέντες ὑπὸ θεοῦ ("and more, to be known by God"): Again, Dunn is helpful here.

> This was the other side of the 'knowledge of God'—that God had chosen to acknowledge Israel . . . to take them into a personal relationship with himself, with the obligations which that

---

10. Dunn, *Galatians*, 224. Keener adds that "knowing God" signified "God's people maintaining their side of the covenant that he had established with them (e.g., Jer. 9:24; 22:16)," and is "equivalent to righteousness and immortality in Wis. 15:3" (*Galatians*, 356n1331).

11. Bruce, *Galatians*, 201.

12. Bruce, *Galatians*, 201.

entailed (Gen. xviii.19; Hos. v.3; xiii.5; Amos iii.2) . . . It is a two-way relationship, of acknowledgement and obligation . . . the Galatians had already begun to experience that personal knowing and being known which were at the heart of Israel's covenant relationship with God, prior to and apart from the [Jewish] law.[13]

4:9. πῶς ἐπιστρέφετε πάλιν ἐπὶ τὰ ἀσθενῆ καὶ πτωχὰ στοιχεῖα οἷς πάλιν ἄνωθεν δουλεύειν θέλετε; ("how is it that you turn back again to the weak and worthless elemental things, to which you desire to be enslaved all over again?"). As Keener notes, "Paul's language is emphatic, three times using words for *again* (despite the failure of most translations to reflect this)."[14] However, the similarity in reversion is not to the same gentile paganism, but to similar religious bondage in the form of Pharisaic Judaism. The apostle is upset over the Galatians' return to religious enslavement.[15] Dunn observes that ἐπιστρέφω ("turn back") was characteristic Jewish idiom for both repentance and apostasy: "The assessment was not merely ironic: in turning *to* the traditional Jewish understanding of the covenant as defined by the [Pharisaic traditions], they were actually turning *away from* the God of Israel's covenant."[16]

On the calendar observances in Galatians 4:10, Dunn asserts, "as with the Sabbath, the issue of the right observance of these feasts was a matter of sectarian dispute within the Judaism of the period . . . This was principally because the calendar by which the dates of these feasts were reckoned (solar

---

13. Dunn, *Galatians*, 225; adaptation added in brackets.

14. Keener, *Galatians*, 357; original emphasis.

15. Dunn offers an important clarification on "law" here: "Paul counted the law as one of these 'elemental forces'. That is to say, the law regarded in the way it typically was within contemporary Judaism, the law being treated as it was by the other missionaries and the judaizing Gentile converts, was functioning in effect as one of those cosmic forces which were then popularly thought to control and dominate life . . . Life under such a power was a life dominated by fear of infringing its taboos and boundaries (cf. Rom. viii.15; Col. ii.20-2; see also on iv.10). Since they had already experienced freedom from precisely such slavery Paul found it hard to credit the reports that they wished to exchange their slavery to things which were in reality no gods for a slavery to the [Pharisaic] law misrepresented to function just like another false god" (*Galatians*, 226; adaptation added in brackets).

16. Dunn, *Galatians*, 225; adaptation added in brackets, original italics. Cf. Moo citing Barrett (1985:61): "'[Paul] virtually equates Judaism with heathenism. To go forward into Judaism is to go backward into heathenism.' Some interpreters, however, take this too far, claiming that Paul in effect demonizes the law, putting its observance in the same category as the pagan religions of his day (see esp. Hübner 1984:33–34) . . . he implies that putting themselves under the law . . . is akin to returning to their impotent pagan religions" (*Galatians*, 277).

or lunar) was not agreed by all parties [cf. *Jub.* 2.9; 6.32-35; *1 Enoch* 82.4-7, 9; 1QS 1.14-15; CD 3.14-15]."[17] Keener explains,

> [T]he Pharisaic movement followed a lunar calendar; the Essenes instead insisted on a solar calendar . . . In *Jubilees*, to miss observing the festivals, new moons, Sabbaths, and Jubilees in particular exemplifies the violation of God's commandments. For them, the solar calendar of 364 days was essential for observing "fixed times." So severe was this division that either side regarded the other as unfaithful to Jewish tradition and identity. Thus, for observers of the solar calendar, the lunar calendar was corrupt, and those who observed it were like ignorant *gentiles*! Only the solar calendar was accurate; those who did not observe it were sinners. Pharisaism's successors, however, declared that it is the gentiles who reckon by the sun. Feelings about getting the fixed days of the calendar correct obviously ran high on both sides. Paul's opponents apparently bought into such feelings.[18]

As ben Mordechai explains, the Galatians were being pressured to observe the *halachic* practices of the Jewish elders regarding *yamim* (days), *chodashim* (months), *mo'adim* (festivals), and *shanim* (years); "in other words, to be extra careful about keeping and guarding the Pharisaic halacha of the day in all matters pertaining to the fixed oral traditions of those Jews troubling the Galatians."[19] In the rabbinic *halacha* of Paul's time, each of these categories of the Mosaic law had "piles of oral traditions and decrees attached to them, essentially making all these biblical observances void by the sheer fact that the written Torah never spoke of such detail, nor is there any divine commandment requiring the people of Israel to observe such suffocating particulars, as mandated by Rabbinic law."[20]

[12] Γίνεσθε ὡς ἐγώ, ὅτι κἀγὼ ὡς ὑμεῖς, ἀδελφοί, δέομαι ὑμῶν. οὐδέν με ἠδικήσατε·
[12] I beg of you, brethren, become as I *am*, for I also *have* become as you *are*. You have done me no wrong

This first imperative of the epistle is both a summary of the apostle's argument thus far and a programmatic exhortation for the remainder of the letter. Paul pleads with the Galatians to free themselves from the Pharisaic

---

17. Dunn, *Galatians*, 229. The term παρατηρέω ("observe") in 4:10 was used for scrupulous religious observance of the Sabbath and festival days in *Ant.* 3.91; 11.294; 14.264 (Keener, *Galatians*, 364).

18. Keener, *Galatians*, 363-64.

19. ben Mordechai, *Galatians*, 327.

20. ben Mordechai, *Galatians*, 327.

traditions of the Jewish law. By calling them "brothers" (cf. 1:2, 11) the apostle was reminding the Galatians that they were already part of the family of God without having undergone the rite of circumcision and proselyte conversion into Judaism. Paul has "also *become* as you" (κἀγὼ ὡς ὑμεῖς) by abandoning his "former manner of life in Judaism" (1:13) and "ancestral traditions" (1:14; cf. 2:17; 1 Cor 9:19–23). The statement οὐδέν με ἠδικήσατε ("you did not injure me") indicates that the Galatians did not mistreat the apostle during his ministry among them. Rather than actively opposing and rejecting him and his teaching, they actually accepted his gospel (1:9). Based on this strong verb ἀδικέω (*do wrong, injure, harm*), what follows in 4:13–20 is best understood in the light of the persecution and suffering Paul endured for abandoning the purity traditions of Pharisaic Judaism.

A. J. Goddard and S. A. Cummins explain,

> Paul's appeal in 4.12a concerns the fact that, in the face of the current opposition, the Galatians have ceased to follow his paradigmatic example of faithfulness in suffering—itself based upon that of Christ (2.19–20)—and have instead accepted the demands of the Agitators and begun to Judaize. Having originally embraced Paul's gospel and pattern of life (e.g., 4.14, 15, 18) they have now succumbed and fallen back into slavery (4.8–11) such that Paul despairs of them ever again modelling themselves on him and so having Christ formed in them (4.11, 19–20; cf. 1 Cor. 11.1). Thus, this verse is consonant with other such appeals in which Paul exhorts his churches to imitate him in his faithful suffering (e.g. 1 Thess. 1.6; Phil. 3.17; 1 Cor. 4.16).[21]

¹³ οἴδατε δὲ ὅτι δι' ἀσθένειαν τῆς σαρκὸς εὐηγγελισάμην ὑμῖν τὸ πρότερον, ¹⁴ καὶ τὸν πειρασμὸν ὑμῶν ἐν τῇ σαρκί μου οὐκ ἐξουθενήσατε οὐδὲ ἐξεπτύσατε, ἀλλὰ ὡς ἄγγελον θεοῦ ἐδέξασθέ με, ὡς Χριστὸν Ἰησοῦν.

¹³ but you know that it was because of a bodily illness that I preached the gospel to you the first time; ¹⁴ and that which was a trial to you in my bodily condition you did not despise or loathe, but you received me as an angel of God, as Christ Jesus *Himself*.

Contrary to many commentators, Goddard and Cummins have argued convincingly that Galatians 4:12–20 is not an "opaque parenthetical and personal appeal which is of uncertain relation to the letter's more weighty theological argumentation," but a coherent argument that addresses the

---

21. Goddard and Cummins, "Ill or Ill-Treated?," 99–100.

persecution and suffering Paul faced for abandoning Pharisaic Judaism and not some unspecified personal illness.[22]

> Paul's remarks in 4.13-15 allude to a context of conflict and persecution within which he first established a relationship with the Galatians. That such conflict, suffering and persecution is also a current problem for Paul is confirmed by 5.11, and that Paul believes the Galatians' present difficulties stem from such hostility is a recurring theme throughout the epistle (e.g. 1.7-8; 3.4; 4.17, 29-30; 5.1, 7-12, 15; 6.12).[23]

Accordingly, the phrase δι' ἀσθένειαν τῆς σαρκὸς in 4:13 indicates that Paul's evangelism among the gentiles was because of bodily injury he endured due to hostile persecution. On 4:14 Goddard and Cummins contend,

> Given the theological significance of πειρασμός, and by analogy with Paul's remarks in 1 Thess. 3.4-5 in particular, it may be suggested that in Gal. 4.14 the apostle is likewise reminding the Galatians that when he first ministered among them there was a distinct danger that they would fall away from God because of the attendant threat of opposition and persecution . . . the focal point of the Galatians' πειρασμός is Paul's own flesh/body: ἐν τῇ σαρκί μου . . . this temptation in Paul's flesh/body must be understood in relation to persecution. Thus, for example, Paul concludes his letter with the injunction 'Henceforth let no one cause me trouble, because I bear the marks of Jesus in my body (ἐν τῷ σώματί μου)' (6.17). Although σάρξ is here replaced with σῶμα, there is an obvious parallel with 4.14a, and Paul is indisputably referring to marks of persecution about which the Galatians appear to have some knowledge . . . the other text of note is Col. 1.24 where Paul claims to 'fill up the shortfall of the sufferings of Christ ἐν τῇ σαρκί μου' . . . it employs the identical phrase ἐν τῇ σαρκί μου in reference to the apostle's suffering and affliction in the course of his apostolic ministry.[24]

In other words, "Paul's own persecution—the evidence of which was visible on his body—likewise constituted a 'test' for the Galatians as to whether or not they, under the threat of comparable hardship, would remain faithful to the gospel and its apostle."[25]

---

22. Goddard and Cummins, "Ill or Ill-Treated?," 93-94.
23. Goddard and Cummins, "Ill or Ill-Treated?," 99.
24. Goddard and Cummins, "Ill or Ill-Treated?," 104-5.
25. Goddard and Cummins, "Ill or Ill-Treated?," 107.

Instead of "despising or loathing" (4:14) the apostle on account of the bodily injury he suffered while being persecuted for his gospel, the Galatians gladly recognized Paul's divine commission and authority, and fully accepted him as a representative of the Messiah.

> ¹⁵ ποῦ οὖν ὁ μακαρισμὸς ὑμῶν; μαρτυρῶ γὰρ ὑμῖν ὅτι εἰ δυνατὸν τοὺς ὀφθαλμοὺς ὑμῶν ἐξορύξαντες ἐδώκατέ μοι. ¹⁶ ὥστε ἐχθρὸς ὑμῶν γέγονα ἀληθεύων ὑμῖν; ¹⁷ ζηλοῦσιν ὑμᾶς οὐ καλῶς, ἀλλὰ ἐκκλεῖσαι ὑμᾶς θέλουσιν, ἵνα αὐτοὺς ζηλοῦτε· ¹⁸ καλὸν δὲ ζηλοῦσθαι ἐν καλῷ πάντοτε καὶ μὴ μόνον ἐν τῷ παρεῖναί με πρὸς ὑμᾶς. ¹⁹ τέκνα μου, οὓς πάλιν ὠδίνω μέχρις οὗ μορφωθῇ Χριστὸς ἐν ὑμῖν· ²⁰ ἤθελον δὲ παρεῖναι πρὸς ὑμᾶς ἄρτι καὶ ἀλλάξαι τὴν φωνήν μου, ὅτι ἀποροῦμαι ἐν ὑμῖν.
>
> ¹⁵ Where then is that sense of blessing you had? For I bear you witness that, if possible, you would have plucked out your eyes and given them to me. ¹⁶ So have I become your enemy by telling you the truth? ¹⁷ They eagerly seek you, not commendably, but they wish to shut you out so that you will seek them. ¹⁸ But it is good always to be eagerly sought in a commendable manner, and not only when I am present with you. ¹⁹ My children, with whom I am again in labor until Christ is formed in you ²⁰ but I could wish to be present with you now and to change my tone, for I am perplexed about you.

As the Galatians weakened under the pressure of Paul's opponents to undergo circumcision and the process of proselyte conversion, the apostle asks what has become of their former capacity to experience blessing in the midst of conflict and persecution. Goddard and Cummins demonstrate that the language of "gouging out your eyes" (τοὺς ὀφθαλμοὺς ὑμῶν ἐξορύξαντες) in 4:15 is found in Jewish and Greco-Roman literature (cf. Judg 16:21; 1 Sam 11:2; 4 Macc. 5:29–30; Josephus, *Ant.* 6.71; Dionysius Halicarnassensis, *Antiquitates Romanae* 5.54.2; Lucian, *Deorum Concilium* 5.1.5; Plutarch, *Artaxerxes* 14.5) as a common form of torture, and in later Christian literature as a means of executing Christian martyrs.[26] In succumbing to the pressure of Paul's opponents, "It is they, not Paul, who have become enemies of the truth, a situation that can only be rectified if they once again become like him: faithful as Christ in the face of persecution and suffering (4.12a)."[27]

The Jewish sense of 4:17 is obscured in most English translations: "They are zealous (ζηλοῦσιν) toward you but not commendably; rather they want to exclude you so that you may be zealous (ζηλοῦτε) toward them."

---

26. Goddard and Cummins, "Ill or Ill-Treated?," 112n71, 74–75.
27. Goddard and Cummins, "Ill or Ill-Treated?," 112.

Goddard and Cummins rightly connect the "zeal" language of 4:17 to Paul's former extreme zeal "for my ancestral traditions" (1:14).

> [E]lsewhere it is clear that Paul can and does use ζηλ- terminology in describing a passionate commitment to a cause which may even take the form of violent action—his own former life as a zealous Pharisee being a case in point. In this instance Paul is concerned that the zeal is resulting in the exclusion of the Galatians from Paul (4.16), Christ (5.4) and/or God (1.6), and in a concomitant misplaced zeal on behalf of the Agitators and their Torah-based 'gospel' (1.6–9).[28]

Dunn helpfully explains that ἐκκλείω ("exclude") in 4:17 is "very well suited to describe the typical attitude of the Jewish zealot—that is, to draw the boundary line sharply and clearly between the people of the covenant so as to exclude those not belonging to Israel . . . or . . . to exclude all Gentiles other than proselytes from Christ, the Jewish Messiah, and from the eschatological community of his people."[29]

> In the Galatian churches, then, the tactic of the other missionaries had clearly been to draw again these firm boundaries as laid down by the Torah, and to point out the (to them) inevitable corollary: that the Gentile converts were still outside them . . . by demonstrating what membership of the covenant people actually involved ('the works of the law'), they hoped to incite a godly desire for that membership in those whose God-fearing had already shown the seriousness of their wish to be numbered among Abraham's heirs. They hoped to convert the Galatians not simply to Judaism but to Judaism as they understood it. By showing 'zeal for the covenant' themselves, they hoped to spark off an equivalent zeal among the Galatians.[30]

The beginning statement of 4:18 has proven to be enigmatic for many commentators. Literally, Paul states, "but it is always good to be zealous in good" (καλὸν δὲ ζηλοῦσθαι ἐν καλῷ πάντοτε). After addressing the errant and misguided zeal of his Pharisaic opponents in 4:17, the apostle clarifies that being "zealous in good," to be zealous in obeying the biblical law of God from the heart, "is always good . . . and not only when I am present with you" (4:18).[31]

---

28. Goddard and Cummins, "Ill or Ill-Treated?," 114–15.
29. Dunn, *Galatians*, 238.
30. Dunn, *Galatians*, 238.
31. Dunn: "zealots like Phinehas would also no doubt have seen their zeal as an expression of 'the zeal of God'—note particularly Deut. iv.24 and vi.15" (*Galatians*, 239).

Paul's statement in 4:19, "I am again in labor until Christ is formed in you" (πάλιν ὠδίνω μέχρις οὗ μορφωθῇ Χριστὸς ἐν ὑμῖν) concerns the apostle's work of shaping the Galatians' lives of faithfulness to God according to the righteousness taught and lived out by the Messiah instead of the religious system of Pharisaic Judaism.

Keener offers an intriguing insight on the eschatological imagery of Paul's birth pang language:

> What is most intriguing is that Paul uses "birth pang" language in two adjacent paragraphs, in Gal. 4:19 and in 4:27. Given that Paul uses cognates of this language elsewhere only rarely (Rom. 8:22; 1 Thess. 5:3), the proximity of these references is likely no coincidence. As a messianic Jew, part of Israel's righteous remnant, and perhaps as part of Jesus's movement more generally, Paul is part of Zion travailing to bring forth eschatological Zion.[32] The delivered remnant gives birth to the full restored people of God (Isa. 66:7–13; cf. Rev. 12:1–5, 17; 21:2).[33]

> [21] Λέγετέ μοι, οἱ ὑπὸ νόμον θέλοντες εἶναι, τὸν νόμον οὐκ ἀκούετε; [22] γέγραπται γὰρ ὅτι Ἀβραὰμ δύο υἱοὺς ἔσχεν, ἕνα ἐκ τῆς παιδίσκης καὶ ἕνα ἐκ τῆς ἐλευθέρας. [23] ἀλλ' ὁ μὲν ἐκ τῆς παιδίσκης κατὰ σάρκα γεγέννηται, ὁ δὲ ἐκ τῆς ἐλευθέρας δι' ἐπαγγελίας. [24] ἅτινά ἐστιν ἀλληγορούμενα· αὗται γάρ εἰσιν δύο διαθῆκαι, μία μὲν ἀπὸ ὄρους Σινᾶ εἰς δουλείαν γεννῶσα, ἥτις ἐστὶν Ἁγάρ.

> [21] Tell me, you who want to be under law, do you not listen to the law? [22] For it is written that Abraham had two sons, one by the bondwoman and one by the free woman. [23] But the son by the bondwoman was born according to the flesh, and the son by the free woman through the promise. [24] This is allegorically speaking, for these *women* are two covenants: one *proceeding* from Mount Sinai bearing children who are to be slaves; she is Hagar.

Being "under law" (ὑπὸ νόμον) in 4:21 involves the scrupulous observance of "days and months and seasons and years" (4:10) and "the works of the law" (3:10), practices spelled out in the "ancestral traditions" of Pharisaic Judaism (1:13–14). In 4:21 Paul ironically questions those wanting to undergo proselyte conversion and come under *Jewish* law whether they "listen to *the* [biblical] law [of God]" (τὸν νόμον οὐκ ἀκούετε;).[34]

---

32. Keener cites Acts 13:47 here (*Galatians*, 394n1707).

33. Keener, *Galatians*, 394.

34. As in 3:2, "listen/hear" in 4:21 probably has the Hebraic sense of שמע, "listening that leads to understanding and obedience ... Paul wants the Galatians to 'learn' what

As Longenecker suggests, "The Judaizers had evidently contemporized the Hagar-Sarah story in their argument to prove that since the promises were made to Abraham and his seed, who was Sarah's son Isaac, Gentile Christians had no share in the promise unless they submitted to the Mosaic law given to Isaac's posterity and were circumcised."[35]

4:24. ἅτινά ἐστιν ἀλληγορούμενα ("which are allegorized"): Paul is applying elements of the biblical Hagar-Sarah account as a tool to ministry circumstances in his time to argue against his opponents.[36] The verb ἀλληγορέω here carries the general sense of "taken figuratively or analogously" and should not be defined technically (e.g., Philonic/rabbinic allegory, theological typology). Evidently, the Hagar-Sarah account of Abraham's two sons was being used by Paul's opponents in Galatia to support their insistence upon circumcision and proselyte conversion. The apostle sought to refute their argument by demonstrating how the same Hagar-Sarah narrative supports his gospel message of salvation through the faithfulness of the Messiah.

4:24. αὗται γάρ εἰσιν δύο διαθῆκαι ("for these *women* are two covenants"): According to Bruce these two covenants are the Sinai and Abrahamic covenants.[37] For Longenecker the two covenants "are the Old Covenant that is Torah-centered, under which the Judaizers were attempting to subsume the faith of Galatian Christians, and the New Covenant that is Christ-centered, which Paul proclaimed."[38] Dunn suggests, "two ways of understanding the one covenant purpose of God through Abraham and for his seed."[39] Similar to Dunn's view, Paul seems to be distinguishing between two ways of understanding the same Sinai covenant: the legalistic Jewish law of Pharisaic Judaism versus heart faithfulness to the law of God as taught and embodied by the Messiah (and "faithful" Abraham, 3:9).

[25] τὸ δὲ Ἁγὰρ Σινᾶ ὄρος ἐστὶν ἐν τῇ Ἀραβίᾳ· συστοιχεῖ δὲ τῇ νῦν Ἰερουσαλήμ, δουλεύει γὰρ μετὰ τῶν τέκνων αὐτῆς. [26] ἡ δὲ ἄνω Ἰερουσαλὴμ ἐλευθέρα ἐστίν, ἥτις ἐστὶν μήτηρ ἡμῶν· [27] γέγραπται γάρ,
Εὐφράνθητι, στεῖρα ἡ οὐ τίκτουσα,

---

the Law is saying" (Moo, *Galatians*, 297).

35. Longenecker, *Galatians*, 207-8.

36. The μέν in 4:23-24 suggests that Paul may be responding to his opponents: "if Paul's use of the Hagar-Sarah story is seen as ad hominem throughout, μέν here [in 4:23] (and in v.24) fits in, acknowledging, as it would, his opponents' rightful emphasis on the differences between the births of the two sons" (Longenecker, *Galatians*, 208).

37. Bruce, *Galatians*, 218; so Moo, *Galatians*, 301; Keener, *Galatians*, 416-17.

38. Longenecker, *Galatians*, 211.

39. Dunn, *Galatians*, 249.

> ῥῆξον καὶ βόησον, ἡ οὐκ ὠδίνουσα·
> ὅτι πολλὰ τὰ τέκνα τῆς ἐρήμου μᾶλλον ἢ τῆς ἐχούσης τὸν ἄνδρα.
> ²⁵ Now this Hagar is Mount Sinai in Arabia and corresponds to the present Jerusalem, for she is in slavery with her children. ²⁶ But the Jerusalem above is free; she is our mother. ²⁷ For it is written,
>> "Rejoice, barren woman who does not bear;
>> Break forth and shout, you who are not in labor;
>> For more numerous are the children of the desolate
>> Than of the one who has a husband."

In Paul's analogy, Hagar and Mount Sinai represent "the present Jerusalem for she is in slavery with her children" (4:25). Bruce specifies, "it is not so much the literal city that is meant as the whole legal system of Judaism, which had its world-centre in Jerusalem."⁴⁰

Why does Paul associate Hagar with Mount Sinai in 4:25? Bruce recreates a likely argument Paul's opponents would have used to pressure the Galatians:

> Abraham had two sons, one by a slave and one by a free woman ... Isaac was the ancestor of the chosen people; the Ishmaelites are Gentiles. The Jews are the children of the free woman; the Gentiles are children of the slave woman. The Jews have received the liberating knowledge of the law; the Gentiles are in bondage to ignorance and sin. The Jews are the people of the covenant ... the Gentiles of Galatia could not be sons of Abraham by natural descent, as Isaac was; yet there was hope for them: they could be adopted into Abraham's family by circumcision and so enjoy the covenant mercies promised to Abraham and his descendants.⁴¹

Yet Paul inverts their argument by contending that they are the ones who are enslaved to their own religious traditions in the Jewish law (cf. 3:13, 23–25; 4:1–12, 17, 21).⁴² It is actually the people of the Pharisaic law who are the offspring of the slave woman while the true children of the free woman, including gentile believers, are those who have been liberated from Pharisaic Judaism by the gospel of justification through the faithfulness of Messiah.⁴³

---

40. Bruce, *Galatians*, 220.

41. Bruce, *Galatians*, 218–19.

42. The theme of bondage "under Jewish law" (ὑπὸ νόμον) in 4:21 is carried into the term παιδίσκη ("bondwoman") in 4:22 which Paul gets from the description of Hagar in LXX Gen 16:1.

43. Keener: "They are spiritual Ishmaelites, circumcised yet missing the very fulfillment that the law had promised" (*Galatians*, 401).

Moreover, while Paul's opponents likely emphasized their association with Mount Sinai since Isaac's descendants through Jacob were the original recipients of the Sinai covenant, the apostle seems to wryly point out that the location of Mount Sinai is in fact more closely associated with Hagar the gentile slave woman. According to Longenecker,

> It is McNamara's thesis, which he convincingly argues in some detail, that not only were "most of the significant episodes of the desert wanderings and of the further Jewish traditions" centered in and around the Nabatean capital Petra, but also that the giving of the law on Mt. Sinai was believed by some to have taken place in that region; and so Paul, who himself may have resided in this region during his postconversion sojourn in Arabia mentioned in Gal 1:17, perhaps had this constellation of ideas in mind when saying "Now Hagar is (or, 'represents') Mt. Sinai in Arabia" (ibid., 27-41). Basing his argument on Jewish tradition as drawn principally from the Targums, but also referring to Arabic place names and Paul's own word association, McNamara concludes: Hagar, in fact, would be a very suitable designation for Sinai, and would be all the more appropriate if Sinai were believed to be in the vicinity of Petra, associated in the Jewish interpreted Bible [the Targums] with the dwelling place of Hagar, the bondwoman, and her son Ishmael. There was also a place named Hagra or Hagar (with an initial *heth*) in that area, and this name may also have been read or pronounced as Hagra or Hagar [with an initial *he*]. In fact, it is quite conceivable that this very place, Hagar, was regarded in some sections of Jewish tradition as the mount of revelation. Hagar, in fact, may have been a designation for Mount Sinai in the vicinity of Petra and at the heart of Arabia (ibid., 36).[44]

4:26. ἡ δὲ ἄνω Ἰερουσαλὴμ ἐλευθέρα ἐστίν ("but the Jerusalem above is free"). Longenecker helps explain the deep significance of "the heavenly Jerusalem" throughout Scripture:

> References to a "heavenly Jerusalem" are to be found in embryonic form in the Jewish Scriptures (e.g., Ps 87:3; Isa 54 [the opening verse of which Paul quotes in 4:27]; Ezek 40-48 [also Exod 25:40; 1 Chr 28:19]), in Jewish wisdom literature (e.g., Sir 36:13ff.; Tob 13), and in more developed form in the apocalyptic writings of Second Temple Judaism (cf. *1 Enoch* 53.6; 90.28-29;

---

44. Longenecker, *Galatians*, 212; Longenecker cites Martin McNamara, "'To de (Hagar) Sina." Bruce: "The 'Hagarites' [Heb. *hagrîm, hagrī'îm*] are referred to as an Arab group in 1 Ch. 5:10, 19f.; 27:31; Ps. 83:6" (*Galatians*, 220).

> 2 *Enoch* 55.2; *Pss. Sol.* 17:33; 4 Ezra 7:26; 8:52; 10:25-28; 2 *Apoc. Bar.* 4.2-6; 32.2; 59.4; also of relevance here are 1QM 12.1-2 and 4QShirShab, which speak of angelic ministry in a heavenly temple). The idea of a "heavenly Jerusalem" in contrast to the present Jerusalem appears a number of times in rabbinic literature as well (e.g., *b. Ta.an.* 5a; *b.Ḥag.* 12b; *Gen. Rab.* 55.7; 69.7; *Num. Rab.* 4.13; *Midr. Pss.* 30.1; 122.4; *Cant. Rab.* 3.10; 4.4; *Pesiq. R.* 40.6), though without reflecting negatively on Judaism itself. This concept of a "heavenly" or "new" Jerusalem also epitomized the hopes of Jewish Christians, as in Heb 11:10, 14-16; 12:22; 13:14; and Rev 3:12; 21:2, where the full realization of God's kingdom and Christ's reign is set out in terms of a "heavenly" or "new" Jerusalem that was looked forward to by the patriarchs.[45]

4:26. ἥτις ἐστὶν μήτηρ ἡμῶν ("she is our mother") echoes LXX Psalm 87:5 [86:5]: μήτηρ Σιών ἐρεῖ τις, "'Zion is my mother,' one will say."[46] The allusion to Psalm 87:5 in Galatians 4:26 is crucial for properly understanding Paul's Hagar-Sarah allegory in this unit. According to Ronald Allen, Psalm 87:4 celebrates an ethnically diverse gathering of peoples in the Jerusalem temple to worship the God of Israel: "With the Jewish believers were peoples from a variety of places and cultures, a prefiguring of the complex of peoples from the world who now worship the Savior in the church, and ultimately that varied population that will inhabit Jerusalem in the glorious coming kingdom of the Savior."[47]

> The wording of [Ps 87] verse 4 . . . might better be rendered "as those who know Me." Among those who entered the gates of Zion were individuals from Egypt and Babylon, from Philistia, Tyre, and Africa. God looks out on His courts, and with great joy He sees those who have been born in foreign places but who are now found among His people. More surprising than anything else in this psalm is what God said three times about these people: "This one was born there" (vv.4-6). This repetition is remarkable, given the psalm's penchant for terseness. Amazingly God imputes to foreign-born believers that they are the same as the native-born peoples of Israel. This strongly repeated idea conveys the dramatic message of this undeservedly obscure psalm, the message of being born again. These people who had come to faith in Yahweh as proselytes had been born in a variety

---

45. Longenecker, *Galatians*, 214; adaptations added in brackets.

46. Bruce, *Galatians*, 221; Dunn, *Galatians*, 254 (Dunn also lists Isa 50:1; 51:18; Jer 50:12; Hos 4:5; 4 Ezra 10:7; 2 Bar. 3:1; SB 3.574).

47. Allen, "Psalm 87," 139.

of places, among ethnic peoples, across the known world. But in their coming to faith in the living God, He, Yahweh, declared them born "again." They were "born there," that is, in Zion.[48]

Thus the vision of Psalm 87 is not of gentile believers undergoing a process of proselyte conversion and being bound "under the law" (Gal 4:21) of Pharisaic Judaism since "the Jerusalem above is free" (Gal 4:26). In Psalm 87:4-6 God is the one who decrees the status of Zion citizenship to gentile worshipers who already "know me" (Ps 87:4). As in Psalm 87, the gentile believers in Galatia are citizens and born-again sons of "the Jerusalem above" (Gal 4:26), the heavenly Zion, and are thus not enslaved to the Jewish law of "the present Jerusalem" (Gal 4:25) on earth. Psalm 87 envisions a multiracial gathering of ethnically diverse worshipers at the temple in Zion, not gentile proselytes who are legally Jewish according to Pharisaic conversion requirements.

The explanatory γάρ following γέγραπται in 4:27 modifies the preceding statement "she is our mother" in 4:26 since the following citation of Isaiah 54:1 concerns a formerly "barren woman" through whom God will bring forth "numerous children." The apparent connection between the allusion to Psalm 87:5 and Isaiah 54:1 seems to be the imagery of Zion/Jerusalem as the mother of her citizens (cf. Isa 49:20-22).

Longenecker explains how Paul connects Sarah to Jerusalem and Isaiah 54:1 in Galatians 4:27:

> According to the second of the seven *middôt* or interpretive principles ascribed to Rabbi Hillel, when the same word occurs in two separate passages, then the considerations of the one can be applied to the other (*gĕzērâ šāwâ*, or interpretation by verbal analogy). Here the fact that Sarah was barren (cf. στεῖρα in Gen 11:30 LXX) allows Paul to connect Sarah with Isa 54:1, which also contains the word "barren" (cf. στεῖρα in Isa 54:1 LXX). Thus the "barren one" is also the city of Jerusalem, who, though barren, is the wife of the Lord (54:5-8) and should rejoice because she will be rebuilt by the Lord (54:11-12; cf. Tob 13:16-18) and because her sons will be taught by the Lord (54:13).[49]

The imagery of the once barren woman in Isaiah 54:1a ultimately having "sons . . . more numerous than the sons of the married woman" (Isa 54:1b) who "will possess nations and will resettle the desolate cities" (Isa 54:3) recalls God's ancient promises to a once-barren Sarah: "I will bless her and indeed I

---

48. Allen, "Psalm 87," 139.
49. Longenecker, *Galatians*, 215.

will give you a son by her. Then I will bless her, and she shall be *a mother of nations; kings of peoples will come from her*" (Gen 17:16). Like Sarah, the city of Jerusalem in Isaiah 54:1–3, bereft of her children who have been carried into exile in Babylon, will ultimately be restored and blessed with returning children more numerous than those whom she lost. Accordingly, the gentile believers in Galatia who have embraced Paul's gospel of salvation through the faithfulness of Messiah apart from Pharisaic "works of the law" are a part of fulfilling the great visions of Genesis 17:6, Psalm 87, and Isaiah 54:1–3.

Thus Paul responds to his opponents' manipulation of the Hagar-Sarah account in 4:25–27 with a shocking correction and unquestionable biblical support for his gospel message and gentile ministry. Hagar and her son Ishmael, who in fact are more closely connected to the actual location of Mount Sinai, are to be associated with the present city of Jerusalem and her children, including Paul's adversaries, since the present Jerusalem, like the bondwoman Hagar, "is in slavery with her children" under the Jewish law. The point of Paul's allegory in 4:21–27 is clearly spelled out in 4:28—5:1.

> [28] ὑμεῖς δέ, ἀδελφοί, κατὰ Ἰσαὰκ ἐπαγγελίας τέκνα ἐστέ. [29] ἀλλ' ὥσπερ τότε ὁ κατὰ σάρκα γεννηθεὶς ἐδίωκεν τὸν κατὰ πνεῦμα, οὕτως καὶ νῦν. [30] ἀλλὰ τί λέγει ἡ γραφή; Ἔκβαλε τὴν παιδίσκην καὶ τὸν υἱὸν αὐτῆς· οὐ γὰρ μὴ κληρονομήσει ὁ υἱὸς τῆς παιδίσκης μετὰ τοῦ υἱοῦ τῆς ἐλευθέρας. [31] διό, ἀδελφοί, οὐκ ἐσμὲν παιδίσκης τέκνα ἀλλὰ τῆς ἐλευθέρας. [5:1] τῇ ἐλευθερίᾳ ἡμᾶς Χριστὸς ἠλευθέρωσεν· στήκετε οὖν καὶ μὴ πάλιν ζυγῷ δουλείας ἐνέχεσθε.
>
> [28] And you brethren, like Isaac, are children of promise. [29] But as at that time he who was born according to the flesh persecuted him *who was born* according to the Spirit, so it is now also. [30] But what does the Scripture say?
> "Cast out the bondwoman and her son, For the son of the bondwoman shall not be an heir with the son of the free woman."
> [31] So then, brethren, we are not children of a bondwoman, but of the free woman. [5:1] It was for freedom that Christ set us free; therefore keep standing firm and do not be subject again to a yoke of slavery.

4:29. "but as at that time he who was born according to the flesh persecuted him *who was born* according to the Spirit": cf. Judges 8:24; Psalm 83:6 where the descendants of Ishmael attacked the Israelites, the descendants of Isaac (cf. 1 Thess 2:14–16).[50]

Bruce summarizes the point of Paul's application of Genesis 21:12 in Galatians 4:30:

---

50. Bruce, *Galatians*, 223.

[L]egal bondage and spiritual freedom cannot coexist. The inheritance promised to Abraham belongs to the children of the promise who, being believers themselves, are blessed with believing Abraham (3:9). It does not belong to those who, being 'under law', are still in bondage. If it was Paul's opponents who compelled him to take up the story of Ishmael and Isaac, they unintentionally provided him with a wonderful text to undergird the argument of this whole letter.[51]

4:31. οὐκ ἐσμὲν παιδίσκης τέκνα ἀλλὰ τῆς ἐλευθέρας: The apostle's summary of the overarching point of his Hagar-Sarah allegory rephrases 4:28. Those who live out the faithfulness embodied in the Messiah "are Abraham's offspring, heirs according to promise" (3:29), and sons of the free woman, citizens of the heavenly Jerusalem.

In 5:1 Paul sums up and applies, not just the preceding allegory of 4:21-31, but his entire argument in the epistle thus far.[52] As argued before, the "freedom" from the "yoke of slavery" won by the Messiah refers primarily to the purity regulations of Pharisaic Judaism and not the biblical law of God (cf. Acts 15:10; ὑπὸ ζυγὸν δοῦλοι in 1 Tim 6:1; the Messiah's comparably lighter yoke in Matt 11:29-30).[53]

5:1. στήκετε οὖν ("stand fast therefore"): "Paul repeatedly urges his readers to stand fast—in the faith (1 Cor. 16:13), in one spirit (Phil. 1:27), in the Lord (Phil. 4:1; cf. 1 Thes. 3:8)."[54]

5:1. "do not be subject again to a yoke of slavery": The term πάλιν might refer to the temptation of Jewish believers in Galatia to return to the Pharisaic practices of the Jewish law, or it may liken bondage under the Jewish law to the former enslavement of pagan religion (τὰ στοιχεῖα τοῦ κόσμου) for Galatia's gentile believers.

---

51. Bruce, *Galatians*, 225.

52. Longenecker explains why 5:1 should be understood as a concluding summary of 4:21-31 and not as the beginning of a new section/topic: "His use of ἐλευθερία [in 5:1] . . . springs immediately from the statement and vocabulary of 4:31: 'Therefore, brothers, we are not children of the slave woman, but of the free woman.' In fact, the expression τῆς ἐλευθέρας ("of the free woman") that appears throughout the Hagar-Sarah allegory (vv.22, 23, 30, 31) furnishes the linguistic basis for all that follows in chap. 5 regarding the freedom of believers in Christ" (*Galatians*, 223).

53. Bruce recounts how ζυγός (Heb. עֹל) in Jewish literature refers to the obligation to keep the entire Jewish law, including its oral tradition (cf. Nexunya b. Haqqanah in m. Ab. 3.5; Yoxanan b. Zakkai in j. Qidd. 1.2 (59d); Joshua b. Qarḥa in m. Ber. 2.2) (*Galatians*, 226). Dunn: "'The yoke of the law' was probably already current within Judaism as denoting the obligations and privileges of the religious Jew (cf. *m. Abot* iii.5 . . .)" (*Galatians*, 263).

54. Bruce, *Galatians*, 226.

6

Commentary on Galatians 5

⁵:² Ἴδε ἐγὼ Παῦλος λέγω ὑμῖν ὅτι ἐὰν περιτέμνησθε, Χριστὸς ὑμᾶς οὐδὲν ὠφελήσει. ³ μαρτύρομαι δὲ πάλιν παντὶ ἀνθρώπῳ περιτεμνομένῳ ὅτι ὀφειλέτης ἐστὶν ὅλον τὸν νόμον ποιῆσαι. ⁴ κατηργήθητε ἀπὸ Χριστοῦ, οἵτινες ἐν νόμῳ δικαιοῦσθε, τῆς χάριτος ἐξεπέσατε. ⁵ ἡμεῖς γὰρ πνεύματι ἐκ πίστεως ἐλπίδα δικαιοσύνης ἀπεκδεχόμεθα. ⁶ ἐν γὰρ Χριστῷ Ἰησοῦ οὔτε περιτομή τι ἰσχύει οὔτε ἀκροβυστία ἀλλὰ πίστις δι' ἀγάπης ἐνεργουμένη.

⁵:² Behold I, Paul, say to you that if you receive circumcision, Christ will be of no benefit to you. ³ And I testify again to every man who receives circumcision, that he is under obligation to keep the whole Law. ⁴ You have been severed from Christ, you who are seeking to be justified by law; you have fallen from grace. ⁵ For we through the Spirit, by faith, are waiting for the hope of righteousness. ⁶ For in Christ Jesus neither circumcision nor uncircumcision means anything, but faith working through love.

As in 2:3, "circumcision" in this section refers, not to the biblical requirement first described in Genesis 17, but to the official rite that was a part of the sanctioned process of gentile proselyte conversion according to the broader Jewish law and Pharisaic authority. If the Galatian believers underwent proselyte conversion into Pharisaic Judaism, the Messiah's teaching, example, and ministry would become useless. And if they undergo the process of proselyte conversion through the rite of circumcision, they will be obligated to observe the entirety of the Jewish law, including the Pharisaic oral traditions. The phrase ὅλον τὸν νόμον ("the whole law") in 5:3 does not refer to flawless perfectionism, but to everything a religious Jew of Paul's time was expected to do, including the oral traditions of the Jewish elders, the rulings of the Sanhedrin, and every one of the 613 *mitzvot* as interpreted by the Jewish religious leaders of that time.[1] Thus, ὅλον τὸν νόμον in 5:3 does not refer to obeying the biblical law of God, but to compliance with the religious system of Pharisaic Judaism. Having undergone proselyte conversion, the Galatian believers would then come under the spiritual authority of Pharisaic Judaism and thus "be severed from Christ" (5:4).

5:4. τῆς χάριτος ἐξεπέσατε ("you have fallen from grace"): This is an alternate expression to describe the preceding alienation from the Messiah that results from coming under the authority of the Jewish law (5:4a).[2] The explanatory γὰρ at the beginning of the following verse further explains Paul's meaning. In contrast to the legalism of Pharisaic Judaism (5:4), seeking to be justified[3] through the Holy Spirit by faithfulness (5:5) is characterized as τῆς χάριτος. This difference is akin to the grace of the Messiah's light and easy yoke of law (Matt 11:29-30) versus his opponents' "yoke of slavery" (5:1). Moo is helpful when he comments, "[T]he pursuit of the [Pharisaic] law as a means of justification involves an attempt to find security with God by means of human effort, a 'doing' of the law (cf. v.2) that, with whatever attitude it is pursued, introduces into the divine-human relationship a nexus of obligation that is incompatible with the nature of our gracious God."[4]

5:6. The opening γὰρ further explains the gracious nature (τῆς χάριτος, 5:4b) of pursuing justification through the Spirit by faithfulness (5:5) instead of the Jewish law (5:4a). Thus "circumcision" and "uncircumcision" in 5:6 must be interpreted through the lens of Pharisaic Judaism as religious statuses in relation to proselyte conversion (cf. 6:15; 1 Cor 7:19).[5] Paul is not

---

1. Bruce: "If one of them were to say, in answer to his warning, 'In that case, we will keep the whole law', Paul could not have said, 'That is quite impossible', for he himself had kept it all (Phil. 3:6b)" (*Galatians*, 231).

2. Keener rightly notes that "falling" or "stumbling" often designates apostasy (Rom 11:11, 22; 14:4, 13; 1 Cor 8:9, 13; 10:12) (*Galatians*, 454), in keeping with OT imagery.

3. The immediate context indicates that "waiting for the hope of righteousness" in 5:5 refers to final justification at the eschatological judgment.

4. Moo, *Galatians*, 326-27; adaptations added in brackets.

5. E.g., Bruce: "There was ample precedent for Gentiles' acceptance of circumcision as a prelude to full incorporation into Jewish faith and life. In Jud. 14:10 Achior the Ammonite, impressed by the downfall of Holofernes, had himself circumcised (περιετέμετο τὴν σάρκα . . .) there and then and joined the house of Israel, with his family, 'unto this day'. The Idumaeans subdued by John Hyrcanus were allowed to retain their homeland 'provided they had themselves circumcised (εἰ περιτέμνοιντο τὰ αἰδοῖα

addressing Jews or gentiles in general, nor the biblical requirement of circumcision (Gen 17), but whether the Galatian believers undergo the rite of circumcision as a part of proselyte conversion into Pharisaic Judaism.[6] The religious requirements of Pharisaic Judaism concerning "circumcision" are meaningless; what matters before God is "faithfulness [to the law of God!] energized by love [for God and his word]" (πίστις δι' ἀγάπης ἐνεργουμένη).

> [7] Ἐτρέχετε καλῶς· τίς ὑμᾶς ἐνέκοψεν [τῇ] ἀληθείᾳ μὴ πείθεσθαι; [8] ἡ πεισμονὴ οὐκ ἐκ τοῦ καλοῦντος ὑμᾶς. [9] μικρὰ ζύμη ὅλον τὸ φύραμα ζυμοῖ. [10] ἐγὼ πέποιθα εἰς ὑμᾶς ἐν κυρίῳ ὅτι οὐδὲν ἄλλο φρονήσετε· ὁ δὲ ταράσσων ὑμᾶς βαστάσει τὸ κρίμα, ὅστις ἐὰν ᾖ. [11] ἐγὼ δέ, ἀδελφοί, εἰ περιτομὴν ἔτι κηρύσσω, τί ἔτι διώκομαι; ἄρα κατήργηται τὸ σκάνδαλον τοῦ σταυροῦ. [12] ὄφελον καὶ ἀποκόψονται οἱ ἀναστατοῦντες ὑμᾶς.
>
> [7] You were running well; who hindered you from obeying the truth? [8] This persuasion *did* not *come* from Him who calls you. [9] A little leaven leavens the whole lump *of dough*. [10] I have confidence in you in the Lord that you will adopt no other view; but the one who is disturbing you will bear his judgment, whoever he is. [11] But I, brethren, if I still preach circumcision, why am I still persecuted? Then the stumbling block of the cross has been abolished. [12] I wish that those who are troubling you would even mutilate themselves.

The proverbial saying on leaven in 5:9 continues the thought of 5:8. The "persuasion" (5:8) of Paul's opponents for the Galatians to submit to circumcision and the Jewish law "*did* not *come* from" the Messiah, "Him who calls you," who regularly warned, "Beware of the leaven of the Pharisees, which is hypocrisy" (Luke 12:1) and "beware of the leaven. . . . of the teaching of the Pharisees and Sadducees" (Matt 16:12; cf. Mark 8:15). This connection between the Lord and his teaching on leaven in 5:8-9 is reaffirmed by the phrase "in the Lord" in 5:10. As Longenecker states, in using the imagery of leaven in 5:9 Paul draws attention to the "tendency of small

---

. . .) and were willing to follow the Jewish laws' (Josephus, *Ant.* 13.257). It was not unknown, indeed, for a man to accept circumcision from self-regarding motives, with no serious intention of conforming to the Jews' religion; examples are Azizus of Emesa, for a short time husband of Drusilla (Josephus, *Ant.* 20.139), and Polemo of Cilicia, for a short time husband of her elder sister Berenice (*Ant.* 20.145f.). On the other hand, no amount of law-keeping or conformity to Jewish ways mattered in the eyes of stricter Jews unless circumcision had been accepted: only when King Izates of Adiabene had himself circumcised did the Galilaean Eleazar acknowledge him as a true proselyte (*Ant.* 20.44-48)" (*Galatians*, 230-31).

6. For the possibility that ἀκροβυστία in Galatians 5:6; 6:15; and 1 Corinthians 7:19 actually refers to Hellenized irreligious Jews/Israelites, see Hall, "Epispasm," 52-57.

matters to become large concerns and so to dominate a given situation."[7] The progression from "little leaven" to "whole lump" in 5:9 corresponds to the earlier progression from "circumcision" to "the whole law" in 5:3.

The presence of the adverb ἔτι ("yet," "still") with κηρύσσω and its following repetition indicates that there was a time when the apostle "preached circumcision."[8] As Bruce observes, "if Paul had engaged in proselytization among Gentiles before his conversion, he would certainly have preached circumcision then: such a zealot for the traditions would not have viewed circumcision as optional, as something which might be neglected if expediency so directed."[9]

Following the apostle's encounter with the Messiah, however, κηρύσσειν περιτομήν would stand in sharp contrast to κηρύσσειν τὸν Χριστόν ("preach the Messiah," Phil 1:15) and κηρύσσειν Χριστὸν ἐσταυρωμένον ("preach Messiah crucified," 1 Cor 1:23).[10] Similar to Galatians 5:11, the proclamation of a crucified, and thus cursed (Gal 3:13), Messiah is "a stumbling block" for Jews in 1 Corinthians 1:23. The contrast between "proclaiming circumcision" and "proclaiming Messiah" for Paul lay in the competing claims of authority over interpreting the law of God between Pharisaic Judaism and the Messiah. The Lord's confrontation and correction of the errors of the religious authorities of his time led to his crucifixion. The proclamation of circumcision, and thus the confirmation of the authority of Pharisaic Judaism, is "antithetical to and entirely nullifies the preaching of Christ crucified. It is this point that Paul has been making throughout his discussion of the judaizing threat, and so he closes his treatment of that threat with the repetition of this essential antinomy."[11] The potential abolishing of the "stumbling block of the cross" in 5:11 carries the same essential conflict of 2:21: "I do not nullify the grace of God, for if righteousness *comes* through the [Jewish] law, then Christ died needlessly."

5:11. "Why am I still persecuted?": The fact that Paul's opponents are compelling circumcision in 6:12 "so that they will not be persecuted for the cross of Christ" suggests that the persecution Paul has in mind in 5:11 would be from the Jewish religious authorities in general.

[13] Ὑμεῖς γὰρ ἐπ' ἐλευθερίᾳ ἐκλήθητε, ἀδελφοί· μόνον μὴ τὴν ἐλευθερίαν εἰς ἀφορμὴν τῇ σαρκί, ἀλλὰ διὰ τῆς ἀγάπης δουλεύετε ἀλλήλοις. [14] ὁ γὰρ πᾶς νόμος ἐν ἑνὶ λόγῳ πεπλήρωται, ἐν τῷ

---

7. Longenecker, *Galatians*, 231.
8. Longenecker, *Galatians*, 233.
9. Bruce, *Galatians*, 236.
10. Longenecker, *Galatians*, 233.
11. Longenecker, *Galatians*, 233.

Ἀγαπήσεις τὸν πλησίον σου ὡς σεαυτόν. ¹⁵ εἰ δὲ ἀλλήλους δάκνετε καὶ κατεσθίετε, βλέπετε μὴ ὑπ' ἀλλήλων ἀναλωθῆτε.

¹³ For you were called to freedom, brethren; only *do* not *turn* your freedom into an opportunity for the flesh, but through love serve one another. ¹⁴ For the whole Law is fulfilled in one word, in the *statement*, "You shall love your neighbor as yourself." ¹⁵ But if you bite and devour one another, take care that you are not consumed by one another.

That ἐλευθερία ("freedom") in 5:13 does not refer to freedom from the biblical law of God, but to freedom from the religious traditions of Pharisaic Judaism is evident from Paul's citation and application of Leviticus 19:18 in the following verse (Gal 5:14). Paul's statement, "only *do* not *turn* your freedom into an opportunity for the flesh" in 5:13 warns that although the Galatian believers are free from Pharisaic purity regulations, this freedom must not lead to license and a disregard for personal holiness.

The graphic language[12] of 5:15 suggests that the errant teaching of Paul's opponents may have led to "bitter factional infighting . . . sectarian disputes and bitter recriminations":

> [T]he freedom of the Spirit can easily degenerate into the same back-biting power struggles [as in the Maccabean revolt of the 160s BC and the Jewish revolt of 66–70 AD] (cf. ii.4, 12 . . .). This is the lot of those who throw over the law without a principle as penetrating as love of neighbour to guide them and without a genuine commitment to serve one another. Without that the call to freedom can open a floodgate which sweeps away every foundation.[13]

¹⁶ Λέγω δέ, πνεύματι περιπατεῖτε καὶ ἐπιθυμίαν σαρκὸς οὐ μὴ τελέσητε. ¹⁷ ἡ γὰρ σὰρξ ἐπιθυμεῖ κατὰ τοῦ πνεύματος, τὸ δὲ πνεῦμα κατὰ τῆς σαρκός, ταῦτα γὰρ ἀλλήλοις ἀντίκειται, ἵνα μὴ ἃ ἐὰν θέλητε ταῦτα ποιῆτε. ¹⁸ εἰ δὲ πνεύματι ἄγεσθε, οὐκ ἐστὲ ὑπὸ νόμον.

¹⁶ But I say, walk by the Spirit, and you will not carry out the desire of the flesh. ¹⁷ For the flesh sets its desire against the Spirit, and the Spirit against the flesh; for these are in opposition to one another, so that you may not do the things that you please. ¹⁸ But if you are led by the Spirit, you are not under the Law.

---

12. Bruce: "The language which Paul uses suggests a pack of wild animals preying on one another: 'if you keep on biting one another and tearing one another to pieces, take care lest you be annihilated by one another'" (*Galatians*, 242).

13. Dunn, *Galatians*, 293.

Paul's command to "walk by the Spirit" (πνεύματι περιπατεῖτε) in 5:16 is the overarching theme of the entire section that follows: it is elaborated in 5:17–24, restated in 5:25, and applied to the Galatians in 5:26—6:10.[14] The verb περιπατέω regularly bears the Hebraic sense of הלך throughout the OT, to "walk" or "conduct one's life" (cf. *halakah*, rabbinic legislation). To "walk by the Spirit" draws on passages like Ezekiel 11:19-20 ("I will give them one heart and put a new spirit within them. And I will take the heart of stone out of their flesh and give them a heart of flesh, that they may walk in My statutes and keep My ordinances and do them") and Ezekiel 36:26-27 ("I will give you a new heart and put a new spirit within you; and I will remove the heart of stone from your flesh and give you a heart of flesh. I will put My Spirit within you and cause you to walk in My statutes, and you will be careful to observe My ordinances"). Thus, to "walk by the Spirit" in 5:16 is to be empowered by the Spirit of God to "walk in the statutes and observe the ordinances" of God (Ezek 11:19-20; 36:26-27). In Galatians 5:14, the way of the Spirit is to live according to the law of love according to Leviticus 19:18. As Keener points out, "walking by the Spirit" corresponds to "walking with God" (Gen 5:22; 6:9; 17:1; 24:40; 48:15), "walking in righteousness" (Prov 8:20), "walking in God's commandments" (Lev 26:3; 1 Kgs 6:12; 2 Kgs 10:31; Neh 10:29; Ps 78:10; Ezek 20:19), and "walking in God's ways" (Exod 18:20; Deut 26:17; 30:16; Josh 22:5; 1 Kgs 2:3).[15]

In Galatians thus far, the Spirit of God is received by "hearing/obedience of faithfulness" (3:2, 5); received through "faithfulness" (3:14); the Spirit of the Son is sent into believers' hearts (4:6); and believers await final justification through the Spirit by faithfulness (5:5). The "faithfulness" by which the Spirit is received is none other than "the faithfulness of Messiah Jesus" (2:16) that followers emulate. Therefore, rather than some esoteric mystical experience, to "walk by the Spirit" in 5:16 is to live by the statutes and ordinances of the biblical law of God (Ezek 11:19-20; 36:26-27) as demonstrated in "the faithfulness of Messiah Jesus" (Gal 2:16).

With the NRSV, ἐπιθυμίαν σαρκὸς οὐ μὴ τελέσητε in 5:16b is better translated as a prohibition: "do not gratify the desires of the flesh by any means."[16] This prohibition recalls the earlier warning in 5:13: "only *do* not *turn* your freedom into an opportunity for the flesh." This parallel command/prohibition in 5:16 makes better sense of the explanatory (γὰρ) contrasts in the following verse (5:17) and the emphatic οὐ μὴ of the prohibition (5:16b).

14. Longenecker, *Galatians*, 244; Moo, *Galatians*, 352.
15. Keener, *Galatians*, 491–92.
16. Keener, citing Wallace (*Exegetical Syntax*, 469n61, 723), asserts, "prohibitions in the second person in the NT are often in the subjunctive rather than imperative mood, and virtually always when the aorist is used" (*Galatians*, 498).

Similarly in 5:24, "those who belong to Christ Jesus have crucified the flesh with its passions and desires." Elsewhere in Paul, believers are to "put to death the deeds of the body" (Rom 8:13) and "make no provision for the flesh in regard to *its* lusts" (Rom 13:14).

5:17. ἵνα μὴ ἃ ἐὰν θέλητε ταῦτα ποιῆτε ("so that you cannot do what you want") seems to be elaborated upon in Romans 7:14–25 (esp. v. 19: "the good that I want, I do not do, but I practice the very evil that I do not want").

5:18. εἰ δὲ πνεύματι ἄγεσθε, οὐκ ἐστὲ ὑπὸ νόμον ("but if you are led by the Spirit, you are not under the law"): According to ben Mordechai, πνεύματι ἄγεσθε refers to keeping the OT commandments per Ezekiel 36:26–27 while ὑπὸ νόμον refers to "submission to the *takanot, ma'asim, minhagim*, and *halachot* of the Rabbis."[17] Since believers are not subject to "a yoke of slavery" (5:1) and were "called to freedom" from the Pharisaic interpretations of the Jewish law (5:13), this freedom from Jewish purity *halakah* might lead to "an opportunity for the flesh" (5:13). Since this apparent vacuum of authoritative *halakah* seems to have sparked factional infighting (5:15), Paul proceeds to set forth the only true *halakah* for followers of the Messiah in 5:16: "walk by the Spirit." As if to reaffirm the difference between this true *halakah* of the New Covenant and that of Pharisaic Judaism, the apostle reminds his readers in 5:18, "if you are led by the Spirit, you are not under the law."

> [19] φανερὰ δέ ἐστιν τὰ ἔργα τῆς σαρκός, ἅτινά ἐστιν πορνεία, ἀκαθαρσία, ἀσέλγεια, [20] εἰδωλολατρία, φαρμακεία, ἔχθραι, ἔρις, ζῆλος, θυμοί, ἐριθεῖαι, διχοστασίαι, αἱρέσεις, [21] φθόνοι, μέθαι, κῶμοι καὶ τὰ ὅμοια τούτοις, ἃ προλέγω ὑμῖν καθὼς προεῖπον ὅτι οἱ τὰ τοιαῦτα πράσσοντες βασιλείαν θεοῦ οὐ κληρονομήσουσιν. [22] Ὁ δὲ καρπὸς τοῦ πνεύματός ἐστιν ἀγάπη χαρὰ εἰρήνη, μακροθυμία χρηστότης ἀγαθωσύνη, πίστις [23] πραΰτης ἐγκράτεια· κατὰ τῶν τοιούτων οὐκ ἔστιν νόμος. [24] οἱ δὲ τοῦ Χριστοῦ [Ἰησοῦ] τὴν σάρκα ἐσταύρωσαν σὺν τοῖς παθήμασιν καὶ ταῖς ἐπιθυμίαις. [25] εἰ ζῶμεν πνεύματι, πνεύματι καὶ στοιχῶμεν. [26] μὴ γινώμεθα κενόδοξοι, ἀλλήλους προκαλούμενοι, ἀλλήλοις φθονοῦντες.

---

17. ben Mordechai, *Galatians*, 386; original emphasis. ben Mordechai's nuanced understanding of νόμος is crucial for accurately interpreting Paul's argument in the epistle. The existence of Jewish "oral law" and *halakhic* traditions in Paul's time is historically undeniable. Also clear is that for religious Jews, this oral law was reverenced alongside the biblical (written) law in the first century as originating from God and therefore authoritative. Therefore, throughout the factions of Judaism in Paul's time, the people's conception of God's "law" was much broader than only the written OT commandments. Paul's usage of νόμος is nuanced and often includes the Jewish oral law and traditions of his time, a key insight that ensures a more historically accurate understanding of Paul and the NT.

¹⁹ Now the deeds of the flesh are evident, which are: immorality, impurity, sensuality, ²⁰ idolatry, sorcery, enmities, strife, jealousy, outbursts of anger, disputes, dissensions, factions, ²¹ envying, drunkenness, carousing, and things like these, of which I forewarn you, just as I have forewarned you, that those who practice such things will not inherit the kingdom of God. ²² But the fruit of the Spirit is love, joy, peace, patience, kindness, goodness, faithfulness, ²³ gentleness, self-control; against such things there is no law. ²⁴ Now those who belong to Christ Jesus have crucified the flesh with its passions and desires. ²⁵ If we live by the Spirit, let us also walk by the Spirit. ²⁶ Let us not become boastful, challenging one another, envying one another.

5:23. κατὰ τῶν τοιούτων οὐκ ἔστιν νόμος ("against such things there is no law"): The nine fruit of the Spirit enumerated in 5:22–23 exceedingly surpass all legal prescriptions of Pharisaic Judaism. The Jewish law is incapable of producing, enforcing, or regulating this way of the Spirit. This list of biblical virtues is not to be taken as some kind of new Christian law; it is the essence of genuine OT biblical piety and a rich composite of a flowering life lived in heart obedience to the biblical law of God.

5:25. εἰ ζῶμεν πνεύματι, πνεύματι καὶ στοιχῶμεν ("If we live by the Spirit, let us also walk by[18] the Spirit"): For believers who have been crucified with Christ (5:24), since the Spirit of God is the source of our new life, may the Spirit also direct the path of our life through the biblical law of God (cf. Ezek 11:19–20; 36:26–27).

---

18. στοιχέω: *to be in line with, conform to* (Danker et al., "στοιχέω," 946).

7

Commentary on Galatians 6

^{6:1} Ἀδελφοί, ἐὰν καὶ προλημφθῇ ἄνθρωπος ἔν τινι παραπτώματι, ὑμεῖς οἱ πνευματικοὶ καταρτίζετε τὸν τοιοῦτον ἐν πνεύματι πραΰτητος, σκοπῶν σεαυτὸν μὴ καὶ σὺ πειρασθῇς. ² Ἀλλήλων τὰ βάρη βαστάζετε καὶ οὕτως ἀναπληρώσετε τὸν νόμον τοῦ Χριστοῦ.
^{6:1} Brethren, even if anyone is caught in any trespass, you who are spiritual, restore such a one in a spirit of gentleness; *each one looking to yourself, so that you too will not be tempted.* ² Bear one another's burdens, and thereby fulfill the law of Christ.

τὸν νόμον τοῦ Χριστοῦ ("the law of Christ") in 6:2 ought to be interpreted in light of the similar phrase ἔννομος Χριστοῦ ("under the law of Messiah") in 1 Corinthians 9:21. There, ἔννομος Χριστοῦ further clarifies the phrase μὴ ὢν ἄνομος θεοῦ ("not being without the law of God") in the preceding clause, in contrast to "became as a Jew" (ἐγενόμην . . . ὡς Ἰουδαῖος) and "as under the law" (ὡς ὑπὸ νόμον) in 1 Corinthians 9:20. In other words, in 1 Corinthians 9:20–21, "the law of Messiah" is the true and clarified meaning of the biblical law of God in contrast to the Jewish law which Paul no longer finds authoritative (μὴ ὢν αὐτὸς ὑπὸ νόμον, "though not being myself under the [Jewish] law" in 1 Cor 9:20).

Specifically in Galatians 6:2, τὸν νόμον τοῦ Χριστοῦ refers back to the apostle's summary of the law in 5:14: "the whole law is fulfilled in one word, in the *statement*, 'You shall love your neighbor as yourself.'" This use of Leviticus 19:18 is indeed what the Messiah taught in Matthew 22:39–40:

"The second [greatest commandment] is like it, 'You shall love your neighbor as yourself.' On these two commandments depend the whole law and the prophets." Therefore, just as in 1 Corinthians 9:20-21, τὸν νόμον τοῦ Χριστοῦ in Galatians 6:2 refers to the true meaning of the biblical law of God as taught and lived out by the Messiah, in contradistinction to the Jewish law of Pharisaic Judaism.¹ "Bearing one another's burdens" (6:2) fulfills the second greatest commandment of "loving your neighbor as yourself" in Leviticus 19:18 just as the Messiah taught and modeled.²

> ³ εἰ γὰρ δοκεῖ τις εἶναί τι μηδὲν ὤν, φρεναπατᾷ ἑαυτόν. ⁴ τὸ δὲ ἔργον ἑαυτοῦ δοκιμαζέτω ἕκαστος, καὶ τότε εἰς ἑαυτὸν μόνον τὸ καύχημα ἕξει καὶ οὐκ εἰς τὸν ἕτερον· ⁵ ἕκαστος γὰρ τὸ ἴδιον φορτίον βαστάσει.
>
> ³ For if anyone thinks he is something when he is nothing, he deceives himself. ⁴ But each one must examine his own work, and then he will have *reason for* boasting in regard to himself alone, and not in regard to another. ⁵ For each one will bear his own load.

The warning of 6:3 may be aimed at ὑμεῖς οἱ πνευματικοί ("you who are spiritual") in 6:1, the boastful in 5:26, and those responsible for the factional infighting in 5:15. This may be the same group that "wants to be under [Jewish] law" (4:21) and is tempted to "receive circumcision" (5:2).

Since believers are no longer under "a yoke of slavery" (5:1), are "called to freedom" from Pharisaic Judaism (5:13), and "walk/live by the Spirit" (5:16, 25), Paul stresses their personal responsibility in 6:4-5. Free from Pharisaic traditions and rabbinic authority, believers are not to assess or

---

1. Cf. Bruce: "The 'law of Christ' is not essentially different from the commandment of love to one's neighbour (quoted in 5:14), in which 'the whole law' is comprehended. Paul speaks of his commitment to this 'law' in 1 Cor. 9:20, where he describes himself as ἔννομος Χριστοῦ... It may be that Paul speaks of the law of Christ here as a contrast to the law which his converts were being urged to accept... In fine, the 'law of Christ' is for Paul the whole tradition of Jesus' ethical teaching, confirmed by his character and conduct (cf. Rom. 13:14; 2 Cor. 10:1) and reproduced within his people by the power of the Spirit (cf. Rom. 8:2, ὁ ... νόμος τοῦ πνεύματος τῆς ζωῆς ἐν Χριστῷ Ἰησοῦ)" (*Galatians*, 261).

2. Graham Stanton defines τὸν νόμον τοῦ Χριστοῦ in 6:2 as "the law of Moses redefined by Christ, with the 'love commandment' and 'carrying the burdens of others' as its essence; it is fulfilled by Christ in his own self-giving love" ("Law of Christ," 56). Yet, Stanton's definition is unacceptable since his word "redefined" indicates that the Messiah somehow changed the original meaning of the law of God or somehow introduced a novelty. And "fulfilled" (rather than "modeled" or "clarified") suggests that the law of Moses is no longer authoritative or binding for believers today. Perplexingly, Fruchtenbaum insists, "The way they fulfill the law of the Messiah is by fulfilling the commandments of the New Testament, such as bearing one another's burdens" (*Faith Alone*, 56).

judge the "word/deeds" of another; "each one must examine his own work" (6:4) by the standard of "the law of Christ" (6:2). Apart from the regulations of Pharisaic authority and rabbinic *halakah*, "he will have *reason for* boasting in regard to himself alone, and not in regard to another" (6:4; cf. 2 Cor 10:12; the Pharisee in Luke 18:11). Longenecker explains that the warning in 6:4 "is not to live as spiritual people in a state of pride or conceit, always comparing one's own attainments to those of others and so feeling superior, but rather to test one's own actions and so to minimize the possibility of self-deception."[3]

6:5. ἕκαστος γὰρ τὸ ἴδιον φορτίον βαστάσει ("for each one will bear his own load"): As Longenecker observes, in Matthew 23:4 and Luke 11:46 φορτίον ("burden") refers to the legal burdens of Pharisaic tradition while in Matthew 11:30 the term identifies the Messiah's lighter requirements imposed on his disciples versus the heavier "burden" of Pharisaic Judaism.[4] The explanatory γὰρ at the beginning of 6:5 suggests that, in light of the believer's personal responsibility (6:4) in fulfilling the law of Messiah by carrying other's burdens (6:2), the standard by which one fulfills the law of Christ and carries other's burdens is determined by each individual believer and not Pharisaic authority: "each one will bear his own load" (6:5). Paul's use of synonyms for "burden" in 6:2 (βάρος) and 6:5 (φορτίον) is a clever way to underscore the believer's self-determined *halakah* (φορτίον), apart from Jewish law, in fulfilling the law of Messiah by carrying other's burdens (βάρος).

> [6] Κοινωνείτω δὲ ὁ κατηχούμενος τὸν λόγον τῷ κατηχοῦντι ἐν πᾶσιν ἀγαθοῖς. [7] Μὴ πλανᾶσθε, θεὸς οὐ μυκτηρίζεται. ὃ γὰρ ἐὰν σπείρῃ ἄνθρωπος, τοῦτο καὶ θερίσει· [8] ὅτι ὁ σπείρων εἰς τὴν σάρκα ἑαυτοῦ ἐκ τῆς σαρκὸς θερίσει φθοράν, ὁ δὲ σπείρων εἰς τὸ πνεῦμα ἐκ τοῦ πνεύματος θερίσει ζωὴν αἰώνιον. [9] τὸ δὲ καλὸν ποιοῦντες μὴ ἐγκακῶμεν, καιρῷ γὰρ ἰδίῳ θερίσομεν μὴ ἐκλυόμενοι. [10] ἄρα οὖν ὡς καιρὸν ἔχομεν, ἐργαζώμεθα τὸ ἀγαθὸν πρὸς πάντας, μάλιστα δὲ πρὸς τοὺς οἰκείους τῆς πίστεως.

> [6] The one who is taught the word is to share all good things with the one who teaches *him*. [7] Do not be deceived, God is not mocked; for whatever a man sows, this he will also reap. [8] For the one who sows to his own flesh will from the flesh reap corruption, but the one who sows to the Spirit will from the Spirit reap eternal life. [9] Let us not lose heart in doing good, for in due time we will reap if we do not grow weary. [10] So then, while we have opportunity, let us do good to all people, and especially to those who are of the household of the faith.

3. Longenecker, *Galatians*, 277.
4. Longenecker, *Galatians*, 277–78.

6:8. The warning "God is not mocked" (6:7) and the phrases "in due time" (6:9) and "while we have opportunity" (6:10) indicate that the sowing and reaping imagery of 6:7–9 refers to the end-time harvest of judgment spoken of throughout the OT (cf. Isa 17:11; Joel 3:13; Matt 9:37–38; 13:30, 39).

6:8. ὅτι ὁ σπείρων εἰς τὴν σάρκα ἑαυτοῦ ἐκ τῆς σαρκὸς θερίσει φθοράν: As Bruce notes, "The σάρξ here, as in 5:13, 16f., 19, is the unregenerate, 'uncrucified' self. Sowing 'for the flesh' is the practising of such things as are included among 'the works of the flesh' in 5:19–21."[5] Thus "sowing to his own flesh" and "reaping corruption" in 6:8 reaches back to "those who practice such things will not inherit the kingdom of God" in 5:21. To sow εἰς τὸ πνεῦμα, on the other hand, is to cultivate the fruit of the Spirit and reap eternal life (cf. Rom 6:20–23; 8:13). The "eternal life" of 6:8 continues the theme of living by the Spirit (5:16, 18, 22–25) and points ahead to the end-time resurrection.

6:9. τὸ δὲ καλὸν ποιοῦντες μὴ ἐγκακῶμεν ("let us not become weary in doing good"): cf. 2 Thess 3:13. To persevere in "doing good" (6:9) is to "sow to the Spirit" (6:8; cf. Ps 112:9), to obey the biblical law of God like loving one's neighbor as oneself in Leviticus 19:18 (5:14) and thus cultivating the fruit of the Spirit (5:22–23; cf. Eph 2:10; 2 Cor 9:8).

6:10. τοὺς οἰκείους τῆς πίστεως ("the household of faithfulness"): ἡ πίστις has been used throughout the epistle to characterize followers of the Messiah who embrace the faithfulness to God he taught and embodied (2:16) and reject the "works of the law" of Pharisaic Judaism. Thus, "the household of faithfulness" includes even gentile believers whom Paul instructs not to receive circumcision as a part of the proselyte conversion process according to rabbinic *halakah* (cf. Eph 2:19).

> [11] Ἴδετε πηλίκοις ὑμῖν γράμμασιν ἔγραψα τῇ ἐμῇ χειρί. [12] ὅσοι θέλουσιν εὐπροσωπῆσαι ἐν σαρκί, οὗτοι ἀναγκάζουσιν ὑμᾶς περιτέμνεσθαι, μόνον ἵνα τῷ σταυρῷ τοῦ Χριστοῦ μὴ διώκωνται. [13] οὐδὲ γὰρ οἱ περιτεμνόμενοι αὐτοὶ νόμον φυλάσσουσιν ἀλλὰ θέλουσιν ὑμᾶς περιτέμνεσθαι, ἵνα ἐν τῇ ὑμετέρᾳ σαρκὶ καυχήσωνται.
>
> [11] See with what large letters I am writing to you with my own hand. [12] Those who desire to make a good showing in the flesh try to compel you to be circumcised, simply so that they will not be persecuted for the cross of Christ. [13] For those who are circumcised do not even keep the Law themselves, but they desire to have you circumcised so that they may boast in your flesh.

---

5. Bruce, *Galatians*, 265.

As the apostle concludes his epistle, it is as if he grabbed the pen from an amanuensis in 6:11 to write with his own hand what was most urgent and pressing in 6:12–17.

6:12. ὅσοι θέλουσιν εὐπροσωπῆσαι ἐν σαρκί ("those who desire to make a good showing in the flesh"): Flowing from the spirit/flesh antithesis in the immediately preceding context, Paul deftly connects his opponents' hypocritical enforcement of Pharisaic tradition "in the flesh" (6:12) to those who sow to their own "flesh" and reap destruction (6:8), and to those who practice "deeds of the flesh" and thus not inherit the kingdom of God (5:19–21). Those who "compel to be circumcised" in 6:12 recall Peter's compulsion in 2:14, and are most likely part of the same group who taught, "Unless you are circumcised according to the custom of Moses, you cannot be saved" in Acts 15:1. Their motivation is "so that they will not be persecuted for the cross of Christ" (6:12), suggesting that these opponents are fearful of the Jewish religious authorities who rejected the Messiah.[6]

The explanatory γὰρ at the beginning of 6:13 clarifies the hypocrisy of the opponents' desire to "make a good showing in the flesh" (6:12). Despite the outward badge of circumcision, they "do not even keep the law themselves" (6:13). This shocking assessment confirms that "circumcision" in this epistle does not refer to the biblical requirement (Gen 17; Lev 12:3; Exod 12:48) but is shorthand for the ritual process of gentile proselyte conversion according to rabbinic tradition. This explains 6:15 ("neither is circumcision anything, nor uncircumcision, but a new creation") and the otherwise perplexing statement in 1 Corinthians 7:19, "circumcision is nothing, and uncircumcision is nothing, but *what matters is* the keeping of the commandments of God."

The purpose clause ἵνα ἐν τῇ ὑμετέρᾳ σαρκὶ καυχήσωνται ("so that they may boast in your flesh") suggests that Paul had these opponents in mind in his earlier discussion of "boasting" in 6:3–5 and in 5:26: "let us not become boastful, challenging one another, envying one another." As Longenecker explains, "While they undoubtedly claimed to be interested only in Gentile believers being fully accepted by God into the chosen people of Israel, and so full recipients of the blessings of the Abrahamic covenant, Paul accuses them of being primarily motivated by a desire to avoid persecution

---

6. Cf. Longenecker: "What the Judaizers wanted . . . was to lay the religious compulsion of circumcision on Gentile believers in Galatia—thereby bringing Gentile Christians within the orbit of the Jewish nation on a proselyte basis—and so to relieve themselves and Jewish Christendom generally from persecution at the hands of fellow nonbelieving Jews (cf. 1 Thess 2:14b–16)" (*Galatians*, 291).

by being able to boast about gentile Christians being circumcised and so related to the Jewish nation."[7]

¹⁴ ἐμοὶ δὲ μὴ γένοιτο καυχᾶσθαι εἰ μὴ ἐν τῷ σταυρῷ τοῦ κυρίου ἡμῶν Ἰησοῦ Χριστοῦ, δι' οὗ ἐμοὶ κόσμος ἐσταύρωται κἀγὼ κόσμῳ. ¹⁵ οὔτε γὰρ περιτομή τί ἐστιν οὔτε ἀκροβυστία ἀλλὰ καινὴ κτίσις. ¹⁶ καὶ ὅσοι τῷ κανόνι τούτῳ στοιχήσουσιν, εἰρήνη ἐπ' αὐτοὺς καὶ ἔλεος καὶ ἐπὶ τὸν Ἰσραὴλ τοῦ θεοῦ. ¹⁷ Τοῦ λοιποῦ κόπους μοι μηδεὶς παρεχέτω· ἐγὼ γὰρ τὰ στίγματα τοῦ Ἰησοῦ ἐν τῷ σώματί μου βαστάζω. ¹⁸ Ἡ χάρις τοῦ κυρίου ἡμῶν Ἰησοῦ Χριστοῦ μετὰ τοῦ πνεύματος ὑμῶν, ἀδελφοί· ἀμήν.

¹⁴ But may it never be that I would boast, except in the cross of our Lord Jesus Christ, through which the world has been crucified to me, and I to the world. ¹⁵ For neither is circumcision anything, nor uncircumcision, but a new creation. ¹⁶ And those who will walk by this rule, peace and mercy *be* upon them, and upon the Israel of God.
¹⁷ From now on let no one cause trouble for me, for I bear on my body the brand-marks of Jesus.
¹⁸ The grace of our Lord Jesus Christ be with your spirit, brethren. Amen.

6:15. ἀλλὰ καινὴ κτίσις ("but a new creation"): In identifying with the Messiah with wholehearted allegiance (6:14), what matters most for the apostle and the Galatians is not the "circumcision" of proselyte conversion carried out under rabbinic authority (6:15) but "a new creation": pursuing justification through the "faithfulness of the Messiah" and not Pharisaic "works of the law" (2:16); receiving the Holy Spirit through "hearing/obedience of faithfulness" (3:2); and "walking/living by the Spirit" (5:16, 25) to keep the biblical law of God (5:14) and thus produce the fruit of the Spirit (5:22-23) in accordance with ancient prophecy (Ezek 11:19-20; 36:26-27). Significantly, the parallel to "a new creation" in 1 Corinthians 7:19 is "the keeping of the commandments of God" (τήρησις ἐντολῶν θεοῦ). In 2 Corinthians 5:17, "if anyone is in Christ, *he is* a new creature" (εἴ τις ἐν Χριστῷ καινὴ κτίσις).

6:16. τὸν Ἰσραὴλ τοῦ θεοῦ ("the Israel of God") recalls τοὺς οἰκείους τῆς πίστεως ("the household of faithfulness") in 6:10 and refers to all followers of the Messiah, regardless of Pharisaic recognition/authorization, who "walk by this rule" (Paul's instruction in 6:15). The "Israel of God" are those

---

7. Longenecker, *Galatians*, 290-91.

who possess the faithfulness to God of the Messiah (2:16) and Abraham (3:9), the true "sons of God" (3:26) and descendants of Abraham (3:29).

τὸν Ἰσραὴλ τοῦ θεοῦ in 6:16 points ahead to Paul's hope in Romans 11:26 that "all Israel will be saved." This "all Israel" includes "the fullness of the Gentiles coming in" in Romans 11:25, which seems to echo the ancient prophecy of Genesis 48:19: "his younger brother [Ephraim] shall be greater than he, and his descendants shall become a multitude of nations [מְלֹא־הַגּוֹיִם]." In Paul's time the ἐκκλησία of the Messiah in Galatia and Rome existed within the larger ethno-political nation of post-exilic Judea, most of whom rejected the Messiah. Thus, the earliest ἐκκλησία was the faithful remnant of the Messiah's Jewish followers. "Gentile" believers, including hellenized and irreligious Jews/Israelites, were then "grafted into" this believing remnant of Israel by embracing the person/identity, teaching, and atoning sacrifice of the Messiah (Rom 11:17), in fulfillment of the prophecy concerning Ephraim's descendants becoming "a multitude/fullness of nations" (Gen 48:19; Rom 11:25).

On "all Israel will be saved" in Romans 11:26, Jason Staples concludes,

> "all Israel" is a larger entity than just the Jews ... God's plan goes far beyond saving only Judah but extends to the house of Israel as well—*all* Israel will be saved, Paul insists, not just one part. Far from rejecting Israel, God has reached out and saved more of Israel than anyone could have imagined. In fact, God desired to save all Israel so much that he is even incorporating the Gentiles to do it. God's faithfulness to Israel is so great that he has provided to save all—even Gentiles—*in* Israel. God has not moved to a new people but is gathering, restoring, and reconciling even those who were thought to be irretrievably lost. Paul argues that God's covenant-keeping power extends beyond the grave, capable even of bringing life from the dead (Rom 11:15), of producing Israelites from the Gentiles.[8]

---

8. Staples, "Fresh Look at Romans 11:25–27," 390.

Bibliography

REFERENCE WORKS

Brown, Francis, et al. "אֱמוּנָה." In *The Brown-Driver-Briggs Hebrew and English Lexicon*, 53. Peabody, MA: Hendrickson, 1996.
Danker, Frederick W., et al. "γάρ." In *Greek-English Lexicon of the New Testament and Other Early Christian Literature*, 189–90. 3rd ed. Chicago: University of Chicago Press, 2000.
———. "διατάσσω." In *Greek-English Lexicon of the New Testament and Other Early Christian Literature*, 237–38. 3rd ed. Chicago: University of Chicago Press, 2000.
———. "στοιχέω." In *Greek-English Lexicon of the New Testament and Other Early Christian Literature*, 946. 3rd ed. Chicago: University of Chicago Press, 2000.
———. "φραγμός." In *Greek-English Lexicon of the New Testament and Other Early Christian Literature*, 1064. 3rd ed. Chicago: University of Chicago Press, 2000.
Gutbrod, Walter, and Hermann Kleinknecht. "νόμος." In *Theological Dictionary of the New Testament*, edited by Gerhard Kittel, translated by Geoffrey W. Bromiley, 4:1022–85. 10 vols. Grand Rapids: Eerdmans, 1964–76.
Hall, Robert G. "Circumcision." In *The Anchor Bible Dictionary*, edited by David N. Freedman, 1:1025–31. New York: Doubleday, 1992.
Harder, Günther. "στηριγμός." In *Theological Dictionary of the New Testament*. Edited by Gerhard Kittel and Gerhard Friedrich. Translated by Geoffrey W. Bromiley, 7:653–56. 10 vols. Grand Rapids: Eerdmans, 1964–76.
Hays, Richard B. "Galatians." In *New Interpreter's Bible*, 11:183–348. Nashville: Abingdon, 2000.
Hezser, Catherine. "Law, Jewish." In *The Encyclopedia of Ancient History*. 1st edition. Edited by Roger S. Bagnall et al., 7:3947–49. 13 vols. Hoboken, NJ: Blackwell, 2013.
Louw, Johannes P., and Eugene A. Nida. *Greek-English Lexicon of the New Testament: Based on Semantic Domains*. New York: United Bible Societies, 1996.
Michaelis, Wilhelm. "πάσχω." In *Theological Dictionary of the New Testament*, edited by Gerhard Kittel, translated by Geoffrey W. Bromiley, 5:904–24. Grand Rapids: Eerdmans, 1967.

Neusner, Jacob, Alan J. Avery-Peck, and William S. Green, eds. *The Encyclopedia of Judaism*, five volumes. Leiden, The Netherlands: Brill, 2000.
Oepke, Albrecht. "ἄθεσμος." In *Theological Dictionary of the New Testament*, edited by Gerhard Kittel and Gerhard Friedrich, translated by Geoffrey W. Bromiley, 1:167. 10 vols. Grand Rapids: Eerdmans, 1964–76.
Rengstorf, Karl H. "ἀπόστολος." In *Theological Dictionary of the New Testament*, edited by Gerhard Kittel, translated by Geoffrey W. Bromiley, 1:398–447. Grand Rapids: Eerdmans, 1964.
Schneider, Carl. "μεσότοιχον." In *Theological Dictionary of the New Testament*, edited by Gerhard Kittel, 4:625. Grand Rapids: Eerdmans, 1967.
Scott, Jack B. "אָמַן." In *Theological Wordbook of the Old Testament*, edited by R. L. Harris et al., 1:51–53. Chicago: Moody Press, 1980.
Waltke, Bruce K. and M. O'Connor. *An Introduction to Biblical Hebrew Syntax*. Winona Lake, IN: Eisenbrauns, 1990.
Wood, Leon J. "חָרַם." In *Theological Wordbook of the Old Testament*, edited by R. Laird Harris et al., 1:324. 2 vols. Chicago: Moody, 1980.

MONOGRAPHS

Anderson, Jeff. *The Internal Diversification of Second Temple Judaism: An Introduction to the Second Temple Period*. Lanham, MD: University Press of America, 2002.
Barrett, C. K. *The Epistle to the Romans*. Rev. ed. Black's New Testament Commentary. Peabody, MA: Hendrickson, 1991.
Bates, Matthew W. *Salvation by Allegiance Alone*. Grand Rapids: Baker Academic, 2017.
Bauckham, Richard J. *Jude, 2 Peter*. Word Biblical Commentary 50. Edited by David A. Hubbard and Glenn W. Barker. Waco, TX: Word, 1983.
ben Mordechai, Avi. *Galatians: A Torah-Based Commentary in First-Century Hebraic Context*. Haifa, Israel: Millennium 7000 Communications, 2005.
Betz, Hans D. *Galatians*. Hermeneia. Edited by Helmut Koester. Philadelphia: Fortress, 1979.
Blum, Edwin A. "2 Peter." In *Expositor's Bible Commentary*, edited by Frank E. Gæbelein, 12:255–89. Grand Rapids: Zondervan, 1981.
Bock, Darrell L. *Acts*. Baker Exegetical Commentary on the New Testament. Edited by Robert W. Yarbrough and Robert H. Stein. Grand Rapids: Baker Academic, 2007.
Boyarin, Daniel. *A Radical Jew: Paul and the Politics of Identity*. Berkeley: University of California Press, 1994.
Bruce, F. F. *The Epistle to the Galatians*. New International Greek Testament Commentary. Edited by Donald A. Hagner and I. Howard Marshall. Grand Rapids: Eerdmans, 1982.
Carson, Donald A., et al., eds. *Justification and Variegated Nomism*. 2 vols. Grand Rapids: Baker, 2004.
Chamblin, Knox. "The Law of Moses and the Law of Christ." In *Continuity and Discontinuity: Perspectives on the Relationship Between the Old and New Testaments*, edited by John S. Feinberg, 181–202. Wheaton, IL: Crossway, 1988.
Cohen, Shaye J. D. *From the Maccabees to the Mishnah*. 2nd ed. Louisville, KY: Westminster John Knox, 2006.

Cohn-Sherbok, Dan. *Messianic Judaism: A Critical Anthology*. London: Continuum, 2000.

———. *Voices of Messianic Judaism: Confronting Critical Issues Facing a Maturing Movement*. Baltimore: Lederer, 2001.

Das, A. Andrew. *Paul and the Stories of Israel: Grand Thematic Narratives in Galatians*. Minneapolis, MN: Fortress, 2016.

Davids, Peter H. *The Epistle of James*. New International Greek Testament Commentary. Edited by Donald A. Hagner and I. Howard Marshall. Grand Rapids: Eerdmans, 1982.

DeSilva, David A. *Galatians: A Handbook on the Greek Text*. Waco, TX: Baylor University Press, 2014.

Dodd, C. H. *The Bible and the Greeks*. London: Hodder & Stoughton, 1935.

Dunn, James D. G. *Jesus, Paul and the Law: Studies in Mark and Galatians*. London: SPCK, 1990.

———. *The Epistle to the Galatians*. Black's New Testament Commentary. Edited by Henry Chadwick. Grand Rapids: Baker Academic, 1993.

———. *The Epistles to the Colossians and to Philemon*. New International Greek Testament Commentary. Grand Rapids: Eerdmans, 1996.

———. *The New Perspective on Paul*. Rev. ed. Grand Rapids: Eerdmans, 2008.

Eadie, John. *A Commentary on the Greek Text of the Epistle of Paul to the Ephesians*. 2nd ed. New York: Carter, 1861.

Elliott, Mark W., et al., eds. *Galatians and Christian Theology: Justification, the Gospel, and Ethics in Paul's Letter*. Grand Rapids: Baker Academic, 2014.

Fee, Gordon D. *The First Epistle to the Corinthians*. New International Commentary on the New Testament. Grand Rapids: Eerdmans, 1987.

Feinberg, John S, ed. *Continuity and Discontinuity: Perspectives on the Relationship Between the Old and New Testaments*. Wheaton, IL: Crossway, 1988.

Fredriksen, Paula. *From Jesus to Christ: The Origins of the New Testament Images of Jesus*. 2nd ed. New Haven: Yale University Press, 2000.

Fruchtenbaum, Arnold G. *Faith Alone: The Condition of Our Salvation*. San Antonio, TX: Ariel Ministries, 2014.

Garland, David E. *1 Corinthians*. Baker Exegetical Commentary on the New Testament. Grand Rapids: Baker Academic, 2003.

Gaston, Lloyd. *Paul and the Torah*. Vancouver: University of British Columbia Press, 1987.

George, Timothy. *Galatians*. New American Commentary 30. Edited by E. Ray Clendenen. Nashville: B&H Publishing, 1994.

Hagner, Donald A. *Matthew 1–13*. Word Biblical Commentary 33a. Edited by David A. Hubbard and Glenn W. Barker. Dallas, TX: Word, 1993.

Harmon, Matthew S. *She Must and Shall Go Free: Paul's Isaianic Gospel in Galatians*. Beihefte zur Zeitschrift für die neutestamentliche Wissenschaft 168. Berlin: DeGruyter, 2010.

Hawthorne, Gerald F. *Philippians*. Word Biblical Commentary 43. Waco, TX: Word, 1982.

Hegg, Tim. *Paul's Epistle to the Galatians*. Tacoma, WA: TorahResource, 2010.

Hendriksen, William. *Exposition of Ephesians*. New Testament Commentary. Grand Rapids: Baker, 1967.

Hoehner, Harold W. *Ephesians: An Exegetical Commentary*. Grand Rapids: Baker Academic, 2002.
Hurtado, Larry W. *One God, One Lord: Early Christian Devotion and Ancient Jewish Monotheism*. Edinburgh: T. & T. Clark, 1998.
Israel, Isaac. *Galatians: A Messianic Jewish Perspective*. Lexington, KY: Lulu, 2009.
Jewett, Robert. *Romans: A Commentary*. Hermeneia. Minneapolis, MN: Fortress, 2007.
Juster, Daniel. *Jewish Roots: A Foundation of Biblical Theology*. Gaithersburg, MD: Tikkun Ministries, 1986.
Kaiser, Walter C. *Toward Old Testament Ethics*. Grand Rapids: Zondervan, 1983.
Katz, Steven T. "The Rabbinic Response to Christianity." In *The Cambridge History of Judaism: The Late Roman-Rabbinic Period*, edited by Steven T. Katz, 4:259–98. New York: Cambridge University Press, 2006.
Kazen, Thomas. *Jesus and Purity Halakhah: Was Jesus Indifferent to Impurity?* Coniectanea Biblica New Testament Series 38. Edited by Samuel Byrskog. Winona Lake, IN: Eisenbrauns, 2010.
Keener, Craig S. *Galatians: A Commentary*. Grand Rapids: Baker Academic, 2019.
Kinzer, Mark S. *Post-Missionary Messianic Judaism: Redefining Christian Engagement with the Jewish People*. Grand Rapids: Brazos, 2005.
———. *Israel's Messiah and the People of God: A Vision for Messianic Jewish Covenant Fidelity*. Eugene, OR: Wipf & Stock, 2011.
Kruse, Colin G. *Paul's Letter to the Romans*. Pillar New Testament Commentary. Grand Rapids: Eerdmans, 2012.
Lancaster, D. Thomas. *The Holy Epistle to the Galatians*. Marshfield, MO: First Fruits of Zion, 2011.
———. *Restoration: Returning the Torah of Moses to the Disciples of Jesus*. Marshfield, MO: First Fruits of Zion, 2015.
Lapin, Hayim. "The Origins and Development of the Rabbinic Movement in the Land of Israel." In *The Cambridge History of Judaism: The Late Roman-Rabbinic Period*, edited by Steven T. Katz, 4:206–29. New York: Cambridge University Press, 2006.
Lazarus, H. M., et al. *The Soncino Babylonian Talmud: Makkoth, Eduyyoth, Aboth*. Teaneck, NJ: Talmudic, 2012.
Levine, Amy-Jill. *The Misunderstood Jew: The Church and the Scandal of the Jewish Jesus*. New York: HarperCollins, 2006.
Lightfoot, J. B. *St. Paul's Epistle to the Galatians*. Peabody, MA: Hendrickson, 1999.
Lincoln, Andrew T. *Ephesians*. Word Biblical Commentary 42. Dallas, TX: Word, 1990.
Lohse, Eduard. *Colossians and Philemon*. Hermeneia. Minneapolis, MN: Fortress, 1988.
Longenecker, Richard N. *Galatians*. Word Biblical Commentary 41. Edited by Bruce M. Metzger. Dallas, TX: Word, 1990.
Maoz, Baruch. *Judaism Isn't Jewish: A Friendly Critique of the Messianic Movement*. Fearn, Scotland: Mentor, 2003.
Matthews, Kenneth A. *Genesis 11:27—50:26*. New American Commentary 1B. Nashville, TN: Broadman & Holman, 2005.
McKee, John K. *Galatians: For the Practical Messianic*. Richardson, TX: TNN Press, 2012.
Metzger, Bruce M. *Oxford Annotated Apocrypha: The Apocrypha of the Old Testament*. New York: Oxford University Press, 1977.
———. *A Textual Commentary on the Greek New Testament*. 2nd ed. Stuttgart: Deutsche Bibelgesellschaft, 1994.

Meyer, Jason C. *The End of the Law: Mosaic Covenant in Pauline Theology*. NAC Studies in Bible and Theology 6. Edited by E. Ray Clendenen. Nashville: B&H Publishing, 2009.

Moo, Douglas J. *Galatians*. Baker Exegetical Commentary on the New Testament. Edited by Robert W. Yarbrough and Robert H. Stein. Grand Rapids: Baker Academic, 2013.

———. *The Letters to the Colossians and to Philemon*. Pillar New Testament Commentary. Grand Rapids: Eerdmans, 2008.

———. *The Epistle to the Romans*. New International Commentary on the New Testament. Grand Rapids: Eerdmans, 1996.

Nanos, Mark D. *The Irony of Galatians: Paul's Letter in First-Century Context*. Minneapolis, MN: Fortress, 2002.

Nanos, Mark D., ed. *The Galatians Debate: Contemporary Issues in Rhetorical and Historical Interpretation*. Peabody, MA: Hendrickson, 2002.

Nanos, Mark D., and Magnus Zetterholm, eds. *Paul Within Judaism: Restoring the First-Century Context to the Apostle*. Minneapolis: Fortress, 2015.

O'Brien, Peter T. *The Epistle to the Philippians*. New International Greek Testament Commentary. Grand Rapids: Eerdmans, 2013.

Ojewole, Afolarin. "The Seed in Genesis 3:15: an Exegetical and Intertextual Study." PhD diss., Andrews University, 2002.

Ortlund, Dane C. *Zeal Without Knowledge: The Concept of Zeal in Romans 10, Galatians 1, and Philippians 3*. Library of New Testament Studies 472. New York: Bloomsbury T. & T. Clark, 2012.

Porter, Stanley E., ed. *Paul: Jew, Greek, and Roman*. Leiden, Netherlands: Brill, 2008.

Rausch, David A. *Messianic Judaism: Its History, Theology, and Polity*. New York: Mellen Press, 1982.

Reicke, Bo. *The Epistles of James, Peter, and Jude*. Anchor Bible 37. Edited by William F. Albright and David N. Freedman. Garden City, NY: Doubleday, 1980.

Ridderbos, Herman N. *The Gospel of John: A Theological Commentary*. Translated by John Vriend. Grand Rapids: Eerdmans, 1997.

Robinson, John A. T. *Twelve New Testament Studies*. London: SCM Press, 1962.

Robinson, Richard A., ed. *God, Torah, Messiah: The Messianic Jewish Theology of Dr. Louis Goldberg*. San Francisco: Purple Pomegranate, 2009.

Ronning, John L. "The Curse on the Serpent (Genesis 3:15) in Biblical Theology and Hermeneutics." PhD diss., Westminster Theological Seminary, 1997.

Rosner, Brian S. *Paul and the Law: Keeping the commandments of God*. New Studies in Biblical Theology 31. Edited by D. A. Carson. Downers Grove, IL: InterVarsity, 2013.

Rubin, Barry, ed. *The Complete Jewish Study Bible*. Peabody, MA: Hendrickson, 2016.

Rudolph, David J. *A Jew to the Jews: Jewish Contours of Pauline Flexibility in 1 Corinthians 9:19–23*. Wissenschaftliche Untersuchungen zum Neuen Testament 2. Reihe 304. Edited by Jörg Frey. Tübingen: Mohr Siebeck, 2011.

Rudolph, David J., and Joel Willitts, eds. *Introduction to Messianic Judaism: Its Ecclesial Context and Biblical Foundations*. Grand Rapids: Zondervan, 2013.

Sanders, E. P. *Paul and Palestinian Judaism: A Comparison of Patterns of Religion*. Philadelphia: Fortress, 1977.

———. *Paul, the Law, and the Jewish People*. Philadelphia: Fortress, 1983.

Sarna, Nahum. *Genesis*. JPS Torah Commentary. Philadelphia: Jewish Publication Society, 1989.
Schiffman, Lawrence H. *Who Was a Jew? Rabbinic and Halakhic Perspectives on the Jewish Christian Schism*. Hoboken, NJ: KTAV, 1985.
Schreiner, Thomas R. *1, 2 Peter, Jude*. New American Commentary 37. Edited by E. Ray Clendenen. Nashville: B&H Publishing, 2003.
———. *Galatians*. Zondervan Exegetical Commentary on the New Testament. Edited by Clinton E. Arnold. Grand Rapids: Zondervan Publishing, 2010.
Silva, Moisés. *Philippians*. 2nd ed. Baker Exegetical Commentary on the New Testament. Grand Rapids: Baker Academic, 2005.
Soards, Marion L., and Darrell J. Pursiful. *Galatians*. Smyth & Helwys Bible Commentary. Edited by R. Scott Nash. Macon, GA: Smyth & Helwys, 2015.
Steinsaltz, Adin. *The Essential Talmud*. 13th ed. Translated by Chaya Galai. New York: Basic Books, 2006.
Stern, David H. *Jewish New Testament Commentary*. Clarksville, MD: Jewish New Testament Publications, 1992.
Thielman, Frank. *Ephesians*. Baker Exegetical Commentary on the New Testament. Grand Rapids: Baker Academic, 2010.
Thiessen, Matthew. *Contesting Conversion: Genealogy, Circumcision, and Identity in Ancient Judaism and Christianity*. New York: Oxford University Press, 2011.
Thiselton, Anthony C. *The First Epistle to the Corinthians*. New International Greek Testament Commentary. Grand Rapids: Eerdmans, 2013.
Thomas, Robert L. *Evangelical Hermeneutics: The New Versus the Old*. Grand Rapids: Kregel Academic, 2002.
Tomson, Peter J. *Paul and the Jewish Law: Halakha in the Letters of the Apostle to the Gentiles*. Compendia Rerum Iudaicarum ad Novum Testamentum 3/1. Assen, the Netherlands: Van Gorcum: Fortress, 1990.
Torrance, T. F. *Royal Priesthood: A Theology of Ordained Ministry*. 2nd ed. New York: T. & T. Clark, 1993.
Winger, Michael. *By What Law? The Meaning of Nomos in the Letters of Paul*. SBL Dissertation Series 128. Atlanta, GA: Scholars, 1992.
Wright, N. T. *The Climax of the Covenant: Christ and the Law in Pauline Theology*. Edinburgh: T. & T. Clark, 1991.
———. *Justification: God's Plan and Paul's Vision*. Downers Grove, IL: IVP Academic, 2009.
———. *Paul: In Fresh Perspective*. Minneapolis, MN: Fortress, 2005.
Zetterholm, Magnus. *The Formation of Christianity in Antioch: A Sociological Approach to the Separation between Judaism and Christianity*. New York: Routledge, 2003.

ARTICLES

Agnew, Francis H. "On the Origin of the Term *Apostolos*." *Catholic Biblical Quarterly* 38.1 (January 1976) 49–53.
Allen, Ronald B. "Psalm 87, A Song Rarely Sung." *Bibliotheca Sacra* 153 (April–June 1996) 131–40.
Arnold, Clinton E. "Returning to the Domain of the Powers: *Stoicheia* as Evil Spirits in Galatians 4:3,9." *Novum Testamentum* 38.1 (January 1996) 55–76.

Baird, William R. "What Is the Kerygma: A Study of 1 Corinthians 15:3–8 and Galatians 1:11–17." *Journal of Biblical Literature* 76.3 (1957) 181–91.

Balla, Peter. "Is the Law Abolished According to Eph. 2:15?" *European Journal of Theology* 3.1 (1994) 9–16.

Blomberg, Craig L. "The Law in Luke–Acts." *Journal for the Study of the New Testament* 22 (1984) 53–80.

Boyarin, Daniel, and Jonathan Boyarin. "Diaspora: Generation and the Ground of Jewish Identity." *Critical Inquiry* 19.4 (Summer 1993) 693–725.

Boyarin, Daniel. "The Gospel of the *Memra*: Jewish Binitarianism and the Prologue to John." *Harvard Theological Review* 94.3 (July 2001) 243–84.

———. "Beyond Judaisms: Metatron and the Divine Polymorphy of Ancient Judaism." *Journal for the Study of Judaism* 41 (2010) 323–65.

Bruce, F. F. "Is the Paul of Acts the Real Paul?" *Bulletin of the John Rylands Library* 58 (1975–76) 282–305.

———. "The Curse of the Law." In *Paul and Paulinism: Essays in Honour of C. K. Barrett*, edited by M. D. Hooker and S. G. Wilson, 27–36. London: SPCK, 1982.

Bundrick, David R. "*TA STOICHEIA TOU KOSMOU* (Gal 4:3)." *Journal of the Evangelical Theological Society* 34.3 (September 1991) 353–64.

Burer, Michael H. "'Sons of Abraham' in Galatians 3:7 as a Spiritual, Qualitative Designation." *Bibliotheca Sacra* 173.691 (July–September 2016) 337–51.

Campbell, Douglas A. "Galatians 5.11: Evidence of an Early Law-observant Mission by Paul?" *New Testament Studies* 57.3 (2011) 325–47.

Caneday, Ardel. "'Redeemed from the Curse of the Law': The Use of Deut 21:22–23 in Gal 3:13." *Trinity Journal* 10 (1989) 185–209.

Carson, David. "Pauline Inconsistency: Reflections on 1 Corinthians 9:19-23 and Galatians 2:11-14." *Churchman* 100.1 (1986) 6–45.

Charles, J. Daryl. "Garnishing with the 'Greater Righteousness': The Disciple's Relationship to the Law (Matthew 5:17–20)." *Bulletin for Biblical Research* 12.1 (2002) 1–15.

Cohen, Shaye J. D. "Crossing the Boundary and Becoming a Jew." *Harvard Theological Review* 82.1 (1989) 13–33.

Collins, C. John. "Galatians 3:16: What Kind of Exegete was Paul?" *Tyndale Bulletin* 54.1 (2003) 75–86.

Cosgrove, Charles H. "The Law Has Given Sarah No Children." *Novum Testamentum* 29.3 (July 1987) 219–35.

Davies, W. D. "Paul and the Law: Reflections on Pitfalls in Interpretation." *Hastings Law Journal* 29.6 (July 1978) 1459–504.

Davis, Anne. "Allegorically Speaking in Galatians 4:21—5:1." *Bulletin for Biblical Research* 14.2 (2004) 161–74.

Donaldson, Terence L. "The 'Curse of the Law' and the Inclusion of the Gentiles: Galatians 3.13–14." *New Testament Studies* 32.1 (January 1986) 94–112.

Dunn, James D. G. "Works of the Law and the Curse of the Law (Galatians 3.10–14)." *New Testament Studies* 31.4 (October 1985) 523–42.

Easter, Matthew C. "The Pistis Christou Debate: Main Arguments and Responses in Summary." *Currents in Biblical Research* 9.1 (2010) 33–47.

Ehorn, Seth M. "Galatians 1:8 and Paul's Reading of Abraham's Story." *Journal of Theological Studies* 64.2 (October 2013) 439–44.

Emerson, Matthew Y. "Arbitrary Allegory, Typical Typology, or Intertextual Interpretation? Paul's Use of the Pentateuch in Galatians 4:21–31." *Biblical Theology Bulletin* 43.1 (2013) 14–22.

Evans, M. J. "The Law in James." *Vox Evangelica* 13 (1983) 29–40.

Fitzmyer, Joseph A. "The Qumran Scrolls, the Ebionites and Their Literature." *Theological Studies* 16 (1955) 335–72.

Fuller, David P. "Paul and Galatians 3:28." *Theological Students Fellowship Bulletin* 9.2 (November–December 1985) 9–13.

———. "Paul and 'The Works of the Law.'" *Westminster Theological Journal* 38.1 (Fall 1975) 28–42.

Gignilliat, Mark S. "Isaiah's Offspring: Paul's Isaiah 54:1 Quotation in Galatians 4:27." *Bulletin for Biblical Research* 25.2 (2015) 205–23.

Goddard, A. J., and S. A. Cummins. "Ill or Ill-Treated? Conflict and Persecution as the Context of Paul's Original Ministry in Galatia (Galatians 4.12–20)." *Journal for the Study of the New Testament* 52 (1993) 93–126.

Gordon, T. David. "Why Israel Did Not Obtain Torah-Righteousness: A Translation Note on Rom 9:32." *Westminster Theological Journal* 54.1 (Spring 1992) 163–66.

Green, Gene L. "Lexical Pragmatics and Biblical Interpretation." *Journal of the Evangelical Theological Society* 50.4 (December 2007) 799–812.

Grindheim, Sigurd. "Apostate Turned Prophet: Paul's Prophetic Self-Understanding and Prophetic Hermeneutic with Special Reference to Galatians 3:10–12." *New Testament Studies* 53 (2007) 545–65.

Hahn, Scott W. "Covenant, Oath, and the Aqedah: Διαθήκη in Galatians 3:15–18." *Catholic Biblical Quarterly* 67.1 (January 2005) 79–100.

Hall, Robert G. "Epispasm: Circumcision in Reverse." *Bible Review* 8.4 (August 1992) 52–57.

Hamerton-Kelly, R. G. "Sacred Violence and 'Works of Law.' 'Is Christ Then an Agent of Sin?' (Galatians 2:17)." *Catholic Biblical Quarterly* 52.1 (January 1990) 55–75.

Hays, J. Daniel. "Applying the Old Testament Law Today." *Bibliotheca Sacra* 158.629 (January–March 2001) 21–35.

Hegg, Tim. "Can We Speak of 'Law' in the New Testament in Monolithic Terms?" Paper presented at the Northwest regional meeting for the Evangelical Theological Society, Portland, Oregon, April 8, 1995.

Hofius, O. "Gal 1:18: historesai Kephan." *Zeitschrift für die Neutestamentliche Wissenschaft* 75 (1984) 73–84.

Howard, George. "Romans 3:21–31 and the Inclusion of the Gentiles." *Harvard Theological Review* 63.2 (April 1970) 223–33.

Kaiser, Walter C., Jr. "The Eschatological Hermeneutics of 'Epangelicalism': Promise Theology." *Journal of the Evangelical Theological Society* 13.2 (Spring 1970) 91–99.

Kim, Kyu S. "Reframing Paul's Sibling Language in Light of Jewish Epistolary Forms of Address." *HTS Teologiese Studies* 71.1 (2015) 1–8.

King, Daniel H. "Paul and the Tannaim: A Study in Galatians." *Westminster Theological Journal* 45.2 (1983) 340–70.

Knox, John. "On the Meaning of Galatians 1:15." *Journal of Biblical Literature* 106.2 (1987) 301–4.

Korner, Ralph J. "Ekklesia as a Jewish Synagogue Term: Some Implications for Paul's Socio-Religious Location." *Journal of the Jesus Movement in Its Jewish Setting* 2 (2015) 53–78.

Longenecker, Richard N. "The Pedagogical Nature of the Law in Galatians 3:19—4:7." *Journal of the Evangelical Theological Society* 25.1 (March 1982) 53-61.
Lull, David J. "'The Law Was Our Pedagogue': A Study of Galatians 3:19-25." *Journal of Biblical Literature* 105.3 (September 1986) 481-98.
Martin, Neil. "Returning to the *stoicheia tou kosmou*: Enslavement to the Physical Elements in Galatians 4.3 and 9?" *Journal for the Study of the New Testament* 40.4 (2018) 434-52.
Martin, Troy W. "The Syntax of Surprise, Irony, or Shifting of Blame in Gal 1:6-7." *Biblical Research* 54 (2009) 79-98.
McNamara, Martin. "'To de (Hagar) Sina oros estin en te Arabia (Gal. 4:25a) Paul and Petra." *Milltown Studies* 2 (1978) 24-41.
Merkle, Benjamin L. "The Meaning of ἘκκλησΙα in Matthew 16:18 and 18:17." *Bibliotheca Sacra* 167 (July-September 2010) 281-91.
Nanos, Mark D. "The Local Contexts of the Galatians: Toward Resolving a Catch-22." Paper presented at the annual meeting for the Society of Biblical Literature, Denver, Colorado, November 20, 2001.
———. "A Torah-Observant Paul?: What Difference Could it Make for Christian/ Jewish Relations Today?" Paper presented at the annual meeting for Christian Scholars Group on Christian-Jewish Relations, Boston, MA, June 4-6, 2005.
Rabbinowitz, Noel S. "Matthew 23:2-4: Does Jesus Recognize the Authority of the Pharisees and Does He Endorse their *Halakhah*?" *Journal of the Evangelical Theological Society* 46.3 (September 2003) 423-47.
Raisanen, Heikki. "Galatians 2.16 and Paul's Break with Judaism." *New Testament Studies* 31 (October 1985) 543-53.
Roetzel, Calvin J. "Jewish Christian—Gentile Christian Relations: A Discussion of Ephesians 2:15a." *Zeitschrift für die neutestamentliche Wissenschaft* 74.1-2 (1983) 81-89.
Rogland, Max. "Abram's Persistent Faith: Hebrew Verb Semantics in Genesis 15:6." *Westminster Theological Journal* 70 (2008) 239-44.
Rudolph, David J. "Paul's Rule for all the Churches." *Studies in Christian-Jewish Relations* 5.1 (2010) 1-24.
Russell, Walt. "Who Were Paul's Opponents in Galatia?" *Bibliotheca Sacra* 147 (July 1990) 329-50.
———. "Does the Christian have 'Flesh' in Gal 5:13-26?" *Journal of the Evangelical Theological Society* 36.2 (June 1993) 179-87.
Sedaca, David. "Salvation and the People of Israel: Harmonizing a Soteriological Dilemma." *Kesher Journal* 22 (Summer 2008) 1-9.
Schliesser, Benjamin. "'Christ-Faith' as an Eschatological Event (Galatians 3.23-26) A 'Third View' on Πίστις Χριστοῦ." *Journal for the Study of the New Testament* 38.3 (2016) 277-300.
Schreiner, Thomas R. "The Church as the New Israel and the Future of Ethnic Israel." *Studia Biblica et Theologica* 13.1 (April 1983) 17-38.
———. "Is Perfect Obedience to the Law Possible? A Re-Examination of Galatians 3:10." *Journal of the Evangelical Theological Society* 27.2 (June 1984) 151-60.
———. "Israel's Failure to Attain Righteousness in Romans 9:30-10:3." *Trinity Journal* 12 (1991) 209-20.
Shanks, Monte A. "Galatians 5:2-4 in Light of the Doctrine of Justification." *Bibliotheca Sacra* 169.674 (April-June 2012) 188-202.

Smith, Michael J. "The Role of the Pedagogue in Galatians." *Bibliotheca Sacra* 163.650 (April–June 2006) 197–214.

Stanton, Graham N. "What is the Law of Christ?" *Ex Auditu* 17 (2001) 47–59.

Staples, Jason A. "What Do the Gentiles Have to Do with 'All Israel'? A Fresh Look at Romans 11:25–27." *Journal of Biblical Literature* 130.2 (2011) 371–90.

———. "Altered Because of Transgressions? The 'Law of Deeds' in Gal 3,19a." *Zeitschrift für die Neutestamentliche Wissenschaft* 106.1 (2015) 126–35.

Stendahl, Krister. "The Apostle Paul and the Introspective Conscience of the West." *Harvard Theological Review* 56.3 (July 1963) 199–215.

Thatcher, Tom. "The Plot of Gal 3:1–18." *Journal of the Evangelical Theological Society* 40.3 (September 1997) 401–10.

Thomas, Robert L. "The New Testament Use of the Old Testament." *The Master's Seminary Journal* 13.1 (Spring 2002) 79–98.

Tyson, Joseph B. "'Works of Law' in Galatians." *Journal of Biblical Literature* 92.3 (September 1973) 423–31.

Vos, Johan S. "Paul's Argumentation in Galatians 1–2." *Harvard Theological Review* 87.1 (1994) 1–16.

Wallace, Daniel B. "Galatians 3:19–20: A *Crux Interpretum* for Paul's View of the Law." *Westminster Theological Journal* 52 (1990) 225–45.

Wendt, Heidi. "Galatians 3:1 as an Allusion to Textual Prophecy." *Journal of Biblical Literature* 135.2 (2016) 369–89.

Williams, Sam K. "Justification and the Spirit in Galatians." *Journal for the Study of the New Testament* 29 (February 1987) 91–100.

Willitts, Joel. "Context Matters: Paul's Use of Leviticus 18:5 in Galatians 3:12." *Tyndale Bulletin* 54.2 (2003) 105–22.

Wilson, Todd A. "'Under Law' in Galatians: A Pauline Theological Abbreviation." *Journal of Theological Studies* 56.2 (October 2005) 362–92.

Wright, N. T. "Paul, Arabia, and Elijah (Galatians 1:17)." *Journal of Biblical Literature* 115.4 (1996) 683–92.

Young, Norman H. "PAIDAGOGOS: The Social Setting of a Pauline Metaphor." *Novum Testamentum* 29.2 (April 1987) 150–76.

www.ingramcontent.com/pod-product-compliance
Lightning Source LLC
Chambersburg PA
CBHW071453150426
43191CB00008B/1334